The Complete 2023
Keto Diet Cookbook

1600 Tasty, Quick and Foolproof Ketogenic Recipes for Every Day and 30-Day Meal Plan for Everyone

Demi Gill

CONTENTS

Sauces And Dressing Recipes 37

Fish And Seafood Recipes 44

Pork, Beef & Lamb Recipes 58

Desserts And Drinks 101

30 Day Meal Plan 114

Appendix : Recipes Index 116

INTRODUCTION

I was diagnosed with low blood sugar half a year ago, which came as a shock to me considering I was always a fan of consuming fast food and sugary snacks. It was then my doctor recommended me to try out the keto diet. I had heard of it, but never really gave it much of a thought.

I had a difficult time adapting to the keto lifestyle. It seemed like my body was fighting against me. My first few weeks were tough; my cravings for sugary treats plagued me, making it hard to stick to the diet.

I started to research and became determined to stick with it no matter what. I started learning more about how keto can improve many chronic diseases like diabetes and autoimmune disorders, which encouraged me even more. I started seeing improvements in my health which strengthened my commitment further. I bought all the keto friendly food and tried out different recipes every day. This made it easier for me to stay committed and motivated to the diet.

I even gave up alcohol as this was not allowed in a keto lifestyle and found alternative ways to enjoy myself with friends and family. Through sheer determination, dedication, perseverance I was able to reach 4 months of living a keto life and noticed drastic changes in my health for the better.

My friends were also surprised at how well I was doing with the keto diet. They started asking me for advice such as which foods I consume and how much exercise do I do. It soon became something of a passion project for me where I would help them adjust to this new lifestyle by creating meal plans.

Since this journey wasn't easy so I decided that I wanted to share my experience with anyone who is interested in keto diet.

Introduction of Keto Diet

The keto diet, or ketogenic diet, emphasizes high-fat foods and strictly limits carbohydrate intake.

Our basic diet consists carbohydrates that are converted to glucose in the body. Cells burn glucose as a source of energy. But when you switch to a very high-fat, low-carb diet, your body necessarily switches from using glucose to using fatty acids and ketone bodies for energy. This process is called ketosis, which is how the diet gets its name.

The ketogenic diet advocates a high-fat, moderate-protein and low-carbohydrate diet, simulating the body in a state of starvation, so that the body directly burns fat (ketone bodies) instead of carbohydrates (sugar). In other words, the fat you eat becomes the main source of energy, so as to achieve faster fat loss.

Nuts, seeds, full-fat cheese and other dairy products, plain Greek yogurt, non-starchy and fibrous vegetables, oils, and small amounts of meat, eggs, and fish, dominate the ketogenic diet.

You need to strictly limit carbohydrates, including bread and baked goods, sweets, pasta, breakfast cereals, starchy vegetables (such as potatoes, sweet potatoes, corn, and peas), beans, fruit, and beer.

You can stick to a ketogenic diet indefinitely as a weight loss program, cycling it back and forth for short periods of time. Fatty foods are key, protein in moderation, and carbohydrates abstained. Here are some advice on getting started on keto:

● The first step is to educate yourself about carbohydrates and familiarize with good fats.

● Before trying keto, try to find sources of grass-fed meat at the supermarket, and learn about hidden food sources of sugar, like coleslaw at your local restaurant.

● Carb cravings don't go away right away.

● During the first week of cutting out carbs, you may experience symptoms such as muscle aches, headaches, fatigue, and mental confusion -- and, of course, hunger. You can try eating some high-fat snacks.

● As you enter the second and third weeks of the diet, you will slowly feel better and the low-carb, high-fat diet will become a habit.

● By week four, you can expect to lose weight, especially if you've been following your exercise program. Choosing the right foods will be easier when you get used to the ketogenic diet. You'll pay more attention to the skin and fat parts of the poultry than the lean meat.

When your body has ketones through a ketogenic diet, your body breaks down its own stored fat and food fat into ketones for energy instead of using carbohydrates for energy.

Studies have shown that the dynamic balance of fat loss is more conducive to mental health. The best way to lose fat is not to strictly require yourself to maintain an optimal weight, but to adjust your diet with flexibility. After reaching the ideal target weight, set an acceptable floating range for yourself. Within the range, you can arrange your own diet relatively easily. Once you outpace the range, you can adjust to a fat-reducing diet in time. Like skin care or beauty, diet is also one of the important items that need to be corrected regularly.

BASIC KITCHEN CONVERSIONS & EQUIVALENTS

DRY MEASUREMENTS CONVERSION CHART

3 TEASPOONS = 1 TABLESPOON = 1/16 CUP

6 TEASPOONS = 2 TABLESPOONS = 1/8 CUP

12 TEASPOONS = 4 TABLESPOONS = 1/4 CUP

24 TEASPOONS = 8 TABLESPOONS = 1/2 CUP

36 TEASPOONS = 12 TABLESPOONS = 3/4 CUP

48 TEASPOONS = 16 TABLESPOONS = 1 CUP

METRIC TO US COOKING CONVERSIONS

OVEN TEMPERATURES

120 °C = 250 °F

160 °C = 320 °F

180° C = 350 °F

205 °C = 400 °F

220 °C = 425 °F

LIQUID MEASUREMENTS CONVERSION CHART

8 FLUID OUNCES = 1 CUP = 1/2 PINT = 1/4 QUART

16 FLUID OUNCES = 2 CUPS = 1 PINT = 1/2 QUART

32 FLUID OUNCES = 4 CUPS = 2 PINTS = 1 QUART = 1/4 GALLON

128 FLUID OUNCES = 16 CUPS = 8 PINTS = 4 QUARTS = 1 GALLON

BAKING IN GRAMS

1 CUP FLOUR = 140 GRAMS

1 CUP SUGAR = 150 GRAMS

1 CUP POWDERED SUGAR = 160 GRAMS

1 CUP HEAVY CREAM = 235 GRAMS

VOLUME

1 MILLILITER = 1/5 TEASPOON

5 ML = 1 TEASPOON

15 ML = 1 TABLESPOON

240 ML = 1 CUP OR 8 FLUID OUNCES

1 LITER = 34 FL. OUNCES

WEIGHT

1 GRAM = .035 OUNCES

100 GRAMS = 3.5 OUNCES

500 GRAMS = 1.1 POUNDS

1 KILOGRAM = 35 OUNCES

US TO METRIC COOKING CONVERSIONS

1/5 TSP = 1 ML

1 TSP = 5 ML

1 TBSP = 15 ML

1 FL OUNCE = 30 ML

1 CUP = 237 ML

1 PINT (2 CUPS) = 473 ML

1 QUART (4 CUPS) = .95 LITER

1 GALLON (16 CUPS) = 3.8 LITERS

1 OZ = 28 GRAMS

1 POUND = 454 GRAMS

BUTTER

1 CUP BUTTER = 2 STICKS = 8 OUNCES = 230 GRAMS = 8 TABLESPOONS

WHAT DOES 1 CUP EQUAL

1 CUP = 8 FLUID OUNCES

1 CUP = 16 TABLESPOONS

1 CUP = 48 TEASPOONS

1 CUP = 1/2 PINT

1 CUP = 1/4 QUART

1 CUP = 1/16 GALLON

1 CUP = 240 ML

BAKING PAN CONVERSIONS

1 CUP ALL-PURPOSE FLOUR = 4.5 OZ

1 CUP ROLLED OATS = 3 OZ 1 LARGE EGG = 1.7 OZ

1 CUP BUTTER = 8 OZ 1 CUP MILK = 8 OZ

1 CUP HEAVY CREAM = 8.4 OZ

1 CUP GRANULATED SUGAR = 7.1 OZ

1 CUP PACKED BROWN SUGAR = 7.75 OZ

1 CUP VEGETABLE OIL = 7.7 OZ

1 CUP UNSIFTED POWDERED SUGAR = 4.4 OZ

BAKING PAN CONVERSIONS

9-INCH ROUND CAKE PAN = 12 CUPS

10-INCH TUBE PAN = 16 CUPS

11-INCH BUNDT PAN = 12 CUPS

9-INCH SPRINGFORM PAN = 10 CUPS

9 X 5 INCH LOAF PAN = 8 CUPS

9-INCH SQUARE PAN = 8 CUPS

Appetizers, Snacks & Side Dishes

Walnut Butter On Cracker

Servings: 1 | Cooking Time: 0 Minutes

Ingredients:
- 1 tablespoon walnut butter
- 2 pieces Mary's gone crackers

Directions:
1. Spread ½ tablespoon of walnut butter per cracker and enjoy.

Nutrition Info:
- Per Servings 4.0g Carbs, 1.0g Protein, 14.0g Fat, 134 Calories

Bacon Jalapeno Poppers

Servings: 8 | Cooking Time: 10 Minutes

Ingredients:
- 4-ounce cream cheese
- ¼ cup cheddar cheese, shredded
- 1 teaspoon paprika
- 16 fresh jalapenos, sliced lengthwise and seeded
- 16 strips of uncured bacon, cut into half
- Salt and pepper to taste

Directions:
1. Preheat oven to 400oF.
2. In a mixing bowl, mix the cream cheese, cheddar cheese, salt, and paprika until well-combined.
3. Scoop half a teaspoon onto each half of jalapeno peppers.
4. Use a thin strip of bacon and wrap it around the cheese-filled jalapeno half.
5. Place in a single layer in a lightly greased baking sheet and roast for 10 minutes.
6. Serve and enjoy.

Nutrition Info:
- Per Servings 3.2g Carbs, 10.6g Protein, 18.9g Fat, 225 Calories

Pesto Stuffed Mushrooms

Servings: 6 | Cooking Time: 25 Minutes

Ingredients:
- 6 large cremini mushrooms
- 6 bacon slices
- 2 tablespoons basil pesto
- 5 tablespoons low-fat cream cheese softened

Directions:
1. Line a cookie sheet with foil and preheat oven to 375oF.
2. In a small bowl mix well, pesto and cream cheese.
3. Remove stems of mushrooms and discard. Evenly fill mushroom caps with pesto-cream cheese filling.

4. Get one stuffed mushroom and a slice of bacon. Wrap the bacon all over the mushrooms. Repeat process on remaining mushrooms and bacon.
5. Place bacon-wrapped mushrooms on prepared pan and bake for 25 minutes or until bacon is crispy.
6. Let it cool, evenly divide into suggested servings, and enjoy.

Nutrition Info:
- Per Servings 2.0g Carbs, 5.0g Protein, 12.2g Fat, 137.8 Calories

Chocolate Mousse

Servings: 4 | Cooking Time: 0 Minutes

Ingredients:
- 1 large, ripe avocado
- 1/4 cup sweetened almond milk
- 1 tbsp coconut oil
- 1/4 cup cocoa or cacao powder
- 1 tsp vanilla extract

Directions:
1. In a food processor, process all ingredients until smooth and creamy.
2. Transfer to a lidded container and chill for at least 4 hours.
3. Serve and enjoy.

Nutrition Info:
- Per Servings 6.9g Carbs, 1.2g Protein, 11.0g Fat, 125 Calories

Cardamom And Cinnamon Fat Bombs

Servings: 10 | Cooking Time: 3 Minutes

Ingredients:
- ¼ tsp ground cardamom (green)
- ¼ tsp ground cinnamon
- ½ cup unsweetened shredded coconut
- ½ tsp vanilla extract
- 3-oz unsalted butter, room temperature

Directions:
1. Place a nonstick pan on medium fire and toast coconut until lightly browned.
2. In a bowl, mix all ingredients.
3. Evenly roll into 10 equal balls.
4. Let it cool in the fridge.
5. Serve and enjoy.

Nutrition Info:
- Per Servings 0.4g Carbs, 0.4g Protein, 10.0g Fat, 90 Calories

Cranberry Sauce Meatballs

Servings: 2 | Cooking Time: 25 Mins

Ingredients:
- 1 pound lean ground beef
- 1 egg
- 2 tablespoons water
- 1/2 cup cauliflower rice
- 3 tablespoons minced onion
- 1 can jellied cranberry sauce, keto-friendly
- 3/4 cup chili sauce

Directions:
1. Preheat oven to 350 degrees F.
2. Mix the ground beef, egg, water, cauliflower rice and minced onions together until well combined. Form into small meatballs and place on a rack over a foil-lined baking sheet.
3. Bake the meatballs for 20 to 25 minutes, turning halfway through.
4. Combine sauce ingredients in a large saucepan over low heat, toss with meatballs and allow to simmer on low for 1 hour.
5. Serve and garnish with parsley if desired.

Nutrition Info:
- Per Servings 8.6g Carbs, 9.8g Protein, 10.2g Fat, 193 Calories

Zucchini And Cheese Gratin

Servings: 8 | Cooking Time: 15 Minutes

Ingredients:
- 5 tablespoons butter
- 1 onion, sliced
- ½ cup heavy cream
- 4 cups raw zucchini, sliced
- 1 ½ cups shredded pepper Jack cheese
- Salt and pepper to taste

Directions:
1. Place all ingredients in a mixing bowl and give a good stir to incorporate everything.
2. Pour the mixture in a heat-proof baking dish.
3. Place in a 350F preheated oven and bake for 15 minutes.
4. Serve and enjoy.

Nutrition Info:
- Per Servings 5.0g Carbs, 8.0g Protein, 20.0g Fat, 280 Calories

Air Fryer Garlic Chicken Wings

Servings: 4 | Cooking Time: 25 Minutes

Ingredients:
- 16 pieces chicken wings
- ¾ cup almond flour
- 4 tablespoons minced garlic
- ¼ cup butter, melted
- 2 tablespoons Stevia powder
- Salt and pepper to taste

Directions:
1. Preheat oven to 400oF.
2. In a mixing bowl, combine the chicken wings, almond flour, Stevia powder, and garlic. Season with salt and pepper to taste.
3. Place in a lightly greased cookie sheet in an even layer and cook for 25 minutes.
4. Halfway through the cooking time, turnover chicken.
5. Once cooked, place in a bowl and drizzle with melted butter. Toss to coat.
6. Serve and enjoy.

Nutrition Info:
- Per Servings 7.8g Carbs, 23.7g Protein, 26.9g Fat, 365 Calories

Chicken Enchilada Dip

Servings: 16 | Cooking Time:240 Minutes

Ingredients:
- 2 pounds cooked rotisserie chicken, shredded
- 1 cup enchilada sauce
- ½ cup cheddar cheese
- 2 stalk green onions, sliced
- 3 tbsp olive oil
- Salt and pepper to taste

Directions:
1. Place all ingredients in the crockpot except for the green onions.
2. Give a good stir to combine everything.
3. Close the lid and cook on low for 4 hours. Mix well and adjust seasoning to taste.
4. Garnish with green onions.

Nutrition Info:
- Per Servings 1.5g Carbs, 16.2g Protein, 13.6g Fat, 178 Calories

Lemony Fried Artichokes

Servings: 4 | Cooking Time: 20 Minutes

Ingredients:
- 12 fresh baby artichokes
- 2 tbsp lemon juice
- 2 tbsp olive oil
- Salt to taste

Directions:
1. Slice the artichokes vertically into narrow wedges. Drain on paper towels before frying.
2. Heat olive oil in a cast-iron skillet over high heat. Fry the artichokes until browned and crispy. Drain excess oil on paper towels. Sprinkle with salt and lemon juice.

Nutrition Info:
- Per Servings 2.9g Carbs, 2g Protein, 2.4g Fat, 35 Calories

Cheesy Cheddar Cauliflower

Servings: 6 | Cooking Time: 20 Minutes

Ingredients:

- ½ cup butter
- 2 cups half and half cream
- 4 cups cheddar cheese, grated
- 3 cups cauliflower florets
- ½ cup water
- Pepper and salt to taste

Directions:

1. In a heavy-bottomed pot on medium-high fire, melt butter.
2. Stir in cream and cheddar cheese. Add in water. Mix well and cook for 5 minutes.
3. Add cauliflower florets and cook for 6 minutes. Season with pepper.
4. Serve and enjoy.

Nutrition Info:

- Per Servings 9g Carbs, 21g Protein, 42g Fat, 500 Calories

Cajun Spiced Pecans

Servings: 10 | Cooking Time: 10 Minutes

Ingredients:

- 1-pound pecan halves
- ¼ cup butter
- 1 packet Cajun seasoning mix
- ¼ teaspoon ground cayenne pepper
- Salt and pepper to taste

Directions:

1. Place a nonstick saucepan on medium fire and melt butter.
2. Add pecans and remaining ingredients.
3. Sauté for 5 minutes.
4. Remove from fire and let it cool completely.
5. Serve and enjoy.

Nutrition Info:

- Per Servings 6.8g Carbs, 4.2g Protein, 37.3g Fat, 356.5 Calories

Squid Salad With Mint, Cucumber & Chili Dressing

Servings: 4 | Cooking Time: 30 Minutes

Ingredients:

- 4 medium squid tubes, cut into strips
- ½ cup mint leaves
- 2 medium cucumbers, halved and cut in strips
- ½ cup coriander leaves, reserve the stems
- ½ red onion, finely sliced
- Salt and black pepper to taste
- 1 tsp fish sauce
- 1 red chili, roughly chopped
- 1 tsp swerve
- 1 clove garlic
- 2 limes, juiced
- 1 tbsp chopped coriander
- 1tsp olive oil

Directions:

1. In a salad bowl, mix mint leaves, cucumber strips, coriander leaves, and red onion. Season with salt, pepper and a little drizzle of olive oil; set aside. In the mortar, pound the coriander stems, red chili, and swerve into a paste using the pestle. Add the fish sauce and lime juice, and mix with the pestle.
2. Heat a skillet over high heat on a stovetop and sear the squid on both sides to lightly brown, about 5 minutes. Pour the squid on the salad and drizzle with the chili dressing. Toss the ingredients with two spoons, garnish with coriander, and serve the salad as a single dish or with some more seafood.

Nutrition Info:

- Per Servings 2.1g Carbs, 24.6g Protein, 22.5g Fat, 318 Calories

Tart Raspberry Crumble Bar

Servings: 9 | Cooking Time: 55 Minutes

Ingredients:

- 1/2 cup whole toasted almonds
- 1 cup almond flour
- 1 cup cold, unsalted butter, cut into cubes
- 2 eggs, beaten
- 3-ounce dried raspberries
- 1/4 teaspoon salt
- 3 tbsp MCT or coconut oil.

Directions:

1. In a food processor, pulse almonds until chopped coarsely. Transfer to a bowl.
2. Add almond flour and salt into the food processor and pulse until a bit combined. Add butter, eggs, and MCT oil. Pulse until you have a coarse batter. Evenly divide batter into two bowls.
3. In the first bowl of batter, knead well until it forms a ball. Wrap in cling wrap, flatten a bit and chill for an hour for easy handling.
4. In the second bowl of batter, add the raspberries. In a pinching motion, pinch batter to form clusters of streusel. Set aside.
5. When ready to bake, preheat oven to 375oF and lightly grease an 8x8-inch baking pan with cooking spray.
6. Discard cling wrap and evenly press dough on the bottom of the pan, up to 1-inch up the sides of the pan, making sure that everything is covered in dough.
7. Top with streusel.
8. Pop in the oven and bake until golden brown and berries are bubbly around 45 minutes.
9. Remove from oven and cool for 20 minutes before slicing into 9 equal bars.
10. Serve and enjoy or store in a lidded container for 10-days in the fridge.

Nutrition Info:

- Per Servings 3.9g Carbs, 2.8g Protein, 22.9g Fat, 229 Calories

Curry ' N Poppy Devilled Eggs

Servings: 6 | Cooking Time: 8 Minutes

Ingredients:
- ½ cup mayonnaise
- ½ tbsp poppy seeds
- 1 tbsp red curry paste
- 6 eggs
- ¼ tsp salt

Directions:
1. Place eggs in a small pot and add enough water to cover it. Bring to a boil without a cover, lower fire to a simmer and simmer for 8 minutes.
2. Immediately dunk in ice-cold water once done the cooking. Peel eggshells and slice eggs in half lengthwise.
3. Remove yolks and place them in a medium bowl. Add the rest of the ingredients in the bowl except for the egg whites. Mix well.
4. Evenly return the yolk mixture into the middle of the egg whites.
5. Serve and enjoy.

Nutrition Info:
- Per Servings 1.0g Carbs, 6.0g Protein, 19.0g Fat, 200 Calories

Sour Cream And Carrot Sticks

Servings: 3 | Cooking Time: 0 Minutes

Ingredients:
- 1 sweet onion, peeled and minced
- ½ cup sour cream
- 2 tbsp mayonnaise
- 4 tablespoons olive oil
- 4 stalks celery, cut into 3-inch lengths
- Pepper and salt to taste

Directions:
1. In a bowl, whisk well sour cream and mayonnaise until thoroughly combined.
2. Stir in onion and mix well.
3. Let it sit for an hour in the fridge and serve with celery sticks on the side.

Nutrition Info:
- Per Servings 7g Carbs, 3g Protein, 13g Fat, 143 Calories

Roasted Cauliflower With Serrano Ham & Pine Nuts

Servings: 6 | Cooking Time: 30 Minutes

Ingredients:
- 2 heads cauliflower, cut into 1-inch slices
- 2 tbsp olive oil
- Salt and chili pepper to taste
- 1 tsp garlic powder
- 10 slices Serrano ham, chopped
- ¼ cup pine nuts, chopped
- 1 tsp capers
- 1 tsp parsley

Directions:
1. Preheat oven to 450ºF and line a baking sheet with foil.
2. Brush the cauli steaks with olive oil and season with chili pepper, garlic, and salt.
3. Spread the cauli florets on the baking sheet. Roast in the oven for 10 minutes until tender and lightly browned. Remove the sheet and sprinkle the ham and pine nuts all over the cauli. Bake for another 10 minutes until the ham is crispy and a nutty aroma is perceived.
4. Take out, sprinkle with capers and parsley. Serve with ground beef stew and braised asparagus.

Nutrition Info:
- Per Servings 2.5g Carbs, 10g Protein, 10g Fat, 141 Calories

Sautéed Brussels Sprouts

Servings: 4 | Cooking Time: 8 Minutes

Ingredients:
- 2 cups Brussels sprouts, halved
- 1 tablespoon balsamic vinegar
- 4 tablespoons olive oil
- Salt and pepper to taste

Directions:
1. Place a saucepan on medium-high fire and heat oil for a minute.
2. Add all ingredients and sauté for 7 minutes.
3. Season with pepper and salt.
4. Serve and enjoy.

Nutrition Info:
- Per Servings 4.6g Carbs, 1.5g Protein, 16.8g Fat, 162 Calories

Coconut And Chocolate Bars

Servings: 6 | Cooking Time: 30 Minutes

Ingredients:
- 1 tbsp Stevia
- ¾ cup shredded coconut, unsweetened
- ½ cup ground nuts (almonds, pecans, or walnuts)
- ¼ cup unsweetened cocoa powder
- 4 tbsp coconut oil
- Done

Directions:
1. In a medium bowl, mix shredded coconut, nuts, and cocoa powder.
2. Add Stevia and coconut oil.
3. Mix batter thoroughly.
4. In a 9x9 square inch pan or dish, press the batter and for a 30-minutes place in the freezer.
5. Serve and enjoy.

Nutrition Info:
- Per Servings 2.3g Carbs, 1.6g Protein, 17.8g Fat, 200 Calories

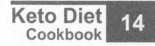

Jalapeno Popper Spread

Servings: 8 | Cooking Time: 3 Mins

Ingredients:
- 2 packages cream cheese, softened; low-carb
- 1 cup. mayonnaise
- 1 can chopped green chilies, drained
- 2 ounces canned diced jalapeno peppers, drained
- 1 cup. grated Parmesan cheese

Directions:
1. Combine cream cheese and mayonnaise in a bowl until incorporated. Add in jalapeno peppers and green chilies. In a microwave safe bowl, spread jalapeno peppers mixture and sprinkle with Parmesan cheese.
2. Microwave jalapeno peppers mixture on High about 3 minutes or until warm.

Nutrition Info:
- Per Servings 1g Carbs, 2.1g Protein, 11.1g Fat, 110 Calories

Bacon Mashed Cauliflower

Servings: 6 | Cooking Time: 40 Minutes

Ingredients:
- 6 slices bacon
- 3 heads cauliflower, leaves removed
- 2 cups water
- 2 tbsp melted butter
- ½ cup buttermilk
- Salt and black pepper to taste
- ¼ cup grated yellow cheddar cheese
- 2 tbsp chopped chives

Directions:
1. Preheat oven to 350ºF. Fry bacon in a heated skillet over medium heat for 5 minutes until crispy. Remove to a paper towel-lined plate, allow to cool, and crumble. Set aside and keep bacon fat.
2. Boil cauli heads in water in a pot over high heat for 7 minutes, until tender. Drain and put in a bowl.
3. Include butter, buttermilk, salt, black pepper, and puree using a hand blender until smooth and creamy. Lightly grease a casserole dish with the bacon fat and spread the mash in it.
4. Sprinkle with cheddar cheese and place under the broiler for 4 minutes on high until the cheese melts. Remove and top with bacon and chopped chives. Serve with pan-seared scallops.

Nutrition Info:
- Per Servings 6g Carbs, 14g Protein, 25g Fat, 312 Calories

Parmesan Crackers

Servings: 6 | Cooking Time: 25 Minutes

Ingredients:
- 1 ⅓ cups coconut flour
- 1 ¼ cup grated Parmesan cheese
- Salt and black pepper to taste
- 1 tsp garlic powder
- ⅓ cup butter, softened
- ⅓ tsp sweet paprika
- ⅓ cup heavy cream
- Water as needed

Directions:
1. Preheat the oven to 350ºF.
2. Mix the coconut flour, parmesan cheese, salt, pepper, garlic powder, and paprika in a bowl. Add in the butter and mix well. Top with the heavy cream and mix again until a smooth, thick mixture has formed. Add 1 to 2 tablespoon of water at this point, if it is too thick.
3. Place the dough on a cutting board and cover with plastic wrap. Use a rolling pin to spread out the dough into a light rectangle. Cut cracker squares out of the dough and arrange them on a baking sheet without overlapping. Bake for 20 minutes and transfer to a serving bowl after.

Nutrition Info:
- Per Servings 0.7g Carbs, 5g Protein, 3g Fat, 115 Calories

Cheesy Cauliflower Bake With Mayo Sauce

Servings: 6 | Cooking Time: 27 Minutes

Ingredients:
- Cooking spray
- 2 heads cauliflower, cut into florets
- ¼ cup melted butter
- Salt and black pepper to taste
- 1 pinch red pepper flakes
- ½ cup mayonnaise
- ¼ tsp Dijon mustard
- 3 tbsp grated pecorino cheese

Directions:
1. Preheat oven to 400ºF and grease a baking dish with cooking spray.
2. Combine the cauli florets, butter, salt, black pepper, and red pepper flakes in a bowl until well mixed. Mix the mayonnaise and Dijon mustard in a bowl, and set aside until ready to serve. Arrange cauliflower florets on the prepared baking dish.
3. Sprinkle with grated pecorino cheese and bake for 25 minutes until the cheese has melted and golden brown on the top. Remove, let sit for 3 minutes to cool, and serve with the mayo sauce.

Nutrition Info:
- Per Servings 2g Carbs, 6g Protein, 35g Fat, 363 Calories

Dill Pickles With Tuna-mayo Topping

Servings: 12 | Cooking Time: 40 Minutes

Ingredients:
- 18 ounces canned and drained tuna
- 6 large dill pickles
- ¼ tsp garlic powder
- ⅓ cup sugar-free mayonnaise
- 1 tbsp onion flakes

Directions:

1. Combine the mayonnaise, tuna, onion flakes, and garlic powder in a bowl. Cut the pickles in half lengthwise. Top each half with tuna mixture. Place in the fridge for 30 minutes before serving.

Nutrition Info:
- Per Servings 1.5g Carbs, 11g Protein, 10g Fat, 118 Calories

Baked Cheese & Spinach Balls

Servings: 8 | Cooking Time: 30 Minutes

Ingredients:
- ⅓ cup crumbled ricotta cheese
- ¼ tsp nutmeg
- ¼ tsp pepper
- 3 tbsp heavy cream
- 1 tsp garlic powder
- 1 tbsp onion powder
- 2 tbsp butter, melted
- ⅓ cup Parmesan cheese
- 2 eggs
- 1 cup spinach
- 1 cup almond flour

Directions:

1. Place all ingredients in a food processor. Process until smooth. Place in the freezer for about 10 minutes. Make balls out of the mixture and arrange them on a lined baking sheet. Bake at 350°F for about 10-12 minutes.

Nutrition Info:
- Per Servings 0.8g Carbs, 8g Protein, 15g Fat, 160 Calories

Old Bay Chicken Wings

Servings: 4 | Cooking Time: 30 Minutes

Ingredients:
- 3 pounds chicken wings
- ¾ cup almond flour
- 1 tablespoon old bay spices
- 1 teaspoon lemon juice, freshly squeezed
- ½ cup butter
- Salt and pepper to taste

Directions:

1. Preheat oven to 400oF.
2. In a mixing bowl, combine all ingredients except for the butter.
3. Place in an even layer in a baking sheet.

4. Bake for 30 minutes. Halfway through the cooking time, shake the fryer basket for even cooking.
5. Once cooked, drizzle with melted butter.

Nutrition Info:
- Per Servings 1.6g Carbs, 52.5g Protein, 59.2g Fat, 700 Calories

Cheesy Green Bean Crisps

Servings: 6 | Cooking Time: 30 Minutes

Ingredients:
- Cooking spray
- ¼ cup shredded pecorino romano cheese
- ¼ cup pork rind crumbs
- 1 tsp garlic powder
- Salt and black pepper to taste
- 2 eggs
- 1 lb green beans, thread removed

Directions:

1. Preheat oven to 425°F and line two baking sheets with foil. Grease with cooking spray and set aside.
2. Mix the pecorino, pork rinds, garlic powder, salt, and black pepper in a bowl. Beat the eggs in another bowl. Coat green beans in eggs, then cheese mixture and arrange evenly on the baking sheets.
3. Grease lightly with cooking spray and bake for 15 minutes to be crispy. Transfer to a wire rack to cool before serving. Serve with sugar-free tomato dip.

Nutrition Info:
- Per Servings 3g Carbs, 5g Protein, 19g Fat, 210 Calories

Tofu Stuffed Peppers

Servings: 8 | Cooking Time: 10 Minutes

Ingredients:
- 1 package firm tofu, crumbled
- 1 onion, finely chopped
- ½ teaspoon turmeric powder
- 1 teaspoon coriander powder
- 8 banana peppers, top-end sliced and seeded
- Salt and pepper to taste
- 3 tablespoons oil

Directions:

1. Preheat oven to 400oF.
2. In a mixing bowl, combine the tofu, onion, coconut oil, turmeric powder, red chili powder, coriander powder, and salt. Mix until well-combined.
3. Scoop the tofu mixture into the hollows of the banana peppers.
4. Place the stuffed peppers in one layer in a lightly greased baking sheet.
5. Cook for 10 minutes.
6. Serve and enjoy.

Nutrition Info:
- Per Servings 4.1g Carbs, 1.2g Protein, 15.6g Fat, 187 Calories

Onion Cheese Muffins

Servings: 6 | Cooking Time: 20 Minutes

Ingredients:
- ¼ cup Colby jack cheese, shredded
- ¼ cup shallots, minced
- 1 cup almond flour
- 1 egg
- 3 tbsp sour cream
- ½ tsp salt
- 3 tbsp melted butter or oil

Directions:
1. Line 6 muffin tins with 6 muffin liners. Set aside and preheat oven to 350oF.
2. In a bowl, stir the dry and wet ingredients alternately. Mix well using a spatula until the consistency of the mixture becomes even.
3. Scoop a spoonful of the batter to the prepared muffin tins.
4. Bake for 20 minutes in the oven until golden brown.
5. Serve and enjoy.

Nutrition Info:
- Per Servings 4.6g Carbs, 6.3g Protein, 17.4g Fat, 193 Calories

Shrimp Fra Diavolo

Servings: 3 | Cooking Time: 5 Minutes

Ingredients:
- 3 tablespoons butter
- 1 onion, diced
- 5 cloves of garlic, minced
- 1 teaspoon red pepper flakes
- ¼ pound shrimps, shelled
- 2 tablespoons olive oil
- Salt and pepper to taste

Directions:
1. Heat the butter and the olive oil in a skillet and sauté the onion and garlic until fragrant.
2. Stir in the red pepper flakes and shrimps. Season with salt and pepper to taste.
3. Stir for 3 minutes.
4. Serve and enjoy.

Nutrition Info:
- Per Servings 4.5g Carbs, 21.0g Protein, 32.1g Fat, 388 Calories

Roasted Stuffed Piquillo Peppers

Servings: 8 | Cooking Time: 20 Minutes

Ingredients:
- 8 canned roasted piquillo peppers
- 1 tbsp olive oil
- 3 slices prosciutto, cut into thin slices
- 1 tbsp balsamic vinegar
- Filling:

- 8 ounces goat cheese
- 3 tbsp heavy cream
- 3 tbsp chopped parsley
- ½ tsp minced garlic
- 1 tbsp olive oil
- 1 tbsp chopped mint

Directions:
1. Mix all filling ingredients in a bowl. Place in a freezer bag, press down and squeeze, and cut off the bottom. Drain and deseed the peppers. Squeeze about 2 tbsp of the filling into each pepper.
2. Wrap a prosciutto slice onto each pepper. Secure with toothpicks. Arrange them on a serving platter. Sprinkle the olive oil and vinegar over.

Nutrition Info:
- Per Servings 2.5g Carbs, 6g Protein, 11g Fat, 132 Calories

Apricot And Soy Nut Trail Mix

Servings: 20 | Cooking Time: 10 Minutes

Ingredients:
- ¼ cup dried apricots, chopped
- 1 cup pumpkin seeds
- ½ cup roasted cashew nuts
- 1 cup roasted, shelled pistachios
- Salt to taste
- 3 tbsp MCT oil or coconut oil

Directions:
1. In a medium mixing bowl, place all ingredients.
2. Thoroughly combine.
3. Bake in the oven for 10 minutes at 3750F.
4. In 20 small zip-top bags, get ¼ cup of the mixture and place in each bag.
5. One zip-top bag is equal to one serving.
6. If properly stored, this can last up to two weeks.

Nutrition Info:
- Per Servings 4.6g Carbs, 5.2g Protein, 10.75g Fat, 129 Calories

Zucchini Gratin With Feta Cheese

Servings: 6 | Cooking Time: 65 Minutes

Ingredients:
- Cooking spray
- 2 lb zucchinis, sliced
- 2 red bell peppers, seeded and sliced
- Salt and black pepper to taste
- 1 ½ cups crumbled feta cheese
- ⅓ cup crumbled feta cheese for topping
- 2 tbsp butter
- ¼ tsp xanthan gum
- ½ cup heavy whipping cream

Directions:
1. Preheat oven to 370°F. Place the sliced zucchinis in a colander over the sink, sprinkle with salt and let sit for 20 minutes.

Transfer to paper towels to drain the excess liquid.

2. Grease a baking dish with cooking spray and make a layer of zucchini and bell peppers in the dish overlapping one on another. Season with black pepper, and sprinkle with some feta cheese. Repeat the layering process a second time.

3. Combine the butter, xanthan gum, and whipping cream in a microwave dish for 2 minutes, stir to mix completely, and pour over the vegetables. Top with remaining feta cheese.

4. Bake the gratin for 45 minutes to be golden brown on top. Cut out slices and serve with kale salad.

Nutrition Info:
- Per Servings 4g Carbs, 14g Protein, 21g Fat, 264 Calories

Balsamic Zucchini

Servings: 4 | Cooking Time: 20 Minutes

Ingredients:
- 3 medium zucchinis, cut into thin slices
- 1/2 cup chopped sweet onion
- 1/2 teaspoon dried rosemary, crushed
- 2 tablespoons balsamic vinegar
- 1/3 cup crumbled feta cheese
- 1/2 teaspoon salt
- 1/4 teaspoon pepper
- 4 tablespoon olive oil

Directions:
1. In a large skillet, heat oil over medium-high heat; sauté zucchini and onion until crisp-tender, 6-8 minutes. Stir in seasonings. Add vinegar; cook and stir 2 minutes. Top with cheese.

Nutrition Info:
- Per Servings 5g Carbs, 4g Protein, 16g Fat, 175 Calories

Party Bacon And Pistachio Balls

Servings: 8 | Cooking Time: 45 Minutes

Ingredients:
- 8 bacon slices, cooked and chopped
- 8 ounces Liverwurst
- ¼ cup chopped pistachios
- 1 tsp Dijon mustard
- 6 ounces cream cheese

Directions:
1. Combine the liverwurst and pistachios in the bowl of your food processor. Pulse until smooth. Whisk the cream cheese and mustard in another bowl. Make 12 balls out of the liverwurst mixture.

2. Make a thin cream cheese layer over. Coat with bacon, arrange on a plate and chill for 30 minutes.

Nutrition Info:
- Per Servings 1.5g Carbs, 7g Protein, 12g Fat, 145 Calories

Garlic Flavored Kale Taters

Servings: 4 | Cooking Time: 20 Minutes

Ingredients:
- 4 cups kale, rinsed and chopped
- 2 cups cauliflower florets, finely chopped
- 2 tbsp almond milk
- 1 clove of garlic, minced
- 3 tablespoons oil
- 1/8 teaspoon black pepper
- cooking spray

Directions:
1. Heat oil in a large skillet and sauté the garlic for 2 minutes. Add the kale until it wilts. Transfer to a large bowl.

2. Add the almond milk. Season with pepper to taste.

3. Evenly divide into 4 and form patties.

4. Lightly grease a baking pan with cooking spray. Place patties on pan. Place pan on the top rack of the oven and broil on low for 6 minutes. Turnover patties and cook for another 4 minutes.

5. Serve and enjoy.

Nutrition Info:
- Per Servings 5g Carbs, 2g Protein, 11g Fat, 117 Calories

Cheese-jalapeno Mushrooms

Servings: 8 | Cooking Time: 20 Mins

Ingredients:
- 2 slices bacon
- 1 package cream cheese, softened; low-carb
- 3 tablespoons shredded Cheddar cheese
- 1 jalapeno pepper, ribs and seeds removed, finely chopped
- 8 mushrooms, stems removed and chopped and caps reserved; keto-friendly
- Salt and pepper to taste
- Cooking spray

Directions:
1. Preheat the oven to 400 degrees F.

2. In a large bowl, combine bacon, cream cheese, cheese, jalapenos, salt and pepper. Mix well.

3. Spoon the bacon filling into each mushroom cap. Then transfer the stuffed mushroom caps to a baking dish or sheet sprayed with cooking spray.

4. Bake until the mushroom caps are cooked, about 15-20 minutes.

5. Serve and enjoy.

Nutrition Info:
- Per Servings 2.5g Carbs, 6.1g Protein, 13.4g Fat, 151 Calories

Fat Burger Bombs

Servings: 6 | Cooking Time: 20 Minutes

Ingredients:

- 12 slices uncured bacon, chopped
- 1 cup almond flour
- 2 eggs, beaten
- ½ pound ground beef
- 3 tablespoons olive oil
- Salt and pepper to taste

Directions:

1. In a mixing bowl, combine all ingredients except for the olive oil.
2. Use your hands to form small balls with the mixture. Place in a baking sheet and allow it to set in the fridge for at least 2 hours.
3. Once 2 hours is nearly up, preheat oven to 400oF.
4. Place meatballs in a single layer in a baking sheet and brush the meatballs with olive oil on all sides.
5. Cook for 20 minutes.

Nutrition Info:

- Per Servings 1.9g Carbs, 19.1g Protein, 40.6g Fat, 448 Calories

Buttered Broccoli

Servings: 6 | Cooking Time: 10 Minutes

Ingredients:

- 1 broccoli head, florets only
- Salt and black pepper to taste
- ¼ cup butter

Directions:

1. Place the broccoli in a pot filled with salted water and bring to a boil. Cook for about 3 minutes.
2. Melt the butter in a microwave. Drain the broccoli and transfer to a plate. Drizzle the butter over and season with some salt and pepper.

Nutrition Info:

- Per Servings 5.5g Carbs, 3.9g Protein, 7.8g Fat, 114 Calories

Simple Tender Crisp Cauli-bites

Servings: 3 | Cooking Time: 10 Minutes

Ingredients:

- 2 cups cauliflower florets
- 2 clove garlic minced
- 4 tablespoons olive oil
- ¼ tsp salt
- ½ tsp pepper

Directions:

1. In a small bowl, mix well olive oil salt, pepper, and garlic.
2. Place cauliflower florets on a baking pan. Drizzle with seasoned oil and toss well to coat.
3. Evenly spread in a single layer and place a pan on the top rack of the oven.

4. Broil on low for 5 minutes. Turnover florets and return to the oven.
5. Continue cooking for another 5 minutes.
6. Serve and enjoy.

Nutrition Info:

- Per Servings 4.9g Carbs, 1.7g Protein, 18g Fat, 183 Calories

Spicy Chicken Cucumber Bites

Servings: 6 | Cooking Time: 5 Minutes

Ingredients:

- 2 cucumbers, sliced with a 3-inch thickness
- 2 cups small dices leftover chicken
- ¼ jalapeño pepper, seeded and minced
- 1 tbsp Dijon mustard
- ⅓ cup mayonnaise
- Salt and black pepper to taste

Directions:

1. Cut mid-level holes in cucumber slices with a knife and set aside. Combine chicken, jalapeno pepper, mustard, mayonnaise, salt, and black pepper to be evenly mixed. Fill cucumber holes with chicken mixture and serve.

Nutrition Info:

- Per Servings 0g Carbs, 10g Protein, 14g Fat, 170 Calories

Roasted String Beans, Mushrooms & Tomato Plate

Servings: 4 | Cooking Time: 32 Minutes

Ingredients:

- 2 cups strings beans, cut in halves
- 1 lb cremini mushrooms, quartered
- 3 tomatoes, quartered
- 2 cloves garlic, minced
- 3 tbsp olive oil
- 3 shallots, julienned
- ½ tsp dried thyme
- Salt and black pepper to season

Directions:

1. Preheat oven to 450ºF. In a bowl, mix the strings beans, mushrooms, tomatoes, garlic, olive oil, shallots, thyme, salt, and pepper. Pour the vegetables in a baking sheet and spread them all around.
2. Place the baking sheet in the oven and bake the veggies for 20 to 25 minutes.

Nutrition Info:

- Per Servings 6g Carbs, 6g Protein, 2g Fat, 121 Calories

Keto "cornbread"

Servings: 8 | Cooking Time: 30 Minutes

Ingredients:

- 1 ¼ cups coconut milk
- 4 eggs, beaten
- 4 tbsp baking powder
- ½ cup almond meal
- 3 tablespoons olive oil

Directions:

1. Prepare 8 x 8-inch baking dish or a black iron skillet then add shortening.
2. Put the baking dish or skillet inside the oven on 425oF and leave there for 10 minutes.
3. In a bowl, add coconut milk and eggs then mix well. Stir in the rest of the ingredients.
4. Once all ingredients are mixed, pour the mixture into the heated skillet.
5. Then cook for 15 to 20 minutes in the oven until golden brown.

Nutrition Info:

- Per Servings 2.6g Carbs, 5.4g Protein, 18.9g Fat, 196 Calories

Cheesy Lettuce Rolls

Servings: 6 | Cooking Time: 10 Minutes

Ingredients:

- ½ pound gouda cheese, grated
- ½ pound feta cheese, crumbled
- 1 tsp taco seasoning mix
- 2 tbsp olive oil
- 1 ½ cups guacamole
- 1 cup buttermilk
- A head lettuce

Directions:

1. Mix both types of cheese with taco seasoning mix. Set pan over medium heat and warm olive oil. Spread the shredded cheese mixture all over the pan. Fry for 5 minutes, turning once.
2. Arrange some of the cheese mixture on each lettuce leaf, top with buttermilk and guacamole, then roll up, folding in the ends to secure and serve.

Nutrition Info:

- Per Servings 4.9g Carbs, 19.5g Protein, 30g Fat, 370 Calories

Pecorino-mushroom Balls

Servings: 4 | Cooking Time: 20 Minutes

Ingredients:

- 2 tbsp butter, softened
- 2 garlic cloves, minced
- 2 cups portobello mushrooms, chopped
- 4 tbsp blanched almond flour
- 4 tbsp ground flax seeds
- 4 tbsp hemp seeds
- 4 tbsp sunflower seeds
- 1 tbsp cajun seasonings
- 1 tsp mustard
- 2 eggs, whisked
- ½ cup pecorino cheese

Directions:

1. Set a pan over medium-high heat and warm 1 tablespoon of butter. Add in mushrooms and garlic and sauté until there is no more water in mushrooms.
2. Place in pecorino cheese, almond flour, hemp seeds, mustard, eggs, sunflower seeds, flax seeds, and Cajun seasonings. Create 4 burgers from the mixture.
3. In a pan, warm the remaining butter; fry the burgers for 7 minutes. Flip them over with a wide spatula and cook for 6 more minutes. Serve while warm.

Nutrition Info:

- Per Servings 7.7g Carbs, 16.8g Protein, 30g Fat, 370 Calories

Spinach And Ricotta Gnocchi

Servings: 4 | Cooking Time: 13 Minutes

Ingredients:

- 3 cups chopped spinach
- 1 cup ricotta cheese
- 1 cup Parmesan cheese , grated
- ¼ tsp nutmeg powder
- 1 egg, cracked into a bowl
- Salt and black pepper
- Almond flour, on standby
- 2 ½ cups water
- 2 tbsp butter

Directions:

1. To a bowl, add the ricotta cheese, half of the parmesan cheese, egg, nutmeg powder, salt, spinach, almond flour, and pepper. Mix well. Make quenelles of the mixture using 2 tbsp and set aside.
2. Bring the water to boil over high heat on a stovetop, about 5 minutes. Place one gnocchi onto the water, if it breaks apart; add some more flour to the other gnocchi to firm it up.
3. Put the remaining gnocchi in the water to poach and rise to the top, about 2 minutes. Remove the gnocchi with a perforated spoon to a serving plate.
4. Melt the butter in a microwave and pour over the gnocchi. Sprinkle with the remaining parmesan cheese and serve with a green salad.

Nutrition Info:

- Per Servings 4.1g Carbs, 6.5g Protein, 8.3g Fat, 125 Calories

Spicy Devilled Eggs With Herbs

Servings: 4 | Cooking Time: 30 Minutes

Ingredients:
- 12 large eggs
- 1 ½ cups water
- 6 tbsp mayonnaise
- Salt and chili pepper to taste
- 1 tsp mixed dried herbs
- ½ tsp sugar-free Worcestershire sauce
- ¼ tsp Dijon mustard
- A pinch of sweet paprika
- Chopped parsley to garnish
- Ice water Bath

Directions:

1. Pour the water into a saucepan, add the eggs, and bring to boil on high heat for 10 minutes. Cut the eggs in half lengthways and remove the yolks into a medium bowl. Use a fork to crush the yolks.

2. Add the mayonnaise, salt, chili pepper, dried herbs, Worcestershire sauce, mustard, and paprika. Mix together until a smooth paste has formed. Then, spoon the mixture into the piping bag and fill the egg white holes with it. Garnish with the chopped parsley and serve immediately.

Nutrition Info:
- Per Servings 0.4g Carbs, 6.7g Protein, 9.3g Fat, 112 Calories

French Fried Butternut Squash

Servings: 6 | Cooking Time: 20 Minutes

Ingredients:
- 1 medium butternut squash
- 1 tablespoon chopped fresh thyme
- 1 tablespoon chopped fresh rosemary
- 4 tablespoons olive oil
- 1/2 teaspoon salt
- Cooking spray

Directions:

1. Heat oven to 425oF. Lightly coat a baking sheet with cooking spray.

2. Peel skin from butternut squash and cut into even sticks, about 1/2-inch-wide and 3 inches long.

3. In a medium bowl, combine the squash, oil, thyme, rosemary, and salt; mix until the squash is evenly coated.

4. Spread onto the baking sheet and roast for 10 minutes.

5. Remove the baking sheet from the oven and shake to loosen the squash.

6. Return to oven and continue to roast for 10 minutes or until golden brown.

7. Serve and enjoy.

Nutrition Info:
- Per Servings 1g Carbs, 1g Protein, 9g Fat, 86 Calories

Crispy Keto Pork Bites

Servings: 3 | Cooking Time: 30 Minutes

Ingredients:
- ½ pork belly, sliced to thin strips
- 1 tablespoon butter
- 1 onion, diced
- 4 tablespoons coconut cream
- Salt and pepper to taste

Directions:

1. Place all ingredients in a mixing bowl and allow to marinate in the fridge for 2 hours.

2. When 2 hours is nearly up, preheat oven to 400oF and lightly grease a cookie sheet with cooking spray.

3. Place the pork strips in an even layer on the cookie sheet.

4. Roast for 30 minutes and turnover halfway through cooking.

Nutrition Info:
- Per Servings 1.9g Carbs, 19.1g Protein, 40.6g Fat, 448 Calories

Herb Cheese Sticks

Servings: 4 | Cooking Time: 15 Minutes

Ingredients:
- 1 cup pork rinds, crushed
- 1 tbsp Italian herb mix
- 1 egg
- 1 lb swiss cheese, cut into sticks
- Cooking spray

Directions:

1. Preheat oven to 350ºF and line a baking sheet with parchment paper. Combine pork rinds and herb mix in a bowl to be evenly mixed and beat the egg in another bowl. Coat the cheese sticks in egg and then generously dredge in pork rind mixture. Arrange on baking sheet. Bake for 4 to 5 minutes, take out after, let cool for 2 minutes, and serve with marinara sauce.

Nutrition Info:
- Per Servings 0g Carbs, 8g Protein, 17.3g Fat, 188 Calories

Italian-style Chicken Wraps

Servings: 8 | Cooking Time: 20 Minutes

Ingredients:
- ¼ tsp garlic powder
- 8 ounces provolone cheese
- 8 raw chicken tenders
- Salt and black pepper to taste
- 8 prosciutto slices

Directions:

1. Pound the chicken until half an inch thick. Season with salt, black pepper, and garlic powder. Cut the provolone cheese into 8 strips. Place a slice of prosciutto on a flat surface. Place one chicken tender on top. Top with a provolone strip.

2. Roll the chicken and secure with previously soaked skewers. Grill the wraps for 3 minutes per side.

Nutrition Info:
- Per Servings 0.7g Carbs, 17g Protein, 10g Fat, 174 Calories

Devilled Eggs With Sriracha Mayo

Servings: 4 | Cooking Time: 15 Minutes

Ingredients:

- 8 large eggs
- 3 cups water
- Ice water bath
- 3 tbsp sriracha sauce
- 4 tbsp mayonnaise
- Salt to taste
- ¼ tsp smoked paprika

Directions:

1. Bring eggs to boil in salted water in a pot over high heat, and then reduce the heat to simmer for 10 minutes. Transfer eggs to an ice water bath, let cool completely and peel the shells.

2. Slice the eggs in half height wise and empty the yolks into a bowl. Smash with a fork and mix in sriracha sauce, mayonnaise, and half of the paprika until smooth.

3. Spoon filling into a piping bag with a round nozzle and fill the egg whites to be slightly above the brim. Garnish with remaining paprika and serve immediately.

Nutrition Info:

- Per Servings 1g Carbs, 4g Protein, 19g Fat, 195 Calories

Keto-approved Trail Mix

Servings: 8 | Cooking Time: 3 Minutes

Ingredients:

- ¼ cup salted pumpkin seeds
- ½ cup slivered almonds
- ¾ cup roasted pecan halves
- ¼ cup unsweetened cranberries
- ¾ cup toasted coconut flakes

Directions:

1. In a skillet, place almonds and pecans. Heat for 2-3 minutes and let it cool.

2. Once cooled, in a large resealable plastic bag, combine all ingredients.

3. Seal and shake vigorously to mix.

4. Serve and enjoy.

Nutrition Info:

- Per Servings 8.0g Carbs, 4.4g Protein, 14.4g Fat, 184 Calories

Cheesy Chicken Fritters With Dill Dip

Servings: 4 | Cooking Time: 40 Minutes + Cooling Time

Ingredients:

- 1 lb chicken breasts, thinly sliced
- 1 ¼ cup mayonnaise
- ¼ cup coconut flour
- 2 eggs
- Salt and black pepper to taste
- 1 cup grated mozzarella cheese
- 4 tbsp chopped dill
- 3 tbsp olive oil
- 1 cup sour cream
- 1 tsp garlic powder
- 1 tbsp chopped parsley
- 2 tbsp finely chopped onion

Directions:

1. In a bowl, mix 1 cup of the mayonnaise, 3 tbsp of dill, sour cream, garlic powder, onion, and salt. Cover the bowl with plastic wrap and refrigerate for 30 minutes.

2. Mix the chicken, remaining mayonnaise, coconut flour, eggs, salt, pepper, mozzarella, and remaining dill, in a bowl. Cover the bowl with plastic wrap and refrigerate it for 2 hours. After the marinating time is over, remove from the fridge.

3. Place a skillet over medium fire and heat the olive oil. Fetch 2 tablespoons of chicken mixture into the skillet, use the back of a spatula to flatten the top. Cook for 4 minutes, flip, and fry for 4 more.

4. Remove onto a wire rack and repeat the cooking process until the batter is finished, adding more oil as needed. Garnish the fritters with parsley and serve with dill dip.

Nutrition Info:

- Per Servings 0.8g Carbs, 12g Protein, 7g Fat, 151 Calories

Coconut Ginger Macaroons

Servings: 6 | Cooking Time: 20 Minutes

Ingredients:

- 2 fingers ginger root, peeled and pureed
- 6 egg whites
- 1 cup finely shredded coconut
- ¼ cup swerve
- A pinch of chili powder
- 1 cup water
- Angel hair chili to garnish

Directions:

1. Preheat the oven to 350°F and line a baking sheet with parchment paper. Set aside.

2. Then, in a heatproof bowl, whisk the ginger, egg whites, shredded coconut, swerve, and chili powder.

3. Bring the water to boil in a pot over medium heat and place the heatproof bowl on the pot. Then, continue whisking the mixture until it is glossy, about 4 minutes. Do not let the bowl touch the water or be too hot so that the eggs don't cook.

4. Spoon the mixture into the piping bag after and pipe out 40 to 50 little mounds on the lined baking sheet. Bake the macaroons in the middle part of the oven for 15 minutes.

5. Once they are ready, transfer them to a wire rack, garnish them with the angel hair chili, and serve.

Nutrition Info:

- Per Servings 0.3g Carbs, 6.8g Protein, 3.5g Fat, 97 Calories

Vegan, Vegetable & Meatless Recipes

Vegan, Vegetable & Meatless Recipes

Vegetable Tempura

Servings: 4 | Cooking Time: 17 Minutes

Ingredients:
- ½ cup coconut flour + extra for dredging
- Salt and black pepper to taste
- 3 egg yolks
- 2 red bell peppers, cut into strips
- 1 squash, peeled and cut into strips
- 1 broccoli, cut into florets
- 1 cup Chilled water
- Olive oil for frying
- Lemon wedges to serve
- Sugar-free soy sauce to serve

Directions:
1. In a deep frying pan or wok, heat the olive oil over medium heat. Beat the eggs lightly with ½ cup of coconut flour and water. The mixture should be lumpy. Dredge the vegetables lightly in some flour, shake off the excess flour, dip it in the batter, and then into the hot oil.
2. Fry in batches for 1 minute each, not more, and remove with a perforated spoon onto a wire rack. Sprinkle with salt and pepper and serve with the lemon wedges and soy sauce.

Nutrition Info:
- Per Servings 0.9g Carbs, 3g Protein, 17g Fat, 218 Calories

Creamy Cucumber Avocado Soup

Servings: 4 | Cooking Time: 15 Minutes

Ingredients:
- 4 large cucumbers, seeded, chopped
- 1 large avocado, peeled and pitted
- Salt and black pepper to taste
- 2 cups water
- 1 tbsp cilantro, chopped
- 3 tbsp olive oil
- 2 limes, juiced
- 2 tsp minced garlic
- 2 tomatoes, evenly chopped
- 1 chopped avocado for garnish

Directions:
1. Pour the cucumbers, avocado halves, salt, pepper, olive oil, lime juice, cilantro, water, and garlic in the food processor. Puree the ingredients for 2 minutes or until smooth.
2. Pour the mixture in a bowl and top with avocado and tomatoes. Serve chilled with zero-carb bread.

Nutrition Info:
- Per Servings 4.1g Carbs, 3.7g Protein, 7.4g Fat, 170 Calories

Cauliflower & Mushrooms Stuffed Peppers

Servings: 4 | Cooking Time: 40 Minutes

Ingredients:
- 1 head cauliflower
- 4 bell peppers
- 1 cup mushrooms, sliced
- 1 ½ tbsp oil
- 1 onion, chopped
- 1 cup celery, chopped
- 1 garlic cloves, minced
- 1 tsp chili powder
- 2 tomatoes, pureed
- Sea salt and pepper, to taste

Directions:
1. To prepare cauliflower rice, grate the cauliflower into rice-size. Set in a kitchen towel to attract and remove any excess moisture. Set oven to 360ºF.
2. Lightly oil a casserole dish. Chop off bell pepper tops, do away with the seeds and core. Line a baking pan with a parchment paper and roast the peppers for 18 minutes until the skin starts to brown.
3. Warm the oil over medium heat. Add in garlic, celery, and onion and sauté until soft and translucent. Stir in chili powder, mushrooms, and cauliflower rice. Cook for 6 minutes until the cauliflower rice becomes tender. Split the cauliflower mixture among the bell peppers. Set in the casserole dish. Combine pepper, salt, and tomatoes. Top the peppers with the tomato mixture. Bake for 10 minutes.

Nutrition Info:
- Per Servings 8.4g Carbs, 1.6g Protein, 4.8g Fat, 77 Calories

Easy Vanilla Granola

Servings: 6 | Cooking Time: 1 Hour

Ingredients:
- ½ cup hazelnuts, chopped
- 1 cup walnuts, chopped
- ⅓ cup flax meal
- ⅓ cup coconut milk
- ⅓ cup poppy seeds
- ⅓ cup pumpkin seeds
- 8 drops stevia
- ⅓ cup coconut oil, melted
- 1 ½ tsp vanilla paste
- 1 tsp ground cloves
- 1 tsp grated nutmeg
- 1 tsp lemon zest
- ⅓ cup water

Directions:

1. Set oven to 300°F. Line a parchment paper to a baking sheet. Combine all ingredients. Spread the mixture onto the baking sheet in an even layer. Bake for 55 minutes, as you stir at intervals of 15 minutes. Let cool at room temperature.

Nutrition Info:

• Per Servings 5.1g Carbs, 9.3g Protein, 44.9g Fat, 449 Calories

Grilled Spicy Eggplant

Servings: 2 | Cooking Time: 20 Minutes

Ingredients:

• 2 small eggplants, cut into 1/2-inch slices
• 1/4 cup olive oil
• 2 tablespoons lime juice
• 3 teaspoons Cajun seasoning
• Salt and pepper to taste

Directions:

1. Brush eggplant slices with oil. Drizzle with lime juice; sprinkle with Cajun seasoning. Let stand for 5 minutes.
2. Grill eggplant, covered, over medium heat or broil 4 minutes. from heat until tender, 4-5 minutes per side.
3. Season with pepper and salt to taste.
4. Serve and enjoy.

Nutrition Info:

• Per Servings 7g Carbs, 5g Protein, 28g Fat, 350 Calories

Roasted Asparagus With Spicy Eggplant Dip

Servings: 6 | Cooking Time: 35 Minutes

Ingredients:

• 1 ½ pounds asparagus spears, trimmed
• ¼ cup olive oil
• 1 tsp sea salt
• ½ tsp black pepper, to taste
• ½ tsp paprika
• For Eggplant Dip
• ¾ pound eggplants
• 2 tsp olive oil
• ½ cup scallions, chopped
• 2 cloves garlic, minced
• 1 tbsp fresh lemon juice
• ½ tsp chili pepper
• Salt and black pepper, to taste
• ¼ cup fresh cilantro, chopped

Directions:

1. Set the oven to 390°F. Line a parchment paper to a baking sheet. Add asparagus spears to the baking sheet. Toss with oil, paprika, pepper, and salt. Bake until cooked through for 9 minutes.
2. Set the oven to 425 °F. Add eggplants on a lined cookie sheet. Place under the broiler for about 20 minutes; let the eggplants to cool. Peel them and discard the stems. Place a frying pan over medium-high heat and warm olive oil. Add in garlic and onion and sauté until tender.
3. Using a food processor, pulse together black pepper, roasted eggplants, salt, lemon juice, scallion mixture, and chili pepper to mix evenly. Add cilantro for garnishing. Serve alongside roasted asparagus spears.

Nutrition Info:

• Per Servings 9g Carbs, 3.6g Protein, 12.1g Fat, 149 Calories

Spicy Cauliflower Steaks With Steamed Green Beans

Servings: 4 | Cooking Time: 20 Minutes

Ingredients:

• 2 heads cauliflower, sliced lengthwise into 'steaks'
• ¼ cup olive oil
• ¼ cup chili sauce
• 2 tsp erythritol
• Salt and black pepper to taste
• 2 shallots, diced
• 1 bunch green beans, trimmed
• 2 tbsp fresh lemon juice
• 1 cup water
• Dried parsley to garnish

Directions:

1. In a bowl, mix the olive oil, chili sauce, and erythritol. Brush the cauliflower with the mixture. Place them on the grill, close the lid, and grill for 6 minutes. Flip the cauliflower, cook further for 6 minutes.
2. Bring the water to boil over high heat, place the green beans in a sieve and set over the steam from the boiling water. Cover with a clean napkin to keep the steam trapped in the sieve. Cook for 6 minutes. After, remove to a bowl and toss with lemon juice.
3. Remove the grilled caulis to a plate; sprinkle with salt, pepper, shallots, and parsley. Serve with the steamed green beans.

Nutrition Info:

• Per Servings 4g Carbs, 2g Protein, 9g Fat, 118 Calories

Herbed Portobello Mushrooms

Servings: 2 | Cooking Time: 10 Minutes

Ingredients:

• 2 Portobello mushrooms, stemmed and wiped clean
• 1 tsp minced garlic
• ¼ tsp dried rosemary
• 1 tablespoon balsamic vinegar
• ¼ cup grated provolone cheese
• 4 tablespoons olive oil
• Salt and pepper to taste

Directions:

1. In an oven, position rack 4-inches away from the top and preheat broiler.
2. Prepare a baking dish by spraying with cooking spray lightly.

3. Stemless, place mushroom gill side up.
4. Mix well garlic, rosemary, balsamic vinegar, and olive oil in a small bowl. Season with salt and pepper to taste.
5. Drizzle over mushrooms equally.
6. Marinate for at least 5 minutes before popping into the oven and broiling for 4 minutes per side or until tender.
7. Once cooked, remove from oven, sprinkle cheese, return to broiler and broil for a minute or two or until cheese melts.
8. Remove from oven and serve right away.

Nutrition Info:
- Per Servings 21.5g Carbs, 8.6g Protein, 5.1g Fat, 168 Calories

Stuffed Portobello Mushrooms

Servings: 2 | Cooking Time: 30 Minutes

Ingredients:
- 4 portobello mushrooms, stems removed
- 2 tbsp olive oil
- 2 cups lettuce
- 1 cup crumbled blue cheese

Directions:
1. Preheat the oven to 350ºF. Fill the mushrooms with blue cheese and place on a lined baking sheet; bake for 20 minutes. Serve with lettuce drizzled with olive oil.

Nutrition Info:
- Per Servings 5.5g Carbs, 14g Protein, 29g Fat, 334 Calories

Parmesan Roasted Cabbage

Servings: 4 | Cooking Time: 25 Minutes

Ingredients:
- Cooking spray
- 1 large head green cabbage
- 4 tbsp melted butter
- 1 tsp garlic powder
- Salt and black pepper to taste
- 1 cup grated Parmesan cheese
- Grated Parmesan cheese for topping
- 1 tbsp chopped parsley to garnish

Directions:
1. Preheat oven to 400ºF, line a baking sheet with foil, and grease with cooking spray.
2. Stand the cabbage and run a knife from the top to bottom to cut the cabbage into wedges. Remove stems and wilted leaves. Mix the butter, garlic, salt, and black pepper until evenly combined.
3. Brush the mixture on all sides of the cabbage wedges and sprinkle with parmesan cheese.
4. Place on the baking sheet, and bake for 20 minutes to soften the cabbage and melt the cheese. Remove the cabbages when golden brown, plate and sprinkle with extra cheese and parsley. Serve warm with pan-glazed tofu.

Nutrition Info:
- Per Servings 4g Carbs, 17.5g Protein, 19.3g Fat, 268 Calories

Mushroom & Jalapeño Stew

Servings: 4 | Cooking Time: 50 Minutes

Ingredients:
- 2 tsp olive oil
- 1 cup leeks, chopped
- 1 garlic clove, minced
- ½ cup celery, chopped
- ½ cup carrot, chopped
- 1 green bell pepper, chopped
- 1 jalapeño pepper, chopped
- 2 ½ cups mushrooms, sliced
- 1 ½ cups vegetable stock
- 2 tomatoes, chopped
- 2 thyme sprigs, chopped
- 1 rosemary sprig, chopped
- 2 bay leaves
- ½ tsp salt
- ¼ tsp ground black pepper
- 2 tbsp vinegar

Directions:
1. Set a pot over medium-high heat and warm oil. Add in garlic and leeks and sauté until soft and translucent. Add in the pepper, celery, mushrooms, and carrots.
2. Cook as you stir for 12 minutes; stir in a splash of vegetable stock to ensure there is no sticking. Stir in the rest of the ingredients. Set heat to medium; allow to simmer for 25 to 35 minutes or until cooked through. Divide into individual bowls and serve while warm.

Nutrition Info:
- Per Servings 9g Carbs, 2.7g Protein, 2.7g Fat, 65 Calories

Mushroom & Cauliflower Bake

Servings: 4 | Cooking Time: 30 Minutes

Ingredients:
- Cooking spray
- 1 head cauliflower, cut into florets
- 8 ounces mushrooms, halved
- 2 garlic cloves, smashed
- 2 tomatoes, pureed
- ¼ cup coconut oil, melted
- 1 tsp chili paprika paste
- ¼ tsp marjoram
- ½ tsp curry powder
- Salt and black pepper, to taste

Directions:
1. Set oven to 390ºF. Apply a cooking spray to a baking dish. Lay mushrooms and cauliflower in the baking dish. Around the vegetables, scatter smashed garlic. Place in the pureed tomatoes. Sprinkle over melted coconut oil and place in chili paprika paste, curry, black pepper, salt, and marjoram. Roast for 25 minutes, turning once. Place in a serving plate and serve with green salad.

Nutrition Info:
- Per Servings 11.6g Carbs, 5g Protein, 6.7g Fat, 113 Calories

Walnut Tofu Sauté

Servings: 4 | Cooking Time: 15 Minutes

Ingredients:
- 1 tbsp olive oil
- 1 block firm tofu, cubed
- 1 tbsp tomato paste with garlic and onion
- 1 tbsp balsamic vinegar
- Pink salt and black pepper to taste
- ½ tsp mixed dried herbs
- 1 cup chopped raw walnuts

Directions:
1. Heat the oil in a skillet over medium heat and cook the tofu for 3 minutes while stirring to brown.
2. Mix the tomato paste with the vinegar and add to the tofu. Stir, season with salt and black pepper, and cook for another 4 minutes.
3. Add the herbs and walnuts. Stir and cook on low heat for 3 minutes to be fragrant. Spoon to a side of squash mash and a sweet berry sauce to serve.

Nutrition Info:
- Per Servings 4g Carbs, 18g Protein, 24g Fat, 320 Calories

Morning Granola

Servings: 8 | Cooking Time: 1 Hour

Ingredients:
- 1 tbsp coconut oil
- ⅓ cup almond flakes
- ½ cups almond milk
- 2 tbsp sugar
- 1/8 tsp salt
- 1 tsp lime zest
- 1/8 tsp nutmeg, grated
- ½ tsp ground cinnamon
- ½ cup pecans, chopped
- ½ cup almonds, slivered
- 2 tbsp pepitas
- 3 tbsp sunflower seeds
- ¼ cup flax seed

Directions:
1. Set a deep pan over medium-high heat and warm the coconut oil. Add almond flakes and toast for 1 to 2 minutes. Stir in the remaining ingredients. Set oven to 300ºF. Lay the mixture in an even layer onto a baking sheet lined with a parchment paper. Bake for 1 hour, making sure that you shake gently in intervals of 15 minutes. Serve alongside additional almond milk.

Nutrition Info:
- Per Servings 9.2g Carbs, 5.1g Protein, 24.3g Fat, 262 Calories

Zucchini Noodles

Servings: 6 | Cooking Time: 15 Mins

Ingredients:
- 2 cloves garlic, minced
- 2 medium zucchini, cut into noodles with a spiralizer
- 12 zucchini blossoms, pistils removed; cut into strips
- 6 fresh basil leaves, cut into strips, or to taste
- 4 tablespoons olive oil
- Salt to taste

Directions:
1. In a large skillet over low heat, cook garlic in olive oil for 10 minutes until slightly browned. Add in zucchini and zucchini blossoms, stir well.
2. Toss in green beans and season with salt to taste; sprinkle with basil and serve.

Nutrition Info:
- Per Servings 13.5g Carbs, 5.7g Protein, 28.1g Fat, 348 Calories

Brussels Sprouts With Tofu

Servings: 4 | Cooking Time: 20 Minutes

Ingredients:
- 2 tbsp olive oil
- 2 garlic cloves, minced
- ½ cup onion, chopped
- 10 ounces tofu, crumbled
- 2 tbsp water
- 2 tbsp soy sauce
- 1 tbsp tomato puree
- ½ pound Brussels sprouts, quartered
- Sea salt and black pepper, to taste

Directions:
1. Set a saucepan over medium-high heat and warm the oil. Add onion and garlic and cook until tender. Place in the soy sauce, water, and tofu. Cook for 5 minutes until the tofu starts to brown.
2. Add in brussels sprouts; apply pepper and salt for seasoning; reduce heat to low and cook for 13 minutes while stirring frequently. Serve while warm.

Nutrition Info:
- Per Servings 12.1g Carbs, 10.5g Protein, 11.7g Fat, 179 Calories

Scrambled Eggs With Mushrooms And Spinach

Servings: 2 | Cooking Time: 15 Minutes

Ingredients:
- 2 large eggs
- 1 teaspoon butter
- 1/2 cup thinly sliced fresh mushrooms
- 1/2 cup fresh baby spinach, chopped
- 2 tablespoons shredded provolone cheese
- 1/8 teaspoon salt
- 1/8 teaspoon pepper

Directions:

1. In a small bowl, whisk eggs, salt, and pepper until blended. In a small nonstick skillet, heat butter over medium-high heat. Add mushrooms; cook and stir 3-4 minutes or until tender. Add spinach; cook and stir until wilted. Reduce heat to medium.

2. Add egg mixture; cook and stir just until eggs are thickened and no liquid egg remains. Stir in cheese.

Nutrition Info:
- Per Servings 2g Carbs, 14g Protein, 11g Fat, 162 Calories

Zesty Frittata With Roasted Chilies

Servings: 4 | Cooking Time: 17 Minutes

Ingredients:
- 2 large green bell peppers, seeded, chopped
- 4 red and yellow chilies, roasted
- 2 tbsp red wine vinegar
- 1 knob butter, melted
- 8 sprigs parsley, chopped
- 8 eggs, cracked into a bowl
- 4 tbsp olive oil
- ½ cup grated Parmesan
- ¼ cup crumbled goat cheese
- 4 cloves garlic, minced
- 1 cup loosely filled salad leaves

Directions:

1. Preheat the oven to 400ºF. With a knife, seed the chilies, cut into long strips, and pour into a bowl.

2. Mix in the vinegar, butter, half of the parsley, half of the olive oil, and garlic; set aside. In another bowl, whisk the eggs with salt, pepper, bell peppers, parmesan, and the remaining parsley.

3. Now, heat the remaining oil in the cast iron over medium heat and pour the egg mixture along with half of the goat cheese. Let cook for 3 minutes and when it is near done, sprinkle the remaining goat cheese on it, and transfer the cast iron to the oven.

4. Bake the frittata for 4 more minutes, remove and drizzle with the chili oil. Garnish the frittata with salad greens and serve for lunch.

Nutrition Info:
- Per Servings 2.3g Carbs, 6.4g Protein, 10.3g Fat, 153 Calories

Roasted Brussels Sprouts With Sunflower Seeds

Servings: 6 | Cooking Time: 45 Minutes

Ingredients:
- Nonstick cooking spray
- 3 pounds brussels sprouts, halved
- ¼ cup olive oil
- Salt and ground black pepper, to taste
- 1 tsp sunflower seeds
- 2 tbsp fresh chives, chopped

Directions:

1. Set oven to 390ºF. Apply a nonstick cooking spray to a rimmed baking sheet. Arrange sprout halves on the baking sheet. Shake in black pepper, salt, sunflower seeds, and olive oil.

2. Roast for 40 minutes, until the cabbage becomes soft. Apply a garnish of fresh chopped chives.

Nutrition Info:
- Per Servings 8g Carbs, 2.1g Protein, 17g Fat, 186 Calories

Cremini Mushroom Stroganoff

Servings: 4 | Cooking Time: 15 Minutes

Ingredients:
- 3 tbsp butter
- 1 white onion, chopped
- 4 cups cremini mushrooms, cubed
- 2 cups water
- ½ cup heavy cream
- ½ cup grated Parmesan cheese
- 1 ½ tbsp dried mixed herbs
- Salt and black pepper to taste

Directions:

1. Melt the butter in a saucepan over medium heat, sauté the onion for 3 minutes until soft.

2. Stir in the mushrooms and cook until tender, about 3 minutes. Add the water, mix, and bring to boil for 4 minutes until the water reduces slightly.

3. Pour in the heavy cream and parmesan cheese. Stir to melt the cheese. Also, mix in the dried herbs. Season with salt and pepper, simmer for 40 seconds and turn the heat off.

4. Ladle stroganoff over a bed of spaghetti squash and serve.

Nutrition Info:
- Per Servings 1g Carbs, 5g Protein, 28g Fat, 284 Calories

Sautéed Celeriac With Tomato Sauce

Servings: 4 | Cooking Time: 20 Minutes

Ingredients:

- 2 tbsp olive oil
- 1 garlic clove, crushed
- 1 celeriac, sliced
- ¼ cup vegetable stock
- Sea salt and black pepper, to taste
- For the Sauce
- 2 tomatoes, halved
- 2 tbsp olive oil
- ½ cup onions, chopped
- 2 cloves garlic, minced
- 1 chili, minced
- 1 bunch fresh basil, chopped
- 1 tbsp fresh cilantro, chopped
- Salt and black pepper, to taste

Directions:

1. Set a pan over medium-high heat and warm olive oil. Add in garlic and sauté for 1 minute. Stir in celeriac slices, stock and cook until softened. Sprinkle with black pepper and salt; kill the heat. Brush olive oil to the tomato halves. Microwave for 15 minutes; get rid of any excess liquid.

2. Remove the cooked tomatoes to a food processor; add the rest of the ingredients for the sauce and puree to obtain the desired consistency. Serve the celeriac topped with tomato sauce.

Nutrition Info:

- Per Servings 3g Carbs, 0.9g Protein, 13.6g Fat, 135 Calories

Avocado And Tomato Burritos

Servings: 4 | Cooking Time: 5 Minutes

Ingredients:

- 2 cups cauli rice
- Water for sprinkling
- 6 zero carb flatbread
- 2 cups sour cream sauce
- 1 ½ cups tomato herb salsa
- 2 avocados, peeled, pitted, sliced

Directions:

1. Pour the cauli rice in a bowl, sprinkle with water, and soften in the microwave for 2 minutes.

2. On flatbread, spread the sour cream all over and distribute the salsa on top. Top with cauli rice and scatter the avocado evenly on top. Fold and tuck the burritos and cut into two.

Nutrition Info:

- Per Servings 6g Carbs, 8g Protein, 25g Fat, 303 Calories

Tasty Cauliflower Dip

Servings: 4 | Cooking Time: 10 Minutes

Ingredients:

- ¾ pound cauliflower, cut into florets
- ¼ cup olive oil
- Salt and black pepper, to taste
- 1 garlic clove, smashed
- 1 tbsp sesame paste
- 1 tbsp fresh lime juice
- ½ tsp garam masala

Directions:

1. Steam cauliflower until tender for 7 minutes in. Transfer to a blender and pulse until you attain a rice-like consistency.

2. Place in Garam Masala, oil, black paper, fresh lime juice, garlic, salt, and sesame paste. Blend the mixture until well combined. Decorate with some additional olive oil and serve. Otherwise, refrigerate until ready to use.

Nutrition Info:

- Per Servings 4.7g Carbs, 3.7g Protein, 8.2g Fat, 100 Calories

Classic Tangy Ratatouille

Servings: 6 | Cooking Time: 47 Minutes

Ingredients:

- 2 eggplants, chopped
- 3 zucchinis, chopped
- 2 red onions, diced
- 1 can tomatoes
- 2 red bell peppers, cut in chunks
- 1 yellow bell pepper, cut in chunks
- 3 cloves garlic, sliced
- ½ cup basil leaves, chop half
- 4 sprigs thyme
- 1 tbsp balsamic vinegar
- 2 tbsp olive oil
- ½ lemon, zested

Directions:

1. In a casserole pot, heat the olive oil and sauté the eggplants, zucchinis, and bell peppers over medium heat for 5 minutes. Spoon the veggies into a large bowl.

2. In the same pan, sauté garlic, onions, and thyme leaves for 5 minutes and return the cooked veggies to the pan along with the canned tomatoes, balsamic vinegar, chopped basil, salt, and pepper to taste. Stir and cover the pot, and cook the ingredients on low heat for 30 minutes.

3. Open the lid and stir in the remaining basil leaves, lemon zest, and adjust the seasoning. Turn the heat off. Plate the ratatouille and serve with some low carb crusted bread.

Nutrition Info:

- Per Servings 5.6g Carbs, 1.7g Protein, 12.1g Fat, 154 Calories

Creamy Vegetable Stew

Servings: 4 | Cooking Time: 32 Minutes

Ingredients:
- 2 tbsp ghee
- 1 tbsp onion garlic puree
- 4 medium carrots, peeled and chopped
- 1 large head cauliflower, cut into florets
- 2 cups green beans, halved
- Salt and black pepper to taste
- 1 cup water
- 1 ½ cups heavy cream

Directions:
1. Melt ghee in a saucepan over medium heat and sauté onion-garlic puree to be fragrant, 2 minutes.
2. Stir in carrots, cauliflower, and green beans, salt, and pepper, add the water, stir again, and cook the vegetables on low heat for 25 minutes to soften. Mix in the heavy cream to be incorporated, turn the heat off, and adjust the taste with salt and pepper. Serve the stew with almond flour bread.

Nutrition Info:
- Per Servings 6g Carbs, 8g Protein, 26.4g Fat, 310 Calories

Curried Tofu

Servings: 6 | Cooking Time: 15 Minutes

Ingredients:
- 2 cloves of garlic, minced
- 1 onion, cubed
- 12-ounce firm tofu, drained and cubed
- 1 teaspoon curry powder
- 1 tablespoon soy sauce
- ¼ teaspoon pepper
- 5 tablespoons olive oil

Directions:
1. Heat the oil in a skillet over medium flame.
2. Sauté the garlic and onion until fragrant.
3. Stir in the tofu and stir for 3 minutes.
4. Add the rest of the ingredients and adjust the water.
5. Close the lid and allow simmering for 10 minutes.
6. Serve and enjoy.

Nutrition Info:
- Per Servings 4.4g Carbs, 6.2g Protein, 14.1g Fat, 148 Calories

Keto Cauliflower Hash Browns

Servings: 4 | Cooking Time: 30 Mins

Ingredients:
- 1 lb cauliflower
- 3 eggs
- ½ yellow onion, grated
- 2 pinches pepper
- 4 oz. butter, for frying
- What you'll need from the store cupboard:

- 1 tsp salt

Directions:
1. Rinse, trim and grate the cauliflower using a food processor or grater.
2. In a large bowl, add the cauliflower onion and pepper, tossing evenly. Set aside for 5 to 10 minutes.
3. In a large skillet over medium heat, heat a generous amount of butter on medium heat. The cooking process will go quicker if you plan to have room for 3–4 pancakes at a time. Use the oven on low heat to keep the first batches of pancakes warm while you make the others.
4. Place scoops of the grated cauliflower mixture in the frying pan and flatten them carefully until they measure about 3 to 4 inches in diameter.
5. Fry for 4 to 5 minutes on each side. Adjust the heat to make sure they don't burn. Serve.

Nutrition Info:
- Per Servings 5g Carbs, 7g Protein, 26g Fat, 282 Calories

Colorful Vegan Soup

Servings: 6 | Cooking Time: 25 Minutes

Ingredients:
- 2 tsp olive oil
- 1 red onion, chopped
- 2 cloves garlic, minced
- 1 celery stalk, chopped
- 1 head broccoli, chopped
- 1 carrot, sliced
- 1 cup spinach, torn into pieces
- 1 cup collard greens, chopped
- Sea salt and black pepper, to taste
- 2 thyme sprigs, chopped
- 1 rosemary sprig, chopped
- 2 bay leaves
- 6 cups vegetable stock
- 2 tomatoes, chopped
- 1 cup almond milk
- 1 tbsp white miso paste
- ½ cup arugula

Directions:
1. Place a large pot over medium-high heat and warm oil. Add in carrots, celery, onion, broccoli, garlic, and sauté until soft.
2. Place in spinach, salt, rosemary, tomatoes, bay leaves, ground black pepper, collard greens, thyme, and vegetable stock. On low heat, simmer the mixture for 15 minutes while the lid is slightly open.
3. Stir in white miso paste, watercress, and almond milk and cook for 5 more minutes.

Nutrition Info:
- Per Servings 9g Carbs, 2.9g Protein, 11.4g Fat, 142 Calories

Briam With Tomato Sauce

Servings: 4 | Cooking Time: 70 Minutes

Ingredients:
- 3 tbsp olive oil
- 1 large eggplant, halved and sliced
- 1 large onion, thinly sliced
- 3 cloves garlic, sliced
- 5 tomatoes, diced
- 3 rutabagas, peeled and diced
- 1 cup sugar-free tomato sauce
- 4 zucchinis, sliced
- ¼ cup water
- Salt and black pepper to taste
- 1 tbsp dried oregano
- 2 tbsp chopped parsley

Directions:

1. Preheat the oven to 400ºF. Heat the olive oil in a skillet over medium heat and cook the eggplants in it for 6 minutes to brown on the edges. After, remove to a medium bowl.

2. Sauté the onion and garlic in the oil for 3 minutes and add them to the eggplants. Turn the heat off.

3. In the eggplants bowl, mix in the tomatoes, rutabagas, tomato sauce, and zucchinis. Add the water and stir in the salt, pepper, oregano, and parsley. Pour the mixture in the casserole dish. Place the dish in the oven and bake for 45 to 60 minutes. Serve the briam warm on a bed of cauli rice.

Nutrition Info:
- Per Servings 12.5g Carbs, 11.3g Protein, 12g Fat, 365 Calories

Stir-fried Buttery Mushrooms

Servings: 4 | Cooking Time: 15 Minutes

Ingredients:
- 4 tablespoons butter
- 3 cloves of garlic, minced
- 6 ounces fresh brown mushrooms, sliced
- 7 ounces fresh shiitake mushrooms, sliced
- A dash of thyme
- 2 tablespoons olive oil
- Salt and pepper to taste

Directions:
1. Heat the butter and oil in a pot.
2. Sauté the garlic until fragrant, around 2 minutes.
3. Stir in the rest of the ingredients and cook until soft, around 13 minutes.

Nutrition Info:
- Per Servings 8.7g Carbs, 3.8g Protein, 17.5g Fat, 231 Calories

Cauliflower Risotto With Mushrooms

Servings: 4 | Cooking Time: 15 Minutes

Ingredients:
- 2 shallots, diced
- 3 tbsp olive oil
- ¼ cup veggie broth
- ⅓ cup Parmesan cheese
- 4 tbsp butter
- 3 tbsp chopped chives
- 2 pounds mushrooms, sliced
- 4 ½ cups riced cauliflower

Directions:

1. Heat 2 tbsp. oil in a saucepan. Add the mushrooms and cook over medium heat for about 3 minutes. Remove from the pan and set aside.

2. Heat the remaining oil and cook the shallots for 2 minutes. Stir in the cauliflower and broth, and cook until the liquid is absorbed. Stir in the rest of the ingredients.

Nutrition Info:
- Per Servings 8.4g Carbs, 11g Protein, 18g Fat, 264 Calories

Guacamole

Servings: 2 | Cooking Time: 0 Minutes

Ingredients:
- 2 medium ripe avocados
- 1 tablespoon lemon juice
- 1/4 cup chopped tomatoes
- 4 tablespoons olive oil
- 1/4 teaspoon salt
- Pepper to taste

Directions:
1. Peel and chop avocados; place them in a small bowl. Sprinkle with lemon juice.
2. Add tomatoes and salt.
3. Season with pepper to taste and mash coarsely with a fork. Refrigerate until serving.

Nutrition Info:
- Per Servings 10g Carbs, 6g Protein, 56g Fat, 565 Calories

Easy Cauliflower Soup

Servings: 4 | Cooking Time: 15 Minutes

Ingredients:
- 2 tbsp olive oil
- 2 onions, finely chopped
- 1 tsp garlic, minced
- 1 pound cauliflower, cut into florets
- 1 cup kale, chopped
- 4 cups vegetable broth
- ½ cup almond milk
- ½ tsp salt
- ½ tsp red pepper flakes
- 1 tbsp fresh chopped parsley

Directions:

1. Set a pot over medium-high heat and warm the oil. Add garlic and onion and sauté until browned and softened. Place in vegetable broth, kale, and cauliflower; cook for 10 minutes until the mixture boils. Stir in the pepper, salt, and almond milk; simmer the soup while covered for 5 minutes.

2. Transfer the soup to an immersion blender and blend to achieve the required consistency; top with parsley and serve immediately.

Nutrition Info:

• Per Servings 11.8g Carbs, 8.1g Protein, 10.3g Fat, 172 Calories

Pumpkin Bake

Servings: 6 | Cooking Time: 45 Minutes

Ingredients:

• 3 large Pumpkins, peeled and sliced
• 1 cup almond flour
• 1 cup grated mozzarella cheese
• 2 tbsp olive oil
• ½ cup chopped parsley

Directions:

1. Preheat the oven to 350ºF. Arrange the pumpkin slices in a baking dish, drizzle with olive oil, and bake for 35 minutes. Mix the almond flour, cheese, and parsley and when the pumpkin is ready, remove it from the oven, and sprinkle the cheese mixture all over. Place back in the oven and grill the top for 5 minutes.

Nutrition Info:

• Per Servings 5.7g Carbs, 2.7g Protein, 4.8g Fat, 125 Calories

Roasted Leeks And Asparagus

Servings: 12 | Cooking Time: 25 Minutes

Ingredients:

• 3 pounds fresh asparagus, trimmed
• 2 medium leeks (white portion only), halved lengthwise
• 1-1/2 teaspoons dill weed
• 1/2 teaspoon crushed red pepper flakes
• 3 tablespoons melted butter
• 1/4 teaspoon pepper
• 1/2 teaspoon salt
• 4 ½ tablespoons olive oil

Directions:

1. Place asparagus and leeks on an ungreased 15x10x1-inch baking pan. Combine the remaining ingredients; pour over vegetables.

2. Bake at 400F for 20-25 minutes or until tender, stirring occasionally.

Nutrition Info:

• Per Servings 6g Carbs, 3g Protein, 8g Fat, 98 Calories

Butternut Squash And Cauliflower Stew

Servings: 4 | Cooking Time:10 Minutes

Ingredients:

• 3 cloves of garlic, minced
• 1 cup cauliflower florets
• 1 ½ cups butternut squash, cubed
• 2 ½ cups heavy cream
• Pepper and salt to taste
• 3 tbsp coconut oil

Directions:

1. Heat the oil in a pan and saute the garlic until fragrant.
2. Stir in the rest of the ingredients and season with salt and pepper to taste.
3. Close the lid and bring to a boil for 10 minutes.
4. Serve and enjoy.

Nutrition Info:

• Per Servings 10g Carbs, 2g Protein, 38.1g Fat, 385 Calories

Coconut Cauliflower Rice

Servings: 3 | Cooking Time: 15 Minutes

Ingredients:

• 1 head cauliflower, grated
• ½ cup heavy cream
• ¼ cup butter, melted
• 3 cloves of garlic, minced
• 1 onion, chopped
• Salt and pepper to taste

Directions:

1. Place a nonstick saucepan on high fire and heat cream and butter.
2. Saute onion and garlic for 3 minutes.
3. Stir in grated cauliflower. Season with pepper and salt.
4. Cook until cauliflower is tender, around 5 minutes.
5. Turn off fire and let it set for 5 minutes.
6. Serve and enjoy.

Nutrition Info:

• Per Servings 9g Carbs, 3g Protein, 23g Fat, 246 Calories

Sausage Roll

Servings: 6 | Cooking Time: 1 Hour And 15 Minutes

Ingredients:

• 6 vegan sausages (defrosted)
• 1 cup mushrooms
• 1 onion
• 2 fresh sage leaves
• 1 package tofu skin sheet
• Salt and pepper to taste
• 5 tablespoons olive oil

Directions:

1. Preheat the oven to 180°F/356°F assisted.
2. Defrost the vegan sausages.
3. Roughly chop the mushrooms and add them to a food pro-

cessor. Process until mostly broken down. Peel and roughly chop the onions, then add them to the processor along with the defrosted vegan sausages, sage leaves, and a pinch of salt and pepper. Pour in the oil. Process until all the ingredients have mostly broken down, and only a few larger pieces remain.

4. Heat a frying pan on a medium heat. Once hot, transfer the mushroom mixture to the pan and fry for 20 minutes or until almost all of the moisture has evaporated, frequently stirring to prevent the mixture sticking to the pan.

5. Remove the mushroom mixture from the heat and transfer to a plate. Leave to cool completely. Tip: if it's cold outside, we leave the mushroom mixture outdoors, so it cools quicker.

6. Meanwhile, either line a large baking tray with baking paper or (if the pastry already comes wrapped in a sheet of baking paper) roll out the tofu skin onto the tray and cut it in half both lengthways and widthways to create 4 equal-sized pieces of tofu skin.

7. Spoon a quarter of the mushroom mixture along the length of each rectangle of tofu skin and shape the mixture into a log. Add one vegan sausage and roll into a log.

8. Seal the roll by securing the edged with a toothpick.

9. Brush the sausage rolls with olive oil and bake for 40-45 minutes until golden brown. Enjoy!

Nutrition Info:
- Per Servings 3g Carbs, 0.9g Protein, 11g Fat, 113 Calories

Garlicky Bok Choy

Servings: 4 | Cooking Time: 25 Minutes

Ingredients:
- 2 pounds bok choy, chopped
- 2 tbsp almond oil
- 1 tsp garlic, minced
- ½ tsp thyme
- ½ tsp red pepper flakes, crushed
- Salt and black pepper, to the taste

Directions:
1. Add Bok choy in a pot containing salted water and cook for 10 minutes over medium heat. Drain and set aside. Place a sauté pan over medium-high heat and warm the oil.
2. Add in garlic and cook until soft. Stir in the Bok choy, red pepper, black pepper, salt, and thyme and ensure they are heated through. Add more seasonings if needed and serve warm with cauli rice.

Nutrition Info:
- Per Servings 13.4g Carbs, 2.9g Protein, 7g Fat, 118 Calories

Bell Pepper Stuffed Avocado

Servings: 8 | Cooking Time: 10 Minutes

Ingredients:
- 4 avocados, pitted and halved
- 2 tbsp olive oil
- 3 cups green bell peppers, chopped
- 1 onion, chopped
- 1 tsp garlic puree

- Salt and black pepper, to taste
- 1 tsp deli mustard
- 1 tomato, chopped

Directions:
1. From each half of the avocados, scoop out 2 teaspoons of flesh; set aside.
2. Use a sauté pan to warm oil over medium-high heat. Cook the garlic, onion, and bell peppers until tender. Mix in the reserved avocado. Add in tomato, salt, mustard, and black pepper. Separate the mushroom mixture and mix equally among the avocado halves and serve.

Nutrition Info:
- Per Servings 7.4g Carbs, 2.4g Protein, 23.2g Fat, 255 Calories

Keto Enchilada Bake

Servings: 6 | Cooking Time: 20 Minutes

Ingredients:
- 1 package House Foods Organic Extra Firm Tofu
- 1 cup roma tomatoes, chopped
- 1 cup shredded cheddar cheese
- 1 small avocado, pitted and sliced
- ½ cup sour cream
- 5 tablespoons olive oil
- Salt and pepper to taste

Directions:
1. Preheat oven to 350F.
2. Cut tofu into small cubes and sauté with oil and seasoning. Set aside and reserve the oil.
3. Place the tofu in the bottom of a casserole dish.
4. Mix the reserved oil and tomatoes and pour over the tofu.
5. Sprinkle with cheese on top.
6. Bake for 20 minutes.
7. Top with avocado and sour cream toppings.
8. Serve and enjoy.

Nutrition Info:
- Per Servings 6g Carbs, 38g Protein, 40g Fat, 568 Calories

Fried Tofu With Mushrooms

Servings: 2 | Cooking Time: 40 Minutes

Ingredients:
- 12 ounces extra firm tofu, pressed and cubed
- 1 ½ tbsp flax seed meal
- Salt and black pepper, to taste
- 1 tsp garlic clove, minced
- ½ tsp paprika
- 1 tsp onion powder
- ½ tsp ground bay leaf
- 1 tbsp olive oil
- 1 cup mushrooms, sliced
- 1 jalapeño pepper, deveined, sliced

Directions:
1. In a container, add onion powder, tofu, salt, paprika, black

pepper, flaxseed, garlic paste, and bay leaf. While the container is closed, toss the mixture to coat, and allow to marinate for 30 minutes.

2. In a pan, warm oil over medium heat. Cook mushrooms and tofu for 6 minutes, stirring continuously.

Nutrition Info:

• Per Servings 8.1g Carbs, 15.6g Protein, 15.9g Fat, 223 Calories

Paprika 'n Cajun Seasoned Onion Rings

Servings: 6 | Cooking Time: 25 Minutes

Ingredients:

• 1 large white onion
• 2 large eggs, beaten
• ½ teaspoon Cajun seasoning
• ¾ cup almond flour
• 1 ½ teaspoon paprika
• ½ cups coconut oil for frying
• ¼ cup water
• Salt and pepper to taste

Directions:

1. Preheat a pot with oil for 8 minutes.
2. Peel the onion, cut off the top and slice into circles.
3. In a mixing bowl, combine the water and the eggs. Season with pepper and salt.
4. Soak the onion in the egg mixture.
5. In another bowl, combine the almond flour, paprika powder, Cajun seasoning, salt and pepper.
6. Dredge the onion in the almond flour mixture.
7. Place in the pot and cook in batches until golden brown, around 8 minutes per batch.

Nutrition Info:

• Per Servings 3.9g Carbs, 2.8g Protein, 24.1g Fat, 262 Calories

Greek Salad With Poppy Seed Dressing

Servings: 4 | Cooking Time: 3 Hours 15 Minutes

Ingredients:

• For the Dressing
• 1 cup poppy seeds
• 2 cups water
• 2 tbsp green onions, chopped
• 1 garlic clove, minced
• 1 lime, freshly squeezed
• Salt and black pepper, to taste
• ¼ tsp dill, minced
• 2 tbsp almond milk
• For the salad
• 1 head lettuce, separated into leaves
• 3 tomatoes, diced
• 3 cucumbers, sliced
• 2 tbsp kalamata olives, pitted

Directions:

1. Put all dressing ingredients in a food processor and pulse until well incorporated. Add in poppy seeds and mix well. Divide salad ingredients into 4 plates. Add the dressing to each and shake.

Nutrition Info:

• Per Servings 6.7g Carbs, 7.6g Protein, 15.6g Fat, 208 Calories

Stuffed Cremini Mushrooms

Servings: 4 | Cooking Time: 35 Minutes

Ingredients:

• ½ head broccoli, cut into florets
• 1 pound cremini mushrooms, stems removed
• 2 tbsp coconut oil
• 1 onion, finely chopped
• 1 tsp garlic, minced
• 1 bell pepper, chopped
• 1 tsp cajun seasoning mix
• Salt and black pepper, to taste
• 1 cup vegan cheese

Directions:

1. Use a food processor to pulse broccoli florets until become like small rice-like granules.
2. Set oven to 360°F. Bake mushroom caps until tender for 8 to 12 minutes. In a heavy-bottomed skillet, melt the oil; stir in bell pepper, garlic, and onion and sauté until fragrant. Place in pepper, salt, and cajun seasoning mix. Fold in broccoli rice.
3. Equally separate the filling mixture among mushroom caps. Add a topping of vegan cheese and bake for 17 more minutes. Serve warm.

Nutrition Info:

• Per Servings 10g Carbs, 12.7g Protein, 13.4g Fat, 206 Calories

Greek-style Zucchini Pasta

Servings: 4 | Cooking Time: 15 Minutes

Ingredients:

• ¼ cup sun-dried tomatoes
• 5 garlic cloves, minced
• 2 tbsp butter
• 1 cup spinach
• 2 large zucchinis, spiralized
• ¼ cup crumbled feta
• ¼ cup Parmesan cheese, shredded
• 10 kalamata olives, halved
• 2 tbsp olive oil
• 2 tbsp chopped parsley

Directions:

1. Heat the olive oil in a pan over medium heat. Add zoodles, butter, garlic, and spinach. Cook for about 5 minutes. Stir in the olives, tomatoes, and parsley. Cook for 2 more minutes. Add in the cheeses and serve.

Nutrition Info:

• Per Servings 6.5g Carbs, 6.5g Protein, 19.5g Fat, 231 Calories

Spicy Tofu With Worcestershire Sauce

Servings: 4 | Cooking Time: 25 Minutes

Ingredients:
- 2 tbsp olive oil
- 14 ounces block tofu, pressed and cubed
- 1 celery stalk, chopped
- 1 bunch scallions, chopped
- 1 tsp cayenne pepper
- 1 tsp garlic powder
- 2 tbsp Worcestershire sauce
- Salt and black pepper, to taste
- 1 pound green cabbage, shredded
- ½ tsp turmeric powder
- ¼ tsp dried basil

Directions:
1. Set a large skillet over medium-high heat and warm 1 tablespoon of olive oil. Stir in tofu cubes and cook for 8 minutes. Place in scallions and celery; cook for 5 minutes until soft
2. Stir in cayenne, Worcestershire sauce, pepper, salt, and garlic; cook for 3 more minutes; set aside.
3. In the same pan, warm the remaining 1 tablespoon of oil. Add in shredded cabbage and the remaining seasonings and cook for 4 minutes. Mix in tofu mixture and serve while warm.

Nutrition Info:
- Per Servings 8.3g Carbs, 8.1g Protein, 10.3g Fat, 182 Calories

Cream Of Zucchini And Avocado

Servings: 4 | Cooking Time: 35 Minutes

Ingredients:
- 3 tsp vegetable oil
- 1 onion, chopped
- 1 carrot, sliced
- 1 turnip, sliced
- 3 cups zucchinis, chopped
- 1 avocado, peeled and diced
- ¼ tsp ground black pepper
- 4 vegetable broth
- 1 tomato, pureed

Directions:
1. In a pot, warm the oil and sauté onion until translucent, about 3 minutes. Add in turnip, zucchini, and carrot and cook for 7 minutes; add black pepper for seasoning.
2. Mix in pureed tomato, and broth; and boil. Change heat to low and allow the mixture to simmer for 20 minutes. Lift from the heat. In batches, add the soup and avocado to a blender. Blend until creamy and smooth.

Nutrition Info:
- Per Servings 11g Carbs, 2.2g Protein, 13.4g Fat, 165 Calories

Zoodles With Avocado & Olives

Servings: 4 | Cooking Time: 15 Minutes

Ingredients:
- 4 zucchinis, julienned or spiralized
- ½ cup pesto
- 2 avocados, sliced
- 1 cup kalamata olives, chopped
- ¼ cup chopped basil
- 2 tbsp olive oil
- ¼ cup chopped sun-dried tomatoes

Directions:
1. Heat half of the olive oil in a pan over medium heat. Add zoodles and cook for 4 minutes. Transfer to a plate. Stir in pesto, basil, salt, tomatoes, and olives. Top with avocado slices.

Nutrition Info:
- Per Servings 8.4g Carbs, 6.3g Protein, 42g Fat, 449 Calories

Cauliflower Mash

Servings: 4 | Cooking Time: 10 Minutes

Ingredients:
- 1 head of cauliflower
- ¼ tsp, garlic powder
- 1 handful of chives, chopped
- What you'll need from the store cupboard:
- ¼ tsp, salt
- ¼ tsp, ground black pepper

Directions:
1. Bring a pot of water to boil.
2. Chop cauliflower into florets. Place in a pot of boiling water and boil for 5 minutes.
3. Drain well.
4. Place florets in a blender. Add remaining ingredients except for chives and pulse to desired consistency.
5. Transfer to a bowl and toss in chives.
6. Serve and enjoy.

Nutrition Info:
- Per Servings 3.7g Carbs, 1.3g Protein, 0.2g Fat, 18 Calories

Vegetarian Burgers

Servings: 2 | Cooking Time: 20 Minutes

Ingredients:
- 1 garlic cloves, minced
- 2 portobello mushrooms, sliced
- 1 tbsp coconut oil, melted
- 1 tbsp chopped basil
- 1 tbsp oregano
- 2 eggs, fried
- 2 low carb buns
- 2 tbsp mayonnaise
- 2 lettuce leaves

Directions:
1. Combine the melted coconut oil, garlic, herbs, and salt, in a

bowl. Place the mushrooms in the bowl and coat well. Preheat the grill to medium heat. Grill the mushrooms for 2 minutes per side.

2. Cut the low carb buns in half. Add the lettuce leaves, grilled mushrooms, eggs, and mayonnaise. Top with the other bun half.

Nutrition Info:
• Per Servings 8.5g Carbs, 23g Protein, 55g Fat, 637 Calories

Garlic And Greens

Servings: 4 | Cooking Time: 20 Minutes

Ingredients:
• 1-pound kale, trimmed and torn
• 1/4 cup chopped oil-packed sun-dried tomatoes
• 5 garlic cloves, minced
• 2 tablespoons minced fresh parsley
• 1/4 teaspoon salt
• 3 tablespoons olive oil

Directions:
1. In a 6-qt. stockpot, bring 1 inch. of water to a boil. Add kale; cook, covered, 10-15 minutes or until tender. Remove with a slotted spoon; discard cooking liquid.
2. In the same pot, heat oil over medium heat. Add tomatoes and garlic; cook and stir 1 minute. Add kale, parsley and salt; heat through, stirring occasionally.

Nutrition Info:
• Per Servings 9g Carbs, 6g Protein, 13g Fat, 160 Calories

Lemon Grilled Veggie

Servings: 4 | Cooking Time: 20 Minutes

Ingredients:
• 2/3 eggplant
• 1 zucchini
• 10 oz. cheddar cheese
• 20 black olives
• 2 oz. leafy greens
• ½ cup olive oil
• 1 lemon, the juice
• 1 cup mayonnaise
• 4 tbsp almonds
• Salt and pepper

Directions:
1. Cut eggplant and zucchini lengthwise into half inch-thick slices. Season with salt to coat evenly. Set aside for 5-10 minutes.
2. Preheat the oven to 450 degrees F.
3. Pat zucchini and eggplant slices' surface dry with a kitchen towel.
4. Line a baking sheet with parchment paper and place slices on it. Spray with olive oil on top and season with pepper.
5. Bake for 15-20 minutes or until cooked through, flipping halfway.
6. Once done, transfer to a serving platter. Drizzle olive oil

and lemon juice on top.
7. Serve with cheese cubes, almonds, olives, mayonnaise and leafy greens.

Nutrition Info:
• Per Servings 9g Carbs, 21g Protein, 99g Fat, 1013 Calories

Morning Coconut Smoothie

Servings: 4 | Cooking Time: 5 Minutes

Ingredients:
• ½ cup water
• 1 ½ cups coconut milk
• 1 cup frozen cherries
• 4 cup fresh blueberries
• ¼ tsp vanilla extract
• 1 tbsp vegan protein powder

Directions:
1. Using a blender, combine all the ingredients and blend well until you attain a uniform and creamy consistency. Divide in glasses and serve!

Nutrition Info:
• Per Servings 14.9g Carbs, 2.6g Protein, 21.7g Fat, 247 Calories

Cauliflower Mac And Cheese

Servings: 7 | Cooking Time: 45 Minutes

Ingredients:
• 1 cauliflower head, riced
• 1 ½ cups shredded cheese
• 2 tsp paprika
• ¾ tsp rosemary
• 2 tsp turmeric
• 3 eggs
• Olive oil, for frying

Directions:
1. Microwave the cauliflower for 5 minutes. Place it in cheesecloth and squeeze the extra juices out. Place the cauliflower in a bowl. Stir in the rest of the ingredients.
2. Heat the oil in a deep pan until it reaches 360ºF. Add the 'mac and cheese' and fry until golden and crispy. Drain on paper towels before serving.

Nutrition Info:
• Per Servings 2g Carbs, 8.6g Protein, 12g Fat, 160 Calories

Sauces And Dressing Recipes

Sauces And Dressing Recipes

Keto Ranch Dip

Servings: 8 | Cooking Time: 10 Minutes

Ingredients:
- 1 cup egg white, beaten
- 1 lemon juice, freshly squeezed
- Salt and pepper to taste
- 1 teaspoon mustard paste
- 1 cup olive oil
- Salt and pepper to taste

Directions:
1. Add all ingredients to a pot and bring to a simmer. Stir frequently.
2. Simmer for 10 minutes.
3. Adjust seasoning to taste.

Nutrition Info:
- Per Servings 1.2g Carbs, 3.4g Protein, 27.1g Fat, 258 Calories

Ketogenic-friendly Gravy

Servings: 6 | Cooking Time: 10 Minutes

Ingredients:
- 2 tablespoons butter
- 1 white onion, chopped
- ¼ cup coconut milk
- 2 cups bone broth
- 1 tablespoon balsamic vinegar
- Salt and pepper to taste

Directions:
1. Add all ingredients to a pot and bring to a simmer. Stir frequently.
2. Simmer for 10 minutes.
3. Adjust seasoning to taste.

Nutrition Info:
- Per Servings 1.1g Carbs, 0.2g Protein, 6.3g Fat, 59 Calories

Roasted Garlic Lemon Dip

Servings: 3 | Cooking Time: 30 Minutes

Ingredients:
- 3 medium lemons
- 3 cloves garlic, peeled and smashed
- 5 tablespoons olive oil, divided
- 1/2 teaspoon kosher salt
- Pepper to taste
- Salt
- Pepper

Directions:
1. Arrange a rack in the middle of the oven and heat to 400°F.

2. Cut the lemons in half crosswise and remove the seeds. Place the lemons cut-side up in a small baking dish. Add the garlic and drizzle with 2 tablespoons of the oil.
3. Roast until the lemons are tender and lightly browned, about 30 minutes. Remove the baking dish to a wire rack.
4. When the lemons are cool enough to handle, squeeze the juice into the baking dish. Discard the lemon pieces and any remaining seeds. Pour the contents of the baking dish, including the garlic, into a blender or mini food processor. Add the remaining 3 tablespoons oil and salt. Process until the garlic is completely puréed, and the sauce is emulsified and slightly thickened. Serve warm or at room temperature.

Nutrition Info:
- Per Servings 4.8g Carbs, 0.6g Protein, 17g Fat, 165 Calories

Dijon Vinaigrette

Servings: 4 | Cooking Time: 5 Minutes

Ingredients:
- 2 tablespoons Dijon mustard
- Juice of ½ lemon
- 1 garlic clove, finely minced
- 1½ tablespoons red wine vinegar
- Pink Himalayan salt
- Freshly ground black pepper
- 3 tablespoons olive oil

Directions:
1. In a small bowl, whisk the mustard, lemon juice, garlic, and red wine vinegar until well combined. Season with pink Himalayan salt and pepper, and whisk again.
2. Slowly add the olive oil, a little bit at a time, whisking constantly.
3. Keep in a sealed glass container in the refrigerator for up to 1 week.

Nutrition Info:
- Per Servings 1g Carbs, 1g Protein, 11g Fat, 99 Calories

Caesar Dressing

Servings: 4 | Cooking Time: 5 Minutes

Ingredients:
- ½ cup mayonnaise
- 1 tablespoon Dijon mustard
- Juice of ½ lemon
- ½ teaspoon Worcestershire sauce
- Pinch pink Himalayan salt
- Pinch freshly ground black pepper
- ¼ cup grated Parmesan cheese

Directions:
1. In a medium bowl, whisk together the mayonnaise, mustard, lemon juice, Worcestershire sauce, pink Himalayan salt,

and pepper until fully combined.

2. Add the Parmesan cheese, and whisk until creamy and well blended.

3. Keep in a sealed glass container in the refrigerator for up to 1 week.

Nutrition Info:

• Per Servings Calories: 2g Carbs, 2g Protein, 23g Fat, 222 Calories

Keto Thousand Island Dressing

Servings: 10 | Cooking Time: 10 Minutes

Ingredients:

• 1 cup mayonnaise
• 1 tablespoon lemon juice, freshly squeezed
• 4 tablespoons dill pickles, chopped
• 1 teaspoon Tabasco
• 1 shallot chopped finely
• Salt and pepper to taste

Directions:

1. Add all ingredients to a pot and bring to a simmer. Stir frequently.
2. Simmer for 10 minutes.
3. Adjust seasoning to taste.

Nutrition Info:

• Per Servings 2.3g Carbs, 1.7g Protein, 7.8g Fat, 85 Calories

Avocado-lime Crema

Servings: 4 | Cooking Time: 5 Minutes

Ingredients:

• ½ cup sour cream
• ½ avocado
• 1 garlic clove, finely minced
• ¼ cup fresh cilantro leaves
• Juice of ½ lime
• Pinch pink Himalayan salt
• Pinch freshly ground black pepper

Directions:

1. In a food processor (or blender), mix the sour cream, avocado, garlic, cilantro, lime juice, pink Himalayan salt, and pepper until smooth and fully combined.
2. Spoon the sauce into an airtight glass jar and keep in the refrigerator for up to 3 days.

Nutrition Info:

• Per Servings Calories: 2g Carbs, 1g Protein, 8g Fat, 87 Calories

Cheesy Avocado Dip

Cooking Time: 20 Minutes

Ingredients:

• 1/2 medium ripe avocado, peeled and pitted
• 2 crumbled blue cheese
• 1 freshly squeezed lemon juice
• 1/2 kosher salt
• 1/2 cup water

Directions:

1. Scoop the flesh of the avocado into the bowl of a food processor fitted with the blade attachment or blender.
2. Add the blue cheese, lemon juice, and salt. Blend until smooth and creamy, 30 to 40 seconds.
3. With the motor running, add the water and blend until the sauce is thinned and well-combined.

Nutrition Info:

• Per Servings 2.9g Carbs, 3.5g Protein, 7.2g Fat, 86 Calories

Caesar Salad Dressing

Servings: 6 | Cooking Time: 10 Minutes

Ingredients:

• ½ cup olive oil
• 1 tablespoon Dijon mustard
• ½ cup parmesan cheese, grated
• 2/3-ounce anchovies, chopped
• ½ lemon juice, freshly squeezed
• Salt and pepper to taste

Directions:

1. Add all ingredients to a pot and bring to a simmer. Stir frequently.
2. Simmer for 10 minutes.
3. Adjust seasoning to taste.

Nutrition Info:

• Per Servings 1.5g Carbs, 3.4g Protein, 20.7g Fat, 203 Calories

Green Jalapeno Sauce

Servings: 1 | Cooking Time: 0 Minutes

Ingredients:

• ½ avocado
• 1 large jalapeno
• 1 cup fresh cilantro
• 2 tablespoons extra virgin olive oil
• 3 tablespoons water
• Water
• ½ teaspoon salt

Directions:

1. Add all ingredients in a blender.
2. Blend until smooth and creamy.
3. Serve and enjoy.

Nutrition Info:

• Per Servings 10g Carbs, 2.4g Protein, 42g Fat, 407 Calories

Tzatziki

Servings: 4 | Cooking Time: 10 Minutes, Plus At Least 30 Minutes To Chill

Ingredients:
- ½ large English cucumber, unpeeled
- 1½ cups Greek yogurt (I use Fage)
- 2 tablespoons olive oil
- Large pinch pink Himalayan salt
- Large pinch freshly ground black pepper
- Juice of ½ lemon
- 2 garlic cloves, finely minced
- 1 tablespoon fresh dill

Directions:
1. Halve the cucumber lengthwise, and use a spoon to scoop out and discard the seeds.
2. Grate the cucumber with a zester or grater onto a large plate lined with a few layers of paper towels. Close the paper towels around the grated cucumber, and squeeze as much water out of it as you can. (This can take a while and can require multiple paper towels. You can also allow it to drain overnight in a strainer or wrapped in a few layers of cheesecloth in the fridge if you have the time.)
3. In a food processor (or blender), blend the yogurt, olive oil, pink Himalayan salt, pepper, lemon juice, and garlic until fully combined.
4. Transfer the mixture to a medium bowl, and mix in the fresh dill and grated cucumber.
5. I like to chill this sauce for at least 30 minutes before serving. Keep in a sealed glass container in the refrigerator for up to 1 week.

Nutrition Info:
- Per Servings 5g Carbs, 8g Protein, 11g Fat, 149 Calories

Celery-onion Vinaigrette

Servings: 4 | Cooking Time: 0 Minutes

Ingredients:
- 1 tbsp finely chopped celery
- 1 tbsp finely chopped red onion
- 4 garlic cloves, minced
- ½ cup red wine vinegar
- 1 tbsp extra virgin olive oil

Directions:
1. Prepare the dressing by mixing pepper, celery, onion, olive oil, garlic, and vinegar in a small bowl. Whisk well to combine.
2. Let it sit for at least 30 minutes to let flavors blend.
3. Serve and enjoy with your favorite salad greens.

Nutrition Info:
- Per Servings 1.4g Carbs, 0.2g Protein, 3.4g Fat, 41 Calories

Feta Avocado Dip

Servings: 4 | Cooking Time: 0 Minutes

Ingredients:
- 2 avocadoes (mashed)
- ½ cup feta cheese (crumbled)
- 1 plum tomatoes (diced)
- 1 teaspoon garlic (minced)
- ½ lemon (juiced)
- Salt
- Pepper
- 4 tablespoons olive oil

Directions:
1. Fold ingredients together. Do not stir too much to leave chunks of feta and avocado.
2. Serve and enjoy.

Nutrition Info:
- Per Servings 8.1g Carbs, 5g Protein, 19g Fat, 220 Calories

Vegetarian Fish Sauce

Servings: 16 | Cooking Time: 20 Minutes

Ingredients:
- 1/4 cup dried shiitake mushrooms
- 1-2 tbsp tamari (for a depth of flavor)
- 3 tbsp coconut aminos
- 1 ¼ cup water
- 2 tsp sea salt

Directions:
1. To a small saucepan, add water, coconut aminos, dried shiitake mushrooms, and sea salt. Bring to a boil, then cover, reduce heat, and simmer for 15-20 minutes.
2. Remove from heat and let cool slightly. Pour liquid through a fine-mesh strainer into a bowl, pressing on the mushroom mixture with a spoon to squeeze out any remaining liquid.
3. To the bowl, add tamari. Taste and adjust as needed, adding more sea salt for saltiness.
4. Store in a sealed container in the refrigerator for up to 1 month and shake well before use. Or pour into an ice cube tray, freeze, and store in a freezer-safe container for up to 2 months.

Nutrition Info:
- Per Servings 5g Carbs, 0.3g Protein, 2g Fat, 39.1 Calories

Cowboy Sauce

Servings: 6 | Cooking Time: 10 Minutes

Ingredients:
- 1 stick butter
- 2 cloves of garlic, minced
- 1 tablespoon fresh horseradish, grated
- 1 teaspoon dried thyme
- 1 teaspoon paprika powder
- Salt and pepper to taste
- ¼ cup water

Directions:

1. Add all ingredients to a pot and bring to a simmer.
2. Simmer for 10 minutes.
3. Adjust seasoning to taste.

Nutrition Info:

• Per Servings 0.9g Carbs, 1.3g Protein, 20.6g Fat, 194 Calories

Peanut Sauce

Servings: 4 | Cooking Time: 5 Minutes

Ingredients:

• ½ cup creamy peanut butter (I use Justin's)
• 2 tablespoons soy sauce (or coconut aminos)
• 1 teaspoon Sriracha sauce
• 1 teaspoon toasted sesame oil
• 1 teaspoon garlic powder

Directions:

1. In a food processor (or blender), blend the peanut butter, soy sauce, Sriracha sauce, sesame oil, and garlic powder until thoroughly mixed.
2. Pour into an airtight glass container and keep in the refrigerator for up to 1 week.

Nutrition Info:

• Per Servings Calories: 185; Total Fat: 15g; Carbs: 8g; Net Carbs: 6g; Fiber: 2g; Protein: 7g

Simple Tomato Sauce

Servings: 4 | Cooking Time: 20 Minutes

Ingredients:

• 1 can whole peeled tomatoes
• 3 garlic cloves, smashed
• 5 tablespoons olive oil
• Kosher salt
• 2 tablespoons unsalted butter
• Salt

Directions:

1. Purée tomatoes in a food processor until they're as smooth or chunky as you like.
2. Transfer tomatoes to a large Dutch oven or other heavy pot. (Or, use an immersion blender and blend directly in the pot.)
3. Add garlic, oil, and a 5-finger pinch of salt.
4. Bring to a boil and cook, occasionally stirring, until sauce is reduced by about one-third, about 20 minutes. Stir in butter.

Nutrition Info:

• Per Servings 7.6g Carbs, 1.9g Protein, 21.3g Fat, 219 Calories

Alfredo Sauce

Servings: 2 | Cooking Time: 10 Minutes

Ingredients:

• 4 tablespoons butter
• 2 ounces cream cheese
• 1 cup heavy (whipping) cream
• ½ cup grated Parmesan cheese
• 1 garlic clove, finely minced
• 1 teaspoon dried Italian seasoning
• Pink Himalayan salt
• Freshly ground black pepper

Directions:

1. In a heavy medium saucepan over medium heat, combine the butter, cream cheese, and heavy cream. Whisk slowly and constantly until the butter and cream cheese melt.
2. Add the Parmesan, garlic, and Italian seasoning. Continue to whisk until everything is well blended. Turn the heat to medium-low and simmer, stirring occasionally, for 5 to 8 minutes to allow the sauce to blend and thicken.
3. Season with pink Himalayan salt and pepper, and stir to combine.
4. Toss with your favorite hot, precooked, keto-friendly noodles and serve.
5. Keep this sauce in a sealed glass container in the refrigerator for up to 4 days.

Nutrition Info:

• Per Servings 2g Carbs, 5g Protein, 30g Fat, 294 Calories

Artichoke Pesto Dip

Servings: 1 | Cooking Time: 20 Minutes

Ingredients:

• 1 jar marinated artichoke hearts
• 8 ounces cream cheese (at room temperature)
• 4 ounces parmesan cheese (grated)
• 2 tablespoons basil pesto
• ¼ cup shelled pistachio (chopped, optional)

Directions:

1. Preheat oven to 375oF.
2. Drain and chop artichoke hearts.
3. Mix artichokes, cream cheese, parmesan, and pesto.
4. Pour into 4 ramekins evenly.
5. Bake for 15-20 minutes.

Nutrition Info:

• Per Servings 5g Carbs, 8g Protein, 19g Fat, 214 Calories

Fat-burning Dressing

Servings: 6 | Cooking Time: 3 Minutes

Ingredients:

• 2 tablespoons coconut oil
• ¼ cup olive oil
• 2 cloves of garlic, minced
• 2 tablespoons freshly chopped herbs of your choice

- ¼ cup mayonnaise
- Salt and pepper to taste

Directions:

1. Heat the coconut oil and olive oil and sauté the garlic until fragrant in a saucepan.
2. Allow cooling slightly before adding the mayonnaise.
3. Season with salt and pepper to taste.

Nutrition Info:

- Per Servings 0.6g Carbs, 14.1g Protein, 22.5g Fat, 262 Calories

Green Goddess Dressing

Servings: 4 | Cooking Time: 5 Minutes

Ingredients:

- 2 tablespoon buttermilk
- ¼ cup Greek yogurt
- 1 teaspoon apple cider vinegar
- 1 garlic clove, minced
- 1 tablespoon olive oil
- 1 tablespoon fresh parsley leaves

Directions:

1. In a food processor (or blender), combine the buttermilk, yogurt, apple cider vinegar, garlic, olive oil, and parsley. Blend until fully combined.
2. Pour into a sealed glass container and chill in the refrigerator for at least 30 minutes before serving. This dressing will keep in the fridge for up to 1 week.

Nutrition Info:

- Per Servings 1g Carbs, 1g Protein, 6g Fat, 62 Calories

Garlic Aioli

Servings: 4 | Cooking Time: 5 Minutes, Plus 30 Minutes To Chill

Ingredients:

- ½ cup mayonnaise
- 2 garlic cloves, minced
- Juice of 1 lemon
- 1 tablespoon chopped fresh flat-leaf Italian parsley
- 1 teaspoon chopped chives
- Pink Himalayan salt
- Freshly ground black pepper

Directions:

1. In a food processor (or blender), combine the mayonnaise, garlic, lemon juice, parsley, and chives, and season with pink Himalayan salt and pepper. Blend until fully combined.
2. Pour into a sealed glass container and chill in the refrigerator for at least 30 minutes before serving. (This sauce will keep in the fridge for up to 1 week.)

Nutrition Info:

- Per Servings Calories: 3g Carbs, 1g Protein, 22g Fat, 204 Calories

Sriracha Mayo

Servings: 4 | Cooking Time: 5 Minutes

Ingredients:

- ½ cup mayonnaise
- 2 tablespoons Sriracha sauce
- ½ teaspoon garlic powder
- ½ teaspoon onion powder
- ¼ teaspoon paprika

Directions:

1. In a small bowl, whisk together the mayonnaise, Sriracha, garlic powder, onion powder, and paprika until well mixed.
2. Pour into an airtight glass container, and keep in the refrigerator for up to 1 week.

Nutrition Info:

- Per Servings Calories: 2g Carbs, 1g Protein, 22g Fat, 201 Calories

Lemon Tahini Sauce

Servings: 2 | Cooking Time: 5 Minutes

Ingredients:

- 1/2 cup packed fresh herbs, such as parsley, basil, mint, cilantro, dill, or chives
- 1/4 cup tahini
- Juice of 1 lemon
- 1/2 teaspoon kosher salt
- 1 tablespoon water

Directions:

1. Place all the ingredients in the bowl of a food processor fitted with the blade attachment or a blender. Process continuously until the herbs are finely minced, and the sauce is well-blended, 3 to 4 minutes.
2. Serve immediately or store in a covered container in the refrigerator until ready to serve.

Nutrition Info:

- Per Servings 4.3g Carbs, 2.8g Protein, 8.1g Fat, 94 Calories

Chunky Blue Cheese Dressing

Servings: 4 | Cooking Time: 5 Minutes

Ingredients:

- ½ cup sour cream
- ½ cup mayonnaise
- Juice of ½ lemon
- ½ teaspoon Worcestershire sauce
- Pink Himalayan salt
- Freshly ground black pepper
- 2 ounces crumbled blue cheese

Directions:

1. In a medium bowl, whisk the sour cream, mayonnaise, lemon juice, and Worcestershire sauce. Season with pink Himalayan salt and pepper, and whisk again until fully combined.
2. Fold in the crumbled blue cheese until well combined.
3. Keep in a sealed glass container in the refrigerator for up to

1 week.

Nutrition Info:
- Per Servings 3g Carbs, 7g Protein, 32g Fat, 306 Calories

Buttery Dijon Sauce

Servings: 2 | Cooking Time: 0 Minutes

Ingredients:
- 3 parts brown butter
- 1-part vinegar or citrus juice or a combo
- 1-part strong Dijon mustard
- A small handful of flat-leaf parsley (optional)
- 3/4 teaspoon freshly ground pepper
- 1 teaspoon salt

Directions:
1. Add everything to a food processor and blitz until just smooth.
2. You can also mix this up with an immersion blender. Use immediately or store in the refrigerator for up to one day. Blend again before use.

Nutrition Info:
- Per Servings 0.7g Carbs, 0.4g Protein, 34.4g Fat, 306 Calories

Buffalo Sauce

Servings: 8 | Cooking Time: 30 Minutes

Ingredients:
- 8 ounces Cream Cheese (softened)
- ½ cup Buffalo Wing Sauce
- ½ cup Blue Cheese Dressing
- 1 ½ cups Cheddar Cheese (Shredded)
- 1 ¼ cups Chicken Breast (Cooked)

Directions:
1. Preheat oven to 350oF.
2. Blend together buffalo sauce, white salad dressing, cream cheese, chicken, and shredded cheese.
3. Top with any other optional ingredients like blue cheese chunks.
4. Bake for 25-30 minutes

Nutrition Info:
- Per Servings 2.2g Carbs, 16g Protein, 28g Fat, 325 Calories

Avocado Mayo

Servings: 4 | Cooking Time: 5 Minutes

Ingredients:
- 1 medium avocado, cut into chunks
- ½ teaspoon ground cayenne pepper
- Juice of ½ lime
- 2 tablespoons fresh cilantro leaves (optional)
- Pinch pink Himalayan salt
- ¼ cup olive oil

Directions:
1. In a food processor (or blender), blend the avocado, cayenne pepper, lime juice, cilantro, and pink Himalayan salt until all the ingredients are well combined and smooth.
2. Slowly incorporate the olive oil, adding 1 tablespoon at a time, pulsing the food processor in between.
3. Keep in a sealed glass container in the refrigerator for up to 1 week.

Nutrition Info:
- Per Servings 1g Carbs, 1g Protein, 5g Fat, 58 Calories

Greek Yogurt Dressing

Servings: 2 | Cooking Time: 0 Minutes

Ingredients:
- ¼ tsp ground ginger
- ½ tsp prepared mustard
- 2 tbsp low-fat mayonnaise
- ½ cup plain Greek yogurt
- Salt and pepper to taste

Directions:
1. In a bowl, whisk well all ingredients.
2. Adjust seasoning to taste.
3. Serve and enjoy with your favorite salad greens.

Nutrition Info:
- Per Servings 3.5g Carbs, 3.0g Protein, 2.8g Fat, 51 Calories

Fish And Seafood Recipes

Fish And Seafood Recipes

Simple Steamed Salmon Fillets

Servings: 3 | Cooking Time: 15 Minutes

Ingredients:
- 10 oz. salmon fillets
- 2 tbsp. coconut aminos
- 2 tbsp. lemon juice, freshly squeezed
- 1 tsp. sesame seeds, toasted
- 3 tbsp sesame oil
- Salt and pepper to taste

Directions:

1. Place a trivet in a large saucepan and pour a cup or two of water into the pan. Bring to a boil.
2. Place salmon in a heatproof dish that fits inside the saucepan. Season salmon with pepper and salt. Drizzle with coconut aminos, lemon juice, sesame oil, and sesame seeds.
3. Seal dish with foil. Place the dish on the trivet inside the saucepan. Cover and steam for 15 minutes.
4. Serve and enjoy.

Nutrition Info:
- Per Servings 2.6g Carbs, 20.1g Protein, 17.4g Fat, 210 Calories

Cod With Balsamic Tomatoes

Servings: 4 | Cooking Time: 30 Minutes

Ingredients:
- 4 center-cut bacon strips, chopped
- 4 cod fillets
- 2 cups grape tomatoes, halved
- 2 tablespoons balsamic vinegar
- 4 tablespoons olive oil
- 1/2 teaspoon salt
- 1/4 teaspoon pepper

Directions:

1. In a large skillet, heat olive oil and cook bacon over medium heat until crisp, stirring occasionally.
2. Remove with a slotted spoon; drain on paper towels.
3. Sprinkle fillets with salt and pepper. Add fillets to bacon drippings; cook over medium-high heat until fish just begins to flake easily with a fork, 4-6 minutes on each side. Remove and keep warm.
4. Add tomatoes to skillet; cook and stir until tomatoes are softened, 2-4 minutes. Stir in vinegar; reduce heat to medium-low. Cook until sauce is thickened, 1-2 minutes longer.
5. Serve cod with tomato mixture and bacon.

Nutrition Info:
- Per Servings 5g Carbs, 26g Protein, 30.4g Fat, 442 Calories

Bacon And Salmon Bites

Serves: 2 | Cooking Time: 15 Minutes

Ingredients:
- 1 salmon fillets
- 4 bacon slices, halved
- 2 tbsp chopped cilantro
- Seasoning:
- ¼ tsp salt
- 1/8 tsp ground black pepper

Directions:

1. Turn on the oven, then set it to 350 °F, and let it preheat. Meanwhile, cut salmon into bite-size pieces, then wrap each piece with a half slice of bacon, secure with a toothpick and season with salt and black pepper. Take a baking sheet, place prepared salmon pieces on it and bake for 13 to 15 minutes until nicely browned and thoroughly cooked. When done, sprinkle cilantro over salmon and serve.

Nutrition Info:
- 1 g Carbs; 10 g Protein; 9 g Fats; 120 Calories

Bacon Wrapped Mahi-mahi

Serves: 2 | Cooking Time: 12 Minutes

Ingredients:
- 2 fillets of mahi-mahi
- 2 strips of bacon
- ½ of lime, zested
- 4 basil leaves
- ½ tsp salt
- Seasoning:
- ½ tsp ground black pepper
- 1 tbsp avocado oil

Directions:

1. Turn on the oven, then set it to 375 °F and let them preheat. Meanwhile, season fillets with salt and black pepper, top each fillet with 2 basil leaves, sprinkle with lime zest, wrap with a bacon strip and secure with a toothpick if needed. Take a medium skillet pan, place it over medium-high heat, add oil and when hot, place prepared fillets in it and cook for 2 minutes per side. Transfer pan into the oven and bake the fish for 5 to 7 minutes until thoroughly cooked. Serve.

Nutrition Info:
- 1.2 g Carbs; 27.1 g Protein; 11.3 g Fats; 217 Calories

Avocado & Cauliflower Salad With Prawns

Serves:6 | Cooking Time:30 Minutes

Ingredients:
- 1 cauliflower head, florets only
- 1 lb medium-sized prawns
- ¼ cup + 1 tbsp olive oil
- 1 avocado, chopped
- 3 tbsp chopped dill
- ¼ cup lemon juice
- 2 tbsp lemon zest

Directions:
1. Heat 1 tbsp olive oil in a skillet and cook the prawns for 8-10 minutes. Microwave cauliflower for 5 minutes. Place prawns, cauliflower, and avocado in a large bowl. Whisk together the remaining olive oil, lemon zest, juice, dill, and some salt and pepper, in another bowl. Pour the dressing over, toss to combine and serve immediately.

Nutrition Info:
- Per Serves 5g Carbs ; 15g Protein; 17g Fat; 214 Calories

Red Curry Halibut

Servings: 4 | Cooking Time: 15 Minutes

Ingredients:
- 4 halibut fillets, skin removed
- 1 cup chopped tomatoes
- 3 green curry leaves
- 2 tbsp. chopped cilantro
- 1 tbsp. lime juice, freshly squeezed
- 3 tbsp olive oil
- Pepper and salt to taste

Directions:
1. Place a trivet in a large saucepan and pour a cup or two of water into the pan. Bring to a boil.
2. Place halibut in a heatproof dish that fits inside the saucepan. Season halibut with pepper and salt. Drizzle with olive oil. Sprinkle chopped tomatoes, curry leaves, chopped cilantro, and lime juice.
3. Seal dish with foil. Place the dish on the trivet inside the saucepan. Cover and steam for 15 minutes.
4. Serve and enjoy.

Nutrition Info:
- Per Servings 1.8g Carbs, 76.1g Protein, 15.5g Fat, 429 Calories

Coconut Milk Sauce Over Crabs

Servings: 6 | Cooking Time: 20 Minutes

Ingredients:
- 2-pounds crab quartered
- 1 can coconut milk
- 1 thumb-size ginger, sliced
- 1 onion, chopped

- 3 cloves of garlic, minced
- Pepper and salt to taste

Directions:
1. Place a heavy-bottomed pot on medium-high fire and add all ingredients.
2. Cover and bring to a boil, lower fire to a simmer, and simmer for 20 minutes.
3. Serve and enjoy.

Nutrition Info:
- Per Servings 6.3g Carbs, 29.3g Protein, 11.3g Fat, 244.1 Calories

Golden Pompano In Microwave

Servings: 2 | Cooking Time: 11 Minutes

Ingredients:
- ½-lb pompano
- 1 tbsp soy sauce, low sodium
- 1-inch thumb ginger, diced
- 1 lemon, halved
- 1 stalk green onions, chopped
- ¼ cup water
- 1 tsp pepper
- 4 tbsp olive oil

Directions:
1. In a microwavable casserole dish, mix well all ingredients except for pompano, green onions, and lemon.
2. Squeeze half of the lemon in dish and slice into thin circles the other half.
3. Place pompano in the dish and add lemon circles on top of the fish. Drizzle with pepper and olive oil.
4. Cover top of a casserole dish with a microwave-safe plate.
5. Microwave for 5 minutes.
6. Remove from microwave, turn over fish, sprinkle green onions, top with a microwavable plate.
7. Return to microwave and cook for another 3 minutes.
8. Let it rest for 3 minutes more.
9. Serve and enjoy.

Nutrition Info:
- Per Servings 6.3g Carbs, 22.2g Protein, 39.5g Fat, 464 Calories

Seared Scallops With Chorizo And Asiago Cheese

Servings: 4 | Cooking Time: 15 Minutes

Ingredients:
- 2 tbsp ghee
- 16 fresh scallops
- 8 ounces chorizo, chopped
- 1 red bell pepper, seeds removed, sliced
- 1 cup red onions, finely chopped
- 1 cup asiago cheese, grated
- Salt and black pepper to taste

Directions:

1. Melt half of the ghee in a skillet over medium heat, and cook the onion and bell pepper for 5 minutes until tender. Add the chorizo and stir-fry for another 3 minutes. Remove and set aside.

2. Pat dry the scallops with paper towels, and season with salt and pepper. Add the remaining ghee to the skillet and sear the scallops for 2 minutes on each side to have a golden brown color. Add the chorizo mixture back and warm through. Transfer to serving platter and top with asiago cheese.

Nutrition Info:

• Per Servings 5g Carbs, 36g Protein, 32g Fat, 491 Calories

Lemon-rosemary Shrimps

Servings: 4 | Cooking Time: 12 Minutes

Ingredients:

• ½ cup lemon juice, freshly squeezed
• 1 ½ lb. shrimps, peeled and deveined
• 2 tbsp fresh rosemary
• ¼ cup coconut aminos
• 2 tbsp butter
• Pepper to taste
• 4 tbsp olive oil

Directions:

1. Place a nonstick saucepan on medium-high fire and heat oil and butter for 2 minutes.

2. Stir in shrimps and coconut aminos. Season with pepper. Sauté for 5 minutes.

3. Add remaining ingredients and cook for another 5 minutes while stirring frequently.

4. Serve and enjoy.

Nutrition Info:

• Per Servings 3.7g Carbs, 35.8g Protein, 22.4g Fat, 359 Calories

Lemon Garlic Shrimp

Servings: 6 | Cooking Time: 22 Minutes

Ingredients:

• ½ cup butter, divided
• 2 lb shrimp, peeled and deveined
• Pink salt and black pepper to taste
• ¼ tsp sweet paprika
• 1 tbsp minced garlic
• 3 tbsp water
• 1 lemon, zested and juiced
• 2 tbsp chopped parsley

Directions:

1. Melt half of the butter in a large skillet over medium heat, season the shrimp with salt, pepper, paprika, and add to the butter. Stir in the garlic and cook the shrimp for 4 minutes on both sides until pink. Remove to a bowl and set aside.

2. Put the remaining butter in the skillet; include the lemon zest, juice, and water. Cook until the butter has melted, about 1 minute. Add the shrimp, parsley, and adjust the taste with salt

and black pepper. Cook for 2 minutes on low heat. Serve the shrimp and sauce with squash pasta.

Nutrition Info:

• Per Servings 2g Carbs, 13g Protein, 22g Fat, 258 Calories

Lemon Marinated Salmon With Spices

Servings: 2 | Cooking Time: 15 Minutes

Ingredients:

• 2 tablespoons. lemon juice
• 1 tablespoon. yellow miso paste
• 2 teaspoons. Dijon mustard
• 1 pinch cayenne pepper and sea salt to taste
• 2 center-cut salmon fillets, boned; skin on
• 1 1/2 tablespoons mayonnaise
• 1 tablespoon ground black pepper

Directions:

1. In a bowl, combine lemon juice with black pepper. Stir in mayonnaise, miso paste, Dijon mustard, and cayenne pepper, mix well. Pour over salmon fillets, reserve about a tablespoon marinade. Cover and marinate the fish in the refrigerator for 30 minutes.

2. Preheat oven to 450 degrees F. Line a baking sheet with parchment paper.

3. Lay fillets on the prepared baking sheet. Rub the reserved lemon-pepper marinade on fillets. Then season with cayenne pepper and sea salt to taste.

4. Bake in the oven for 10 to 15 minutes until cooked through.

Nutrition Info:

• Per Servings 7.1g Carbs, 20g Protein, 28.1g Fat, 361 Calories

Creamy Hoki With Almond Bread Crust

Servings: 4 | Cooking Time: 50 Minutes

Ingredients:

• 1 cup flaked smoked hoki, bones removed
• 1 cup cubed hoki fillets, cubed
• 4 eggs
• 1 cup water
• 3 tbsp almond flour
• 1 medium white onion, sliced
• 2 cups sour cream
• 1 tbsp chopped parsley
• 1 cup pork rinds, crushed
• 1 cup grated cheddar cheese
• Salt and black pepper to taste
• Cooking spray

Directions:

1. Preheat the oven to 360°F and lightly grease a baking dish with cooking spray.

2. Then, boil the eggs in water in a pot over medium heat to be well done for 12 minutes, run the eggs under cold water and peel the shells. After, place on a cutting board and chop them.

3. Melt the butter in a saucepan over medium heat and sauté

the onion for about 4 minutes. Turn the heat off and stir the almond flour into it to form a roux. Turn the heat back on and cook the roux to be golden brown and stir in the cream until the mixture is smooth. Season with salt and pepper, and stir in the parsley.

4. Spread the smoked and cubed fish in the baking dish, sprinkle the eggs on top, and spoon the sauce over. In a bowl, mix the pork rinds with the cheddar cheese, and sprinkle it over the sauce.

5. Bake the casserole in the oven for 20 minutes until the top is golden and the sauce and cheese are bubbly. Remove the bake after and serve with a steamed green vegetable mix.

Nutrition Info:

• Per Servings 3.5g Carbs, 28.5g Protein, 27g Fat, 386 Calories

Bang Bang Shrimps

Serves: 2 | Cooking Time: 6 Minutes

Ingredients:

• 4 oz shrimps¼ tsp paprika
• ¼ tsp apple cider vinegar
• 2 tbsp sweet chili sauce
• ¼ cup mayonnaise
• Seasoning:
• ¼ tsp salt
• 1/8 tsp ground black pepper
• 2 tsp avocado oil

Directions:

1. Take a medium skillet pan, place it over medium heat, add oil and wait until it gets hot.Season shrimps with salt, black pepper, and paprika until coated, add them to the pan, and cook for 2 to 3 minutes per side until pink and cooked.Take a medium bowl, place mayonnaise in it, and then whisk in vinegar and chili sauce until combined.Add shrimps into the mayonnaise mixture, toss until coated, and then serve.

Nutrition Info:

• 7.2 g Carbs; 13 g Protein; 23.1 g Fats; 290 Calories

Simply Steamed Alaskan Cod

Servings: 2 | Cooking Time: 15 Minutes

Ingredients:

• 1-lb fillet wild Alaskan Cod
• 1 cup cherry tomatoes, halved
• 1 tbsp balsamic vinegar
• 1 tbsp fresh basil chopped
• Salt and pepper to taste
• 5 tbsp olive oil

Directions:

1. In a heat-proof dish that fits inside the saucepan, add all ingredients except for basil. Mix well.

2. Place a large saucepan on the medium-high fire. Place a trivet inside the saucepan and fill pan halfway with water. Cover and bring to a boil.

3. Cover dish with foil and place on a trivet.

4. Cover pan and steam for 10 minutes. Let it rest in pan for another 5 minutes.

5. Serve and enjoy topped with fresh basil.

Nutrition Info:

• Per Servings 4.2g Carbs, 41.0g Protein, 36.6g Fat, 495.2 Calories

Avocado And Salmon

Serves: 2 | Cooking Time: 0 Minutes

Ingredients:

• 1 avocado, halved, pitted
• 2 oz flaked salmon, packed in water
• 1 tbsp mayonnaise
• 1 tbsp grated cheddar cheese
• Seasoning:
• 1/8 tsp salt
• 2 tbsp coconut oil

Directions:

1. Prepare the avocado and for this, cut avocado in half and then remove its seed.Drain the salmon, add it in a bowl along with remaining ingredients, stir well and then scoop into the hollow on an avocado half.Serve.

Nutrition Info:

• 3 g Carbs; 19 g Protein; 48 g Fats; 525 Calories

Pistachio-crusted Salmon

Servings: 4 | Cooking Time: 35 Minutes

Ingredients:

• 4 salmon fillets
• ½ tsp pepper
• 1 tsp salt
• ¼ cup mayonnaise
• ½ cup chopped pistachios
• Sauce
• 1 chopped shallot
• 2 tsp lemon zest
• 1 tbsp olive oil
• A pinch of pepper
• 1 cup heavy cream

Directions:

1. Preheat the oven to 370ºF.

2. Brush the salmon with mayonnaise and season with salt and pepper. Coat with pistachios, place in a lined baking dish and bake for 15 minutes.

3. Heat the olive oil in a saucepan and sauté the shallot for 3 minutes. Stir in the rest of the sauce ingredients. Bring the mixture to a boil and cook until thickened. Serve the fish with the sauce.

Nutrition Info:

• Per Servings 6g Carbs, 34g Protein, 47g Fat, 563 Calories

Flounder With Dill And Capers

Servings: 4 | Cooking Time: 15 Minutes

Ingredients:
- 4 flounder fillets
- 1 tbsp. chopped fresh dill
- 2 tbsp. capers, chopped
- 4 lemon wedges
- 6 tbsp olive oil
- Salt and pepper to taste

Directions:
1. Place a trivet in a large saucepan and pour a cup or two of water into the pan. Bring to a boil.
2. Place flounder in a heatproof dish that fits inside a saucepan. Season snapper with pepper and salt. Drizzle with olive oil on all sides. Sprinkle dill and capers on top of the filet.
3. Seal dish with foil. Place the dish on the trivet inside the saucepan. Cover and steam for 15 minutes.
4. Serve and enjoy with lemon wedges.

Nutrition Info:
- Per Servings 8.6g Carbs, 20.3g Protein, 35.9g Fat, 447 Calories

Lemon Chili Halibut

Servings: 2 | Cooking Time: 15 Minutes

Ingredients:
- 1-lb halibut fillets
- 1 lemon, sliced
- 1 tablespoon chili pepper flakes
- Pepper and salt to taste
- 4 tbsp olive oil

Directions:
1. In a heat-proof dish that fits inside saucepan, place fish. Top fish with chili flakes, lemon slices, salt, and pepper. Drizzle with olive oil. Cover dish with foil
2. Place a large saucepan on the medium-high fire. Place a trivet inside the saucepan and fill the pan halfway with water. Cover and bring to a boil.
3. Place dish on the trivet.
4. Cover pan and steam for 10 minutes. Let it rest in pan for another 5 minutes.
5. Serve and enjoy topped with pepper.

Nutrition Info:
- Per Servings 4.2g Carbs, 42.7g Protein, 58.4g Fat, 675 Calories

Shrimp In Curry Sauce

Servings: 2 | Cooking Time: 25 Minutes

Ingredients:
- ½ ounces grated Parmesan cheese
- 1 tbsp water
- 1 egg, beaten
- ¼ tsp curry powder
- 2 tsp almond flour
- 12 shrimp, shelled
- 3 tbsp coconut oil
- Sauce
- 2 tbsp curry leaves
- 2 tbsp butter
- ½ onion, diced
- ½ cup heavy cream
- ½ ounce cheddar

Directions:
1. Combine all dry ingredients for the batter. Melt the coconut oil in a skillet over medium heat. Dip the shrimp in the egg first, and then coat with the dry mixture. Fry until golden and crispy.
2. In another skillet, melt the butter. Add onion and cook for 3 minutes. Add curry leaves and cook for 30 seconds. Stir in heavy cream and cheddar and cook until thickened. Add the shrimp and coat well. Serve warm.

Nutrition Info:
- Per Servings 4.3g Carbs, 24.4g Protein, 41g Fat, 560 Calories

Enchilada Sauce On Mahi Mahi

Servings: 2 | Cooking Time: 15 Minutes

Ingredients:
- 2 Mahi fillets, fresh
- ¼ cup commercial enchilada sauce
- Pepper to taste

Directions:
1. In a heat-proof dish that fits inside saucepan, place fish and top with enchilada sauce.
2. Place a large saucepan on the medium-high fire. Place a trivet inside the saucepan and fill the pan halfway with water. Cover and bring to a boil.
3. Cover dish with foil and place on a trivet.
4. Cover pan and steam for 10 minutes. Let it rest in pan for another 5 minutes.
5. Serve and enjoy topped with pepper.

Nutrition Info:
- Per Servings 8.9g Carbs, 19.8g Protein, 15.9g Fat, 257 Calories

Shrimp Stuffed Zucchini

Servings: 4 | Cooking Time: 56 Minutes

Ingredients:
- 4 medium zucchinis
- 1 lb small shrimp, peeled, deveined
- 1 tbsp minced onion
- 2 tsp butter
- ¼ cup chopped tomatoes
- Salt and black pepper to taste
- 1 cup pork rinds, crushed
- 1 tbsp chopped basil leaves

- 2 tbsp melted butter

Directions:

1. Preheat the oven to 350ºF and trim off the top and bottom ends of the zucchinis. Lay them flat on a chopping board, and cut a ¼ -inch off the top to create a boat for the stuffing. Scoop out the seeds with a spoon and set the zucchinis aside.

2. Melt the firm butter in a small skillet and sauté the onion and tomato for 6 minutes. Transfer the mixture to a bowl and add the shrimp, half of the pork rinds, basil leaves, salt, and pepper.

3. Combine the ingredients and stuff the zucchini boats with the mixture. Sprinkle the top of the boats with the remaining pork rinds and drizzle the melted butter over them.

4. Place them on a baking sheet and bake them for 15 to 20 minutes. The shrimp should no longer be pink by this time. Remove the zucchinis after and serve with a tomato and mozzarella salad.

Nutrition Info:

- Per Servings 3.2g Carbs, 24.6g Protein, 14.4g Fat, 135 Calories

Baked Cod And Tomato Capers Mix

Serves: 4 | Cooking Time: 25 Minutes

Ingredients:

- 4 cod fillets, boneless
- 2 tablespoons avocado oil
- 1 cup tomato passata
- 2 tablespoons capers, drained
- 2 tablespoons parsley, choppedA pinch of salt and black pepper

Directions:

1. In a roasting pan, combine the cod with the oil and the other ingredients, toss gently, introduce in the oven at 370 °F and bake for 25 minutes.

2. Divide between plates and serve.

Nutrition Info:

- 0.7g carbs; 2g fat; 5g protein; 150 calories

Blackened Fish Tacos With Slaw

Servings: 4 | Cooking Time: 20 Minutes

Ingredients:

- 1 tbsp olive oil
- 1 tsp chili powder
- 2 tilapia fillets
- 1 tsp paprika
- 4 low carb tortillas
- Slaw:
- ½ cup red cabbage, shredded
- 1 tbsp lemon juice
- 1 tsp apple cider vinegar
- 1 tbsp olive oil

Directions:

1. Season the tilapia with chili powder and paprika. Heat the olive oil in a skillet over medium heat.

2. Add tilapia and cook until blackened, about 3 minutes per

side. Cut into strips. Divide the tilapia between the tortillas. Combine all slaw ingredients in a bowl. Split the slaw among the tortillas.

Nutrition Info:

- Per Servings 3.5g Carbs, 13.8g Protein, 20g Fat, 268 Calories

Avocado Tuna Boats

Serves: 2 | Cooking Time: 10 Minutes

Ingredients:

- 4 oz tuna, packed in water, drained1 green onion sliced
- 1 avocado, halved, pitted
- 3 tbsp mayonnaise
- 1/3 tsp salt
- Seasoning:
- ¼ tsp ground black pepper
- ¼ tsp paprika

Directions:

1. Prepare the filling and for this, take a medium bowl, place tuna in it, add green onion, salt, black pepper, paprika and mayonnaise and then stir until well combined.Cut avocado in half lengthwise, then remove the pit and fill with prepared filling.Serve.

Nutrition Info:

- ; 7 g Carbs; 8 g Protein; 19 g Fats; 244 Calories

Trout And Fennel Parcels

Servings: 4 | Cooking Time: 20 Minutes

Ingredients:

- ½ lb deboned trout, butterflied
- Salt and black pepper to season
- 3 tbsp olive oil + extra for tossing
- 4 sprigs rosemary
- 4 sprigs thyme
- 4 butter cubes
- 1 cup thinly sliced fennel
- 1 medium red onion, sliced
- 8 lemon slices
- 3 tsp capers to garnish

Directions:

1. Preheat the oven to 400ºF. Cut out parchment paper wide enough for each trout. In a bowl, toss the fennel and onion with a little bit of olive oil and share into the middle parts of the papers.

2. Place the fish on each veggie mound, top with a drizzle of olive oil each, salt and pepper, a sprig of rosemary and thyme, and 1 cube of butter. Also, lay the lemon slices on the fish. Wrap and close the fish packets securely, and place them on a baking sheet.

3. Bake in the oven for 15 minutes, and remove once ready. Plate them and garnish the fish with capers and serve with a squash mash.

Nutrition Info:

- Per Servings 2.8g Carbs, 17g Protein, 9.3g Fat, 234 Calories

Halibut En Papillote

Servings: 4 | Cooking Time: 15 Minutes

Ingredients:
- 4 halibut fillets
- ½ tbsp. grated ginger
- 1 cup chopped tomatoes
- 1 shallot, thinly sliced
- 1 lemon
- 5 tbsp olive oil
- Salt and pepper to taste

Directions:
1. Slice lemon in half. Slice one lemon in circles.
2. Juice the other half of the lemon in a small bowl. Mix in grated ginger and season with pepper and salt.
3. Place a trivet in a large saucepan and pour a cup or two of water into the pan. Bring to a boil.
4. Get 4 large foil and place one fillet in the middle of each foil. Season with fillet salt and pepper. Drizzle with olive oil. Add the grated ginger, tomatoes, and shallots equally. Fold the foil to create a pouch and crimp the edges.
5. Place the foil containing the fish on the trivet. Cover saucepan and steam for 15 minutes.
6. Serve and enjoy in pouches.

Nutrition Info:
- Per Servings 2.7g Carbs, 20.3g Protein, 32.3g Fat, 410 Calories

Salmon With Pepita And Lime

Servings: 4 | Cooking Time: 15 Minutes

Ingredients:
- 2 tbsp. Pepitas, ground
- ¼ tsp. chili powder
- 1 lb. salmon fillet, cut into 4 portions
- 2 tbsp. lime juice
- Salt and pepper to taste

Directions:
1. Place a trivet in a large saucepan and pour a cup of water into the pan. Bring it to a boil.
2. Place salmon in a heatproof dish that fits inside a saucepan. Drizzle lime juice on the fillet. Season with salt, pepper, and chili powder. Garnish with ground pepitas.
3. Seal dish with foil. Place the dish on the trivet inside the saucepan. Cover and steam for 15 minutes.
4. Serve and enjoy.

Nutrition Info:
- Per Servings 1g Carbs, 24g Protein, 9g Fat, 185 Calories

Chili-lime Shrimps

Servings: 4 | Cooking Time: 10 Minutes

Ingredients:
- 1 ½ lb. raw shrimp, peeled and deveined
- 1 tbsp. chili flakes
- 5 tbsp sweet chili sauce
- 2 tbsp. lime juice, freshly squeezed
- 1 tsp cayenne pepper
- Salt and pepper to taste
- 5 tbsp oil
- 3 tbsp water

Directions:
1. In a small bowl, whisk well chili flakes, sweet chili sauce, cayenne pepper, and water.
2. On medium-high fire, heat a nonstick saucepan for 2 minutes. Add oil to a pan and swirl to coat bottom and sides. Heat oil for a minute.
3. Stir fry shrimp, around 5 minutes. Season lightly with salt and pepper.
4. Stir in sweet chili mixture and toss well shrimp to coat.
5. Turn off fire, drizzle lime juice and toss well to coat.
6. Serve and enjoy.

Nutrition Info:
- Per Servings 1.7g Carbs, 34.9g Protein, 19.8g Fat, 306 Calories

Five-spice Steamed Tilapia

Servings: 4 | Cooking Time: 15 Minutes

Ingredients:
- 1 lb. Tilapia fillets,
- 1 tsp. Chinese five-spice powder
- 3 tablespoons coconut oil
- 3 scallions, sliced thinly
- Salt and pepper to taste

Directions:
1. Place a trivet in a large saucepan and pour a cup of water into the pan. Bring to a boil.
2. Place tilapia in a heatproof dish that fits inside a saucepan. Drizzle oil on tilapia. Season with salt, pepper, and Chinese five-spice powder. Garnish with scallions.
3. Seal dish with foil. Place the dish on the trivet inside the saucepan. Cover and steam for 15 minutes.
4. Serve and enjoy.

Nutrition Info:
- Per Servings 0.9g Carbs, 24g Protein, 12.3g Fat, 201 Calories

Sautéed Savory Shrimps

Servings: 8 | Cooking Time: 15 Minutes

Ingredients:
- 2 pounds shrimp, peeled and deveined
- 4 cloves garlic, minced
- ½ cup chicken stock, low sodium
- 1 tablespoon lemon juice
- Salt and pepper
- 5 tablespoons oil

Directions:
1. Place a heavy-bottomed pot on medium-high fire and heat pot for 3 minutes.
2. Once hot, add oil and stir around to coat pot with oil.
3. Sauté the garlic and corn for 5 minutes.
4. Add remaining ingredients and mix well.
5. Cover and bring to a boil, lower fire to a simmer, and simmer for 5 minutes.
6. Serve and enjoy.

Nutrition Info:
- Per Servings 1.7g Carbs, 25.2g Protein, 9.8g Fat, 182.6 Calories

Rosemary-lemon Shrimps

Servings: 4 | Cooking Time: 8 Minutes

Ingredients:
- 5 tablespoons butter
- ½ cup lemon juice, freshly squeezed
- 1 ½ lb. shrimps, peeled and deveined
- ¼ cup coconut aminos
- 1 tsp rosemary
- Pepper to taste

Directions:
1. Place all ingredients in a large pan on a high fire.
2. Boil for 8 minutes or until shrimps are pink.
3. Serve and enjoy.

Nutrition Info:
- Per Servings 3.7g Carbs, 35.8g Protein, 17.9g Fat, 315 Calories

Blue Cheese Shrimps

Servings: 6 | Cooking Time: 15 Minutes

Ingredients:
- 3 ounces cream cheese, softened
- 2/3 cup minced fresh parsley, divided
- 1/4 cup crumbled blue cheese
- 1/2 teaspoon Creole mustard
- 24 cooked jumbo shrimp, peeled and deveined
- Pepper and salt to taste
- 5 tablespoon olive oil

Directions:
1. In a small bowl, beat cream cheese until smooth. Beat in 1/3 cup parsley, blue cheese, and mustard. Season with pepper and salt as desired. Refrigerate at least 1 hour.
2. Make a deep slit along the back of each shrimp to within 1/4-1/2 inch of the bottom. Stuff with cream cheese mixture; press remaining parsley onto cream cheese mixture.
3. Drizzle with olive oil last.

Nutrition Info:
- Per Servings 1.7g Carbs, 6g Protein, 17.8g Fat, 180 Calories

Steamed Cod With Ginger

Servings: 4 | Cooking Time: 15 Minutes

Ingredients:
- 4 cod fillets, skin removed
- 3 tbsp. lemon juice, freshly squeezed
- 2 tbsp. coconut aminos
- 2 tbsp. grated ginger
- 6 scallions, chopped
- 5 tbsp coconut oil
- Pepper and salt to taste

Directions:
1. Place a trivet in a large saucepan and pour a cup or two of water into the pan. Bring to a boil.
2. In a small bowl, whisk well lemon juice, coconut aminos, coconut oil, and grated ginger.
3. Place scallions in a heatproof dish that fits inside a saucepan. Season scallions mon with pepper and salt. Drizzle with ginger mixture. Sprinkle scallions on top.
4. Seal dish with foil. Place the dish on the trivet inside the saucepan. Cover and steam for 15 minutes.
5. Serve and enjoy.

Nutrition Info:
- Per Servings 10g Carbs, 28.3g Protein, 40g Fat, 514 Calories

Salmon Panzanella

Servings: 4 | Cooking Time: 22 Minutes

Ingredients:
- 1 lb skinned salmon, cut into 4 steaks each
- 1 cucumber, peeled, seeded, cubed
- Salt and black pepper to taste
- 8 black olives, pitted and chopped
- 1 tbsp capers, rinsed
- 2 large tomatoes, diced
- 3 tbsp red wine vinegar
- ¼ cup thinly sliced red onion
- 3 tbsp olive oil
- 2 slices day-old zero carb bread, cubed
- ¼ cup thinly sliced basil leaves

Directions:
1. Preheat a grill to 350ºF and prepare the salad. In a bowl, mix the cucumbers, olives, pepper, capers, tomatoes, wine vinegar, onion, olive oil, bread, and basil leaves. Let sit for the flavors to incorporate.
2. Season the salmon steaks with salt and pepper; grill them on both sides for 8 minutes in total. Serve the salmon steaks warm on a bed of the veggies' salad.

Nutrition Info:
- Per Servings 3.1g Carbs, 28.5g Protein, 21.7g Fat, 338 Calories

Avocado Salad With Shrimp

Serves: 4 | Cooking Time:10 Minutes

Ingredients:
- 2 tomatoes, sliced into cubes
- 2 medium avocados, cut into large pieces
- 3 tablespoons red onion, diced
- ½ large lettuce, chopped
- 2 lbs. shrimp, peeled and deveined
- For the Lime Vinaigrette Dressing
- 2 cloves garlic, minced
- 1 ½ teaspoon Dijon mustard
- 1/3 cup extra virgin olive oil
- salt and pepper to taste
- 1/3 cup lime juice

Directions:

1. Add the peeled and deveined shrimp and 2 quarts of water to a cooking pot and print to a boil, lower the heat and let them simmer for 1-2 minutes until the shrimp is pink. Set aside and let them cool.
2. Next add the chopped lettuce in a large bowl. Then add the avocado, tomatoes, shrimp and red onion.
3. In a small bowl whisk together the Dijon mustard, garlic, olive oil and lime juice. Mix well.
4. Pour the lime vinaigrette dressing over the salad and serve.

Nutrition Info:
- Per serving: 7g Carbs; 43.5g Protein; 17.6g Fat; 377 Calories;

Chipotle Salmon Asparagus

Servings: 2 | Cooking Time: 15 Minutes

Ingredients:
- 1-lb salmon fillet, skin on
- 2 teaspoon chipotle paste
- A handful of asparagus spears, trimmed
- 1 lemon, sliced thinly
- A pinch of rosemary
- Salt to taste
- 5 tbsp olive oil

Directions:

1. In a heat-proof dish that fits inside the saucepan, add asparagus spears on the bottom of the dish. Place fish, top with rosemary, and lemon slices. Season with chipotle paste and salt. Drizzle with olive oil. Cover dish with foil.
2. Place a large saucepan on the medium-high fire. Place a trivet inside the saucepan and fill the pan halfway with water. Cover and bring to a boil.
3. Place dish on the trivet.
4. Cover pan and steam for 10 minutes. Let it rest in pan for another 5 minutes.
5. Serve and enjoy topped with pepper.

Nutrition Info:
- Per Servings 2.8g Carbs, 35.0g Protein, 50.7g Fat, 651 Calories

Baked Codfish With Lemon

Serves: 4 | Cooking Time:25 Minutes

Ingredients:
- 4 fillets codfish
- 1 teaspoon salt
- 1 teaspoon pepper
- 2 tablespoons olive oil
- 2 teaspoons dried basil
- 2 tablespoons melted butter
- 1 teaspoon dried thyme
- 1/3 teaspoon onion powder
- 2 lemons, juiced
- lemon wedges, for garnish

Directions:

1. Preheat the oven to 400°F.
2. In a medium bowl combine the lemon juice, onion powder, olive oil, dried basil and thyme. Stir well. Season the fillets with salt and pepper.
3. Top each fillet into the mixture. Then place the fillets into a medium baking dish, greased with melted butter.
4. Bake the codfish fillets for 15-20 minutes. Serve with fresh lemon wedges. Enjoy!

Nutrition Info:
- Per serving: 3.9g Carbs; 21.2g Protein; 23.6g Fat; 308 Calories

Halibut With Pesto

Servings: 4 | Cooking Time: 15 Minutes

Ingredients:
- 4 halibut fillets
- 1 cup basil leaves
- 2 cloves of garlic, minced
- 1 tbsp. lemon juice, freshly squeezed
- 2 tbsp pine nuts
- 2 tbsp. oil, preferably extra virgin olive oil
- Salt and pepper to taste

Directions:

1. In a food processor, pulse the basil, olive oil, pine nuts, garlic, and lemon juice until coarse. Season with salt and pepper to taste.
2. Place a trivet in a large saucepan and pour a cup or two of water into the pan. Bring to a boil.
3. Place salmon in a heatproof dish that fits inside a saucepan. Season salmon with pepper and salt. Drizzle with pesto sauce.
4. Seal dish with foil. Place the dish on the trivet inside the saucepan. Cover and steam for 15 minutes.
5. Serve and enjoy.

Nutrition Info:
- Per Servings 0.8g Carbs, 75.8g Protein, 8.4g Fat, 401 Calories

Steamed Ginger Scallion Fish

Cooking Time: 15 Minutes

Ingredients:

- 3 tablespoons soy sauce, low sodium
- 2 tablespoons rice wine
- 1 teaspoon minced ginger
- 1 teaspoon garlic
- 1-pound firm white fish
- Pepper to taste
- 4 tbsps sesame oil

Directions:

1. In a heat-proof dish that fits inside the saucepan, add all ingredients. Mix well.
2. Place a large saucepan on the medium-high fire. Place a trivet inside the saucepan and fill the pan halfway with water. Cover and bring to a boil.
3. Cover dish with foil and place on a trivet.
4. Cover pan and steam for 10 minutes. Let it rest in pan for another 5 minutes.
5. Serve and enjoy.

Nutrition Info:

- Per Servings 5.5g Carbs, 44.9g Protein, 23.1g Fat, 409.5 Calories

Red Cabbage Tilapia Taco Bowl

Servings: 4 | Cooking Time: 20 Minutes

Ingredients:

- 2 cups cauli rice
- Water for sprinkling
- 2 tsp ghee
- 4 tilapia fillets, cut into cubes
- ¼ tsp taco seasoning
- Pink salt and chili pepper to taste
- ¼ head red cabbage, shredded
- 1 ripe avocado, pitted and chopped

Directions:

1. Sprinkle cauli rice in a bowl with a little water and microwave for 3 minutes. Fluff after with a fork and set aside. Melt ghee in a skillet over medium heat, rub the tilapia with the taco seasoning, salt, and chili pepper, and fry until brown on all sides, for about 8 minutes in total.
2. Transfer to a plate and set aside. In 4 serving bowls, share the cauli rice, cabbage, fish, and avocado. Serve with chipotle lime sour cream dressing.

Nutrition Info:

- Per Servings 4g Carbs, 16.5g Protein, 23.4g Fat, 269 Calories

Yummy Shrimp Fried Rice

Servings: 6 | Cooking Time: 20 Minutes

Ingredients:

- 4 tablespoons butter, divided
- 4 large eggs, lightly beaten
- 3 cups shredded cauliflower
- 1-pound uncooked medium shrimp, peeled and deveined
- 1/2 teaspoon salt
- 1/4 teaspoon pepper

Directions:

1. In a large skillet, melt 1 tablespoon butter over medium-high heat.
2. Pour eggs into skillet. As eggs set, lift edges, letting uncooked portion flow underneath. Remove eggs and keep warm.
3. Melt remaining butter in the skillet. Add the cauliflower, and shrimp; cook and stir for 5 minutes or until shrimp turn pink.
4. Meanwhile, chop eggs into small pieces. Return eggs to the pan; sprinkle with salt and pepper. Cook until heated through, stirring occasionally. Sprinkle with bacon if desired.

Nutrition Info:

- Per Servings 3.3g Carbs, 13g Protein, 11g Fat, 172 Calories

Coconut Curry Mussels

Servings: 6 | Cooking Time: 25 Minutes

Ingredients:

- 3 lb mussels, cleaned, de-bearded
- 1 cup minced shallots
- 3 tbsp minced garlic
- 1 ½ cups coconut milk
- 2 cups dry white wine
- 2 tsp red curry powder
- ⅓ cup coconut oil
- ⅓ cup chopped green onions
- ⅓ cup chopped parsley

Directions:

1. Pour the wine into a large saucepan and cook the shallots and garlic over low heat. Stir in the coconut milk and red curry powder and cook for 3 minutes.
2. Add the mussels and steam for 7 minutes or until their shells are opened. Then, use a slotted spoon to remove to a bowl leaving the sauce in the pan. Discard any closed mussels at this point.
3. Stir the coconut oil into the sauce, turn the heat off, and stir in the parsley and green onions. Serve the sauce immediately with a butternut squash mash.

Nutrition Info:

- Per Servings 0.3g Carbs, 21.1g Protein, 20.6g Fat, 356 Calories

Seasoned Salmon With Parmesan

Servings: 4 | Cooking Time: 20 Mins

Ingredients:
- 2 lbs. salmon fillet
- 3 minced garlic cloves
- ¼ cup. chopped parsley
- ½ cup. grated parmesan cheese
- Salt and pepper to taste

Directions:
1. Preheat oven to 425 degrees F. Line a baking sheet with parchment paper.
2. Lay salmon fillets on the lined baking sheet, season with salt and pepper to taste.
3. Bake for 10 minutes. Remove from the oven and sprinkle with garlic, parmesan and parsley.
4. Place in the oven to cook for 5 more minutes. Transfer to plates before serving.

Nutrition Info:
- Per Servings 0.6g Carbs, 25g Protein, 12g Fat, 210 Calories

Thyme-sesame Crusted Halibut

Servings: 2 | Cooking Time: 15 Minutes

Ingredients:
- 8 oz. halibut, cut into 2 portions
- 1 tbsp. lemon juice, freshly squeezed
- 1 tsp. dried thyme leaves
- 1 tbsp. sesame seeds, toasted
- Salt and pepper to taste

Directions:
1. Place a trivet in a large saucepan and pour a cup or two of water into the pan. Bring it to a boil.
2. Place halibut in a heatproof dish that fits inside a saucepan. Season with lemon juice, salt, and pepper. Sprinkle with dried thyme leaves and sesame seeds.
3. Seal dish with foil. Place the dish on the trivet inside the saucepan. Cover and steam for 15 minutes.
4. Serve and enjoy.

Nutrition Info:
- Per Servings 4.2g Carbs, 17.5g Protein, 17.7g Fat, 246 Calories

Baked Calamari And Shrimp

Serves: 1 | Cooking Time: 20 Minutes

Ingredients:
- 8 ounces calamari, cut in medium rings
- 7 ounces shrimp, peeled and deveined
- 1 eggs
- 3 tablespoons coconut flour
- 1 tablespoon coconut oil
- 2 tablespoons avocado, chopped
- 1 teaspoon tomato paste
- 1 tablespoon mayonnaise

- A splash of Worcestershire sauce
- 1 teaspoon lemon juice
- 2 lemon slices
- Salt and black pepper to the taste
- ½ teaspoon turmeric

Directions:
1. In a bowl, whisk egg with coconut oil.
2. Add calamari rings and shrimp and toss to coat.
3. In another bowl, mix flour with salt, pepper and turmeric and stir.
4. Dredge calamari and shrimp in this mix, place everything on a lined baking sheet, introduce in the oven at 400 °F and bake for 10 minutes.
5. Flip calamari and shrimp and bake for 10 minutes more.
6. Meanwhile, in a bowl, mix avocado with mayo and tomato paste and mash using a fork.
7. Add Worcestershire sauce, lemon juice, salt and pepper and stir well.
8. Divide baked calamari and shrimp on plates and serve with the sauce and lemon juice on the side.
9. Enjoy!

Nutrition Info:
- 10 carbs; 34 protein; 23 fat; 368 calories

Steamed Chili-rubbed Tilapia

Servings: 4 | Cooking Time: 15 Minutes

Ingredients:
- 1 lb. tilapia fillet, skin removed
- 2 tbsp. chili powder
- 3 cloves garlic, peeled and minced
- 2 tbsp. extra virgin olive oil
- 2 tbsp soy sauce

Directions:
1. Place a trivet in a large saucepan and pour a cup or two of water into the pan. Bring it to a boil.
2. Place tilapia in a heatproof dish that fits inside a saucepan. Drizzle soy sauce and oil on the filet. Season with chili powder and garlic.
3. Seal dish with foil. Place the dish on the trivet inside the saucepan. Cover and steam for 15 minutes.
4. Serve and enjoy.

Nutrition Info:
- Per Servings 2g Carbs, 26g Protein, 10g Fat, 211 Calories

Cedar Salmon With Green Onion

Servings: 5 | Cooking Time: 20 Mins

Ingredients:
- 3 untreated cedar planks
- 1/4 cup. chopped green onions
- 1 tablespoon. grated fresh ginger root
- 1 teaspoon. minced garlic
- 2 salmon fillets, skin removed
- 1/3 cup. olive oil

- 1/3 cup. mayo
- 1 1/2 tablespoons. rice vinegar

Directions:

1. Soak cedar planks in warm water for 1 hour more.
2. Whisk olive oil, rice vinegar, mayo, green onions, ginger, and garlic in a bowl. Marinade salmon fillets to coat completely. Cover the bowl with plastic wrap and marinate for 15 to 60 minutes.
3. Preheat an outdoor grill over medium heat. Lay planks on the center of hot grate Place the salmon fillets onto the planks and remove the marinade. Cover the grill and cook until cooked through, about 20 minutes, or until salmon is done to your liking. Serve the salmon on a platter right off the planks.

Nutrition Info:
- Per Servings 10g Carbs, 18g Protein, 27g Fat, 355 Calories

Baked Salmon With Pistachio Crust

Serves:4 | Cooking Time:35 Minutes

Ingredients:
- 4 salmon fillets
- ¼ cup mayonnaise
- ½ cup ground pistachios
- 1 chopped shallot
- 2 tsp lemon zest
- 1 tbsp olive oil
- A pinch of pepper
- 1 cup heavy cream

Directions:

1. Preheat oven to 375 °F. Brush salmon with mayo and season with salt and pepper. Coat with pistachios. Place in a lined baking dish and bake for 15 minutes. Heat the olive oil in a saucepan and sauté shallot for 3 minutes. Stir in heavy cream and lemon zest. Bring to a boil and cook until thickened. Serve salmon with the sauce.

Nutrition Info:
- Per Serves 6g Carbs; 34g Protein; 47g Fat ; 563 Calories

Air Fryer Seasoned Salmon Fillets

Servings: 4 | Cooking Time: 10 Mins

Ingredients:
- 2 lbs. salmon fillets
- 1 tsp. stevia
- 2 tbsp. whole grain mustard
- 1 clove of garlic, minced
- 1/2 tsp. thyme leaves
- 2 tsp. extra-virgin olive oil
- Cooking spray
- Salt and black pepper to taste

Directions:

1. Preheat your Air Fryer to 390 degrees F.
2. Season salmon fillets with salt and pepper.
3. Add together the mustard, garlic, stevia, thyme, and oil in a bowl, stir to combined well. Rub the seasoning mixture on top

of salmon fillets.
4. Spray the Air Fryer basket with cooking spray and cook seasoned fillets for 10 minutes until crispy. Let it cool before serving.

Nutrition Info:
- Per Servings 14g Carbs, 18g Protein, 10g Fat, 238 Calories

Sicilian-style Zoodle Spaghetti

Servings: 2 | Cooking Time: 10 Minutes

Ingredients:
- 4 cups zoodles (spiralled zucchini)
- 2 ounces cubed bacon
- 4 ounces canned sardines, chopped
- ½ cup canned chopped tomatoes
- 1 tbsp capers
- 1 tbsp parsley
- 1 tsp minced garlic

Directions:

1. Pour some of the sardine oil in a pan. Add garlic and cook for 1 minute. Add the bacon and cook for 2 more minutes. Stir in the tomatoes and let simmer for 5 minutes. Add zoodles and sardines and cook for 3 minutes.

Nutrition Info:
- Per Servings 6g Carbs, 20g Protein, 31g Fat, 355 Calories

Steamed Greek Snapper

Servings: 12 | Cooking Time: 15 Minutes

Ingredients:
- 6 tbsp. olive oil
- 1 clove of garlic, minced
- 2 tbsp. Greek yogurt
- 12 snapper fillets
- Salt and pepper to taste

Directions:

1. In a small bowl, combine the olive oil, garlic, and Greek yogurt. Season with salt and pepper to taste.
2. Place a trivet in a large saucepan and pour a cup or two of water into the pan. Bring to a boil.
3. Place snapper in a heatproof dish that fits inside a saucepan. If needed, cook in batches. Season snapper with pepper and salt and drizzle with olive oil. Slather with yogurt mixture.
4. Seal dish with foil. Place the dish on the trivet inside the saucepan. Cover and steam for 15 minutes.
5. Serve and enjoy.

Nutrition Info:
- Per Servings 0.4g Carbs, 44.8g Protein, 9.8g Fat, 280 Calories

Buttery Almond Lemon Tilapia

Servings: 4 | Cooking Time: 10 Minutes

Ingredients:

- 4 tilapia fillets
- 1/4 cup butter, cubed
- 1/4 cup white wine or chicken broth
- 2 tablespoons lemon juice
- 1/4 cup sliced almonds
- 1/2 teaspoon salt
- 1/4 teaspoon pepper
- 1 tablespoon olive oil

Directions:

1. Sprinkle fillets with salt and pepper. In a large nonstick skillet, heat oil over medium heat.
2. Add fillets; cook until fish just begins to flake easily with a fork, 2-3 minutes on each side. Remove and keep warm.
3. Add butter, wine and lemon juice to the same pan; cook and stir until butter is melted.
4. Serve with fish; sprinkle with almonds.

Nutrition Info:

- Per Servings 2g Carbs, 22g Protein, 19g Fat, 269 Calories

Mustard-crusted Salmon

Servings: 4 | Cooking Time: 15 Minutes

Ingredients:

- 1 ¼ lb. salmon fillets, cut into 4 portions
- 2 tsp. lemon juice
- 2 tbsp. stone-ground mustard
- Lemon wedges, for garnish
- 4 tbsp olive oil
- Salt and pepper to taste

Directions:

1. Place a trivet in a large saucepan and pour a cup of water into the pan. Bring to a boil.
2. Place salmon in a heatproof dish that fits inside saucepan and drizzle with olive oil. Season the salmon fillets with salt, pepper, and lemon juice. Sprinkle with mustard on top and garnish with lemon wedges on top. Seal dish with foil.
3. Place the dish on the trivet inside the saucepan. Cover and steam for 15 minutes.
4. Serve and enjoy.

Nutrition Info:

- Per Servings 2.9g Carbs, 29g Protein, 24.8g Fat, 360 Calories

Baked Fish With Feta And Tomato

Serves: 2 | Cooking Time: 15 Minutes

Ingredients:

- 2 pacific whitening fillets
- 1 scallion, chopped
- 1 Roma tomato, chopped
- 1 tsp fresh oregano
- 1-ounce feta cheese, crumbled
- Seasoning:
- 2 tbsp avocado oil
- 1/3 tsp salt
- 1/4 tsp ground black pepper
- ¼ crushed red pepper

Directions:

1. Turn on the oven, then set it to 400 °F and let it preheat. Take a medium skillet pan, place it over medium heat, add oil and when hot, add scallion and cook for 3 minutes. Add tomatoes, stir in ½ tsp oregano, 1/8 tsp salt, black pepper, red pepper, pour in ¼ cup water and bring it to simmer. Sprinkle remaining salt over fillets, add to the pan, drizzle with remaining oil, and then bake for 10 to 12 minutes until fillets are fork-tender. When done, top fish with remaining oregano and cheese and then serve.

Nutrition Info:

- 8 g Carbs; 26.7 g Protein; 29.5 g Fats; 427.5 Calories

Pork, Beef &
Lamb Recipes

Pork And Cabbage Soup

Servings: 10 | Cooking Time: 50 Minutes

Ingredients:

- 3 lb. pork butt, cut into chunks
- 1 thumb-size ginger, sliced
- 1 head cabbage, cut into quarters
- 1 scallion, green part only
- 1 small onion, chopped
- Pepper and salt to taste
- 3 cups water

Directions:

1. Place all ingredients in a heavy-bottomed pot except for cabbage. Give a good stir and season with salt and pepper to taste.
2. Cover and bring to a boil. Once boiling, lower fire to a simmer and simmer for 30 minutes.
3. Add cabbage and simmer for another 10 minutes.
4. Adjust seasoning to taste.
5. Serve and enjoy.

Nutrition Info:

- Per Servings 4.6g Carbs, 35.2g Protein, 24.7g Fat, 383 Calories

Jalapeno Beef Pot Roasted

Servings: 4 | Cooking Time: 1 Hour 25 Minutes

Ingredients:

- 3½ pounds beef roast
- 4 ounces mushrooms, sliced
- 12 ounces beef stock
- 1 ounce onion soup mix
- ½ cup Italian dressing
- 2 jalapeños, shredded

Directions:

1. Using a bowl, combine the stock with the Italian dressing and onion soup mixture. Place the beef roast in a pan, stir in the stock mixture, mushrooms, and jalapeños; cover with aluminum foil.
2. Set in the oven at 300ºF, and bake for 1 hour. Take out the foil and continue baking for 15 minutes. Allow the roast to cool, slice, and serve alongside a topping of the gravy.

Nutrition Info:

- Per Servings 3.2g Carbs, 87g Protein, 46g Fat, 745 Calories

Beef Italian Sandwiches

Servings: 6 | Cooking Time: 40 Minutes

Ingredients:

- 6 Provolone cheese slices
- 14.5-ounce can beef broth
- 8-ounces giardiniera drained (Chicago-style Italian sandwich mix)
- 3-pounds chuck roast fat trimmed and cut into large pieces
- 6 large lettuce
- Pepper and salt to taste

Directions:

1. Add all ingredients in a pot, except for lettuce and cheese, on high fire, and bring to a boil.
2. Once boiling, lower fire to a simmer and cook for 25 minutes.
3. Adjust seasoning to taste.
4. To make a sandwich, add warm shredded beef in one lettuce leaf and top with cheese.

Nutrition Info:

- Per Servings 3.9g Carbs, 48.6g Protein, 36.4g Fat, 538 Calories

Onion Swiss Steak

Servings: 6 | Cooking Time: 30 Minutes

Ingredients:

- 1 ½ pounds beef round steak, sliced
- 1 medium onion, sliced
- 2 bay leaves
- ¼ cup coconut oil
- 1/2 cup water
- Salt and pepper to taste

Directions:

1. Place all ingredients in a heavy-bottomed pot on high fire and bring to a boil.
2. Once boiling, lower fire to a simmer.
3. Simmer for 30 minutes.
4. Serve and enjoy.

Nutrition Info:

- Per Servings 0.9g Carbs, 19.3g Protein, 25.3g Fat, 308 Calories

Russian Beef Gratin

Servings: 5 | Cooking Time: 45 Minutes

Ingredients:

- 2 tsp onion flakes
- 2 pounds ground beef
- 2 garlic cloves, minced
- Salt and ground black pepper, to taste
- 1 cup mozzarella cheese, shredded
- 2 cups fontina cheese, shredded
- 1 cup Russian dressing
- 2 tbsp sesame seeds, toasted
- 20 dill pickle slices
- 1 iceberg lettuce head, torn

Directions:

1. Set a pan over medium heat, place in the beef, garlic, salt, onion flakes, and pepper, and cook for 5 minutes. Remove and set to a baking dish, stir in half of the Russian dressing, mozzarella cheese, and spread 1 cup of the fontina cheese.
2. Lay the pickle slices on top, spread over the remaining fontina cheese and sesame seeds, place in the oven at 350°F, and bake for 20 minutes. Split the lettuce on serving plates, apply a topping of beef gratin, and the remaining Russian dressing.

Nutrition Info:

- Per Servings 5g Carbs, 41g Protein, 48g Fat, 584 Calories

Baked Pork Meatballs In Pasta Sauce

Servings: 6 | Cooking Time: 45 Minutes

Ingredients:

- 2 lb ground pork
- 1 tbsp olive oil
- 1 cup pork rinds, crushed
- 3 cloves garlic, minced
- ½ cup coconut milk
- 2 eggs, beaten
- ½ cup grated Parmesan cheese
- ½ cup grated asiago cheese
- Salt and black pepper to taste
- ¼ cup chopped parsley
- 2 jars sugar-free marinara sauce
- ½ tsp Italian seasoning
- 1 cup Italian blend kinds of cheeses
- Chopped basil to garnish
- Cooking spray

Directions:

1. Preheat the oven to 400°F, line a cast iron pan with foil and oil it with cooking spray. Set aside.
2. Combine the coconut milk and pork rinds in a bowl. Mix in the ground pork, garlic, Asiago cheese, Parmesan cheese, eggs, salt, and pepper, just until combined. Form balls of the mixture and place them in the prepared pan. Bake in the oven for 20 minutes at a reduced temperature of 370°F.
3. Transfer the meatballs to a plate. Remove the foil and pour in half of the marinara sauce. Place the meatballs back in the pan and pour the remaining marinara sauce all over them.

Sprinkle all over with the Italian blend cheeses, drizzle the olive oil on them, and then sprinkle with Italian seasoning.
4. Cover the pan with foil and put it back in the oven to bake for 10 minutes. After, remove the foil, and continue cooking for 5 minutes. Once ready, take out the pan and garnish with basil. Serve on a bed of squash spaghetti.

Nutrition Info:

- Per Servings 4.1g Carbs, 46.2g Protein, 46.8g Fat, 590 Calories

Pork Burgers With Caramelized Onion Rings

Servings: 6 | Cooking Time: 20 Minutes

Ingredients:

- 2 lb ground pork
- Pink salt and chili pepper to taste
- 3 tbsp olive oil
- 1 tbsp butter
- 1 white onion, sliced into rings
- 1 tbsp balsamic vinegar
- 3 drops liquid stevia
- 6 low carb burger buns, halved
- 2 firm tomatoes, sliced into rings

Directions:

1. Combine the pork, salt and chili pepper in a bowl and mold out 6 patties.
2. Heat the olive oil in a skillet over medium heat and fry the patties for 4 to 5 minutes on each side until golden brown on the outside. Remove onto a plate and sit for 3 minutes.
3. Meanwhile, melt butter in a skillet over medium heat, sauté the onions for 2 minutes to be soft, and stir in the balsamic vinegar and liquid stevia.
4. Cook for 30 seconds stirring once or twice until caramelized. In each bun, place a patty, top with some onion rings and 2 tomato rings. Serve the burgers with cheddar cheese dip.

Nutrition Info:

- Per Servings 7.6g Carbs, 26g Protein, 32g Fat, 445 Calories

Beef With Dilled Yogurt

Servings: 6 | Cooking Time: 25 Minutes

Ingredients:

- ¼ cup almond milk
- 2 pounds ground beef
- 1 onion, grated
- 5 zero carb bread slices, torn
- 1 egg, whisked
- ¼ cup fresh parsley, chopped
- Salt and black pepper, to taste
- 2 garlic cloves, minced
- ¼ cup fresh mint, chopped
- 2 ½ tsp dried oregano
- ¼ cup olive oil
- 1 cup cherry tomatoes, halved

- 1 cucumber, sliced
- 1 cup baby spinach
- 1½ tbsp lemon juice
- 1 cup dilled Greek yogurt

Directions:

1. Place the torn bread in a bowl, add in the milk, and set aside for 3 minutes. Squeeze the bread, chop, and place into a bowl. Stir in the beef, salt, mint, onion, parsley, pepper, egg, oregano, and garlic.

2. Form balls out of this mixture and place on a working surface. Set a pan over medium heat and warm half of the oil; fry the meatballs for 8 minutes. Flip occasionally, and set aside in a tray.

3. In a salad plate, combine the spinach with the cherry tomatoes and cucumber. Mix in the remaining oil, lemon juice, black pepper, and salt. Spread dilled yogurt over, and top with meatballs to serve.

Nutrition Info:

- Per Servings 8.3g Carbs, 27g Protein, 22.4g Fat, 408 Calories

Moroccan Beef Stew

Servings: 4 | Cooking Time: 40 Minutes

Ingredients:

- 1 medium onion, chopped coarsely
- 2-lbs London broil roast, chopped into 2-inch cubes
- ¼ cup prunes
- 1 ¼ teaspoons curry powder
- ½ teaspoon ground cinnamon
- ½ teaspoon salt
- 2 cups water

Directions:

1. Add all ingredients in a pot on high fire and bring to a boil.
2. Once boiling, lower fire to a simmer and cook for 35 minutes.
3. Adjust seasoning to taste.
4. Serve and enjoy.

Nutrition Info:

- Per Servings 8.3g Carbs, 40.6g Protein, 49.6g Fat, 658 Calories

Meatballs With Ranch-buffalo Sauce

Servings: 10 | Cooking Time: 30 Minutes

Ingredients:

- 1 packet Ranch dressing dry mix
- 1 bottle red-hot wings buffalo sauce
- 1 bag frozen Rosina Italian Style Meatballs
- 5 tablespoons butter
- 1 cup water
- Pepper and salt to taste

Directions:

1. Add all ingredients in a pot on high fire and bring to a boil.
2. Once boiling, lower fire to a simmer and cook for 25 min-

utes.
3. Adjust seasoning to taste.
4. Serve and enjoy.

Nutrition Info:

- Per Servings 1.2g Carbs, 36.0g Protein, 27.9g Fat, 400 Calories

Italian Beef Ragout

Servings: 4 | Cooking Time: 1 Hour 52 Minutes

Ingredients:

- 1 lb chuck steak, trimmed and cubed
- 2 tbsp olive oil
- Salt and black pepper to taste
- 2 tbsp almond flour
- 1 medium onion, diced
- ½ cup dry white wine
- 1 red bell pepper, seeded and diced
- 2 tsp sugar-free Worcestershire sauce
- 4 oz tomato puree
- 3 tsp smoked paprika
- 1 cup beef broth
- Thyme leaves to garnish

Directions:

1. First, lightly dredge the meat in the almond flour and set aside. Place a large skillet over medium heat, add 1 tablespoon of oil to heat and then sauté the onion, and bell pepper for 3 minutes. Stir in the paprika, and add the remaining olive oil.

2. Add the beef and cook for 10 minutes in total while turning them halfway. Stir in white wine, let it reduce by half, about 3 minutes, and add Worcestershire sauce, tomato puree, and beef broth.

3. Let the mixture boil for 2 minutes, then reduce the heat to lowest and let simmer for 1 ½ hours; stirring now and then. Adjust the taste and dish the ragout. Serve garnished with thyme leaves.

Nutrition Info:

- Per Servings 4.2g Carbs, 36.6g Protein, 21.6g Fat, 328 Calories

Spanish Frittata

Servings: 6 | Cooking Time: 26 Minutes

Ingredients:

- 3 large eggs, beaten
- ½ chorizo sausage, sliced
- ½ zucchini, sliced
- A dash of oregano
- A dash of Spanish paprika
- Pepper and salt to taste
- 3 tablespoons olive oil

Directions:

1. Preheat the air fryer for 5 minutes.
2. Combine all ingredients in a mixing bowl until well-incorporated.

3. Pour into a greased baking dish that will fit in the air fryer basket.
4. Place the baking dish in the air fryer.
5. Close and cook for 15 minutes at 350F.

Nutrition Info:
- Per Servings 0.5g Carbs, 1.8g Protein, 9.4g Fat, 93 Calories

Mustard-lemon Beef

Servings: 4 | Cooking Time: 25 Minutes

Ingredients:
- 2 tbsp olive oil
- 1 tbsp fresh rosemary, chopped
- 2 garlic cloves, minced
- 1½ pounds beef rump steak, thinly sliced
- Salt and black pepper, to taste
- 1 shallot, chopped
- ½ cup heavy cream
- ½ cup beef stock
- 1 tbsp mustard
- 2 tsp Worcestershire sauce
- 2 tsp lemon juice
- 1 tsp erythritol
- 2 tbsp butter
- A sprig of rosemary
- A sprig of thyme

Directions:
1. Using a bowl, combine 1 tbsp of oil with pepper, garlic, rosemary, and salt. Toss in the beef to coat, and set aside for some minutes. Heat a pan with the rest of the oil over medium-high heat, place in the beef steak, cook for 6 minutes, flipping halfway through; set aside and keep warm.
2. Set the pan to medium heat, stir in the shallot, and cook for 3 minutes; stir in the stock, Worcestershire sauce, erythritol, thyme, cream, mustard, and rosemary, and cook for 8 minutes.
3. Stir in the butter, lemon juice, pepper, and salt. Get rid of the rosemary and thyme, and remove from heat. Arrange the beef slices on serving plates, sprinkle over the sauce, and enjoy.

Nutrition Info:
- Per Servings 5g Carbs, 32g Protein, 30g Fat, 435 Calories

Mexican Beef Chili

Servings: 4 | Cooking Time: 45 Minutes

Ingredients:
- 1 onion, chopped
- 2 pounds ground beef
- 15 oz canned tomatoes with green chilies, chopped
- 6 ounces tomato paste
- ½ cup pickled jalapeños, chopped
- 1 tsp chipotle chili paste
- 4 tbsp garlic, minced
- 3 celery stalks, chopped
- 2 tbsp coconut aminos
- Salt and black pepper, to taste

- A pinch of cayenne pepper
- 2 tbsp cumin
- 1 tsp onion powder
- 1 tsp garlic powder
- 1 bay leaf
- 1 tsp chopped cilantro

Directions:
1. Heat a pan over medium-high heat, add in the onion, celery, garlic, beef, black pepper, and salt, and cook until the meat browns. Stir in jalapeños, tomato paste, canned tomatoes with green chilies, salt, garlic powder, bay leaf, onion powder, cayenne, coconut aminos, chipotle chili paste, and cumin, and cook for 30 minutes while covered. Remove and discard bay leaf. Serve in bowls sprinkled with cilantro.

Nutrition Info:
- Per Servings 5g Carbs, 17g Protein, 26g Fat, 437 Calories

Classic Italian Bolognese Sauce

Servings: 5 | Cooking Time: 35 Minutes

Ingredients:
- 1 pound ground beef
- 2 garlic cloves
- 1 onion, chopped
- 1 tsp oregano
- 1 tsp sage
- 1 tsp marjoram
- 1 tsp rosemary
- 7 oz canned chopped tomatoes
- 1 tbsp olive oil

Directions:
1. Heat olive oil in a saucepan. Add onion and garlic and cook for 3 minutes. Add beef and cook until browned, about 4-5 minutes. Stir in the herbs and tomatoes. Cook for 15 minutes. Serve with zoodles.

Nutrition Info:
- Per Servings 5.9g Carbs, 26g Protein, 20g Fat, 318 Calories

Chicken Broth Beef Roast

Servings: 5 | Cooking Time: 2h Mins

Ingredients:
- 2 1/2 pounds boneless beef chuck roast, cut into 2-inch cubes
- 2 onions, chopped
- 2 teaspoons caraway seeds, crushed
- 4 cups chicken broth, divided
- 2 tablespoons Hungarian paprika
- 1/2 teaspoon ground thyme
- 2 tablespoons balsamic vinegar
- salt and ground black pepper to taste
- 3 cloves garlic, crushed
- 2 tablespoons olive oil

Directions:
1. Heat olive oil in a large skillet over high heat; cook and

stir beef with salt and black pepper about 5 minutes per batch. Transfer to a large stockpot and reserve drippings in the skillet.

2. Stir onions and 1/2 teaspoon salt into the reserved drippings on Medium, and cook about 5 minutes. Transfer to the stockpot with beef.

3. Whisk the paprika, caraway seeds, black pepper and thyme in the skillet over medium heat and saute for 3 minutes.

4. Add 1 cup chicken broth and stir; transfer to the beef and onion mixture.

5. In the stockpot over high heat, stir 3 cups chicken broth into beef mixture. Add garlic, vinegar and 1/2 teaspoon salt, bring to a boil. Reduce heat to low and simmer 1 1/2 to 2 hours. Serve and enjoy.

Nutrition Info:
- Per Servings 13.4g Carbs, 36g Protein, 41.2g Fat, 573 Calories

Garlic Beef & Egg Frittata

Servings: 4 | Cooking Time: 30 Minutes

Ingredients:
- 3 eggs, beaten
- 3 cloves of garlic, minced
- 1 onion, chopped
- ½ pound lean ground beef
- 1 stalk green onion, sliced
- 2 tablespoons olive oil
- A dash of salt
- ¼ tsp pepper

Directions:
1. Place a small cast iron pan on medium fire and heat for 2 minutes.
2. Add beef and crumble. Cook for 5 minutes.
3. Add onion and garlic, continue cooking beef until browned, around 5 minutes more. Discard any fat.
4. Season with pepper and salt.
5. Spread beef in the pan and lower fire to low.
6. Meanwhile, whisk eggs in a bowl. Pour over meat, cover, and cook for 10 minutes on low.
7. Place pan in the oven and broil on low for 3 minutes. Let it set for 5 minutes.
8. Serve and enjoy topped with green onions.

Nutrition Info:
- Per Servings 3.8g Carbs, 22.7g Protein, 20.5g Fat, 294 Calories

Beef And Butternut Squash Stew

Servings: 4 | Cooking Time: 40 Minutes

Ingredients:
- 3 tsp olive oil
- 1 pound ground beef
- 1 cup beef stock
- 14 ounces canned tomatoes with juice
- 1 tbsp stevia
- 1 pound butternut squash, chopped

- 1 tbsp Worcestershire sauce
- 2 bay leaves
- Salt and ground black pepper, to taste
- 3 tbsp fresh parsley, chopped
- 1 onion, chopped
- 1 tsp dried sage
- 1 tbsp garlic, minced

Directions:
1. Set a pan over medium heat and heat olive oil, stir in the onion, garlic, and beef, and cook for 10 minutes. Add in butternut squash, Worcestershire sauce, bay leaves, stevia, beef stock, canned tomatoes, and sage, and bring to a boil. Reduce heat, and simmer for 20 minutes.
2. Adjust the seasonings. Split into bowls and enjoy.

Nutrition Info:
- Per Servings 7.3g Carbs, 32g Protein, 17g Fat, 343 Calories

Sausage Links With Tomatoes & Pesto

Servings: 8 | Cooking Time: 15 Minutes

Ingredients:
- 8 pork sausage links, sliced
- 1 lb mixed cherry tomatoes, cut in half
- 4 cups baby spinach
- 1 tbsp olive oil
- 1 pound Monterrey Jack cheese, cubed
- 2 tbsp lemon juice
- 1 cup basil pesto
- Salt and black pepper, to taste

Directions:
1. Set a pan over medium heat and warm oil, place in the sausage slices, and cook each side for 4 minutes. In a salad bowl, combine the spinach with Monterrey jack cheese, salt, pesto, pepper, cherry tomatoes, and lemon juice, and toss well to coat. Toss in the sausage pieces to coat and enjoy.

Nutrition Info:
- Per Servings 6.8g Carbs, 18g Protein, 26g Fat, 365 Calories

Beef Meatballs

Servings: 5 | Cooking Time: 45 Minutes

Ingredients:
- ½ cup pork rinds, crushed
- 1 egg
- Salt and black pepper, to taste
- 1½ pounds ground beef
- 10 ounces canned onion soup
- 1 tbsp almond flour
- ¼ cup free-sugar ketchup
- 3 tsp Worcestershire sauce
- ½ tsp dry mustard
- ¼ cup water

Directions:
1. Using a bowl, combine ⅓ cup of the onion soup with the beef, pepper, pork rinds, egg, and salt. Heat a pan over medi-

um-high heat, shape 12 meatballs from the beef mixture, place them into the pan, and brown on both sides.

2. In a bowl, combine the rest of the soup with the almond flour, dry mustard, ketchup, Worcestershire sauce, and water. Pour this over the beef meatballs, cover the pan, and cook for 20 minutes as you stir occasionally. Split among serving bowls and enjoy.

Nutrition Info:
- Per Servings 7g Carbs, 25g Protein, 18g Fat, 332 Calories

Bacon Stew With Cauliflower

Servings: 6 | Cooking Time: 40 Minutes

Ingredients:
- 8 ounces mozzarella cheese, grated
- 2 cups chicken broth
- ½ tsp garlic powder
- ½ tsp onion powder
- Salt and black pepper, to taste
- 4 garlic cloves, minced
- ¼ cup heavy cream
- 3 cups bacon, chopped
- 1 head cauliflower, cut into florets

Directions:

1. In a pot, combine the bacon with broth, cauliflower, salt, heavy cream, pepper, garlic powder, cheese, onion powder, and garlic, and cook for 35 minutes, share into serving plates, and enjoy.

Nutrition Info:
- Per Servings 6g Carbs, 33g Protein, 25g Fat, 380 Calories

Venison Tenderloin With Cheese Stuffing

Servings: 8 | Cooking Time: 30 Minutes

Ingredients:
- 2 pounds venison tenderloin
- 2 garlic cloves, minced
- 2 tbsp chopped almonds
- ½ cup gorgonzola
- ½ cup feta cheese
- 1 tsp chopped onion
- ½ tsp Sea salt

Directions:

1. Preheat your grill to medium. Slice the tenderloin lengthwise to make a pocket for the filling. Combine the rest of the ingredients in a bowl. Stuff the tenderloin with the filling. Shut the meat with skewers and grill for as long as it takes to reach your desired density.

Nutrition Info:
- Per Servings 1.7g Carbs, 25g Protein, 12g Fat, 194 Calories

Beef Cheeseburger Casserole

Servings: 6 | Cooking Time: 30 Minutes

Ingredients:
- 2 lb ground beef
- Pink salt and black pepper to taste
- 1 cup cauli rice
- 2 cups chopped cabbage
- 14 oz can diced tomatoes
- ¼ cup water
- 1 cup shredded colby jack cheese

Directions:

1. Preheat oven to 370ºF and grease a baking dish with cooking spray. Put beef in a pot and season with salt and black pepper and cook over medium heat for 6 minutes until no longer pink. Drain the grease. Add cauli rice, cabbage, tomatoes, and water. Stir and bring to boil covered for 5 minutes to thicken the sauce. Adjust taste with salt and black pepper.

2. Spoon the beef mixture into the baking dish and spread evenly. Sprinkle with cheese and bake in the oven for 15 minutes until cheese has melted and it's golden brown. Remove and cool for 4 minutes and serve with low carb crusted bread.

Nutrition Info:
- Per Servings 5g Carbs, 20g Protein, 25g Fat, 385 Calories

Beef Stovies

Servings: 4 | Cooking Time: 60 Minutes

Ingredients:
- 1 lb ground beef
- 1 large onion, chopped
- 6 parsnips, peeled and chopped
- 1 large carrot, chopped
- 1 tbsp olive oil
- 1 clove garlic, minced
- Salt and black pepper to taste
- 1 cup chicken broth
- ¼ tsp allspice
- 2 tsp rosemary leaves
- 1 tbsp sugar-free Worcestershire sauce
- ½ small cabbage, shredded

Directions:

1. Heat the oil in a skillet over medium heat and cook the beef for 4 minutes. Season with salt and pepper, and occasionally stir while breaking the lumps in it.

2. Add the onion, garlic, carrots, rosemary, and parsnips. Stir and cook for a minute, and pour the chicken broth, allspice, and Worcestershire sauce in it. Stir the mixture and cook the ingredients on low heat for 40 minutes.

3. Stir in the cabbage, season with salt and pepper, and cook the ingredients further for 2 minutes. After, turn the heat off, plate the stovies, and serve with wilted spinach and collards.

Nutrition Info:
- Per Servings 3g Carbs, 14g Protein, 18g Fat, 316 Calories

Grilled Lamb On Lemony Sauce

Servings: 4 | Cooking Time: 25 Minutes

Ingredients:
- 8 lamb chops
- 2 tbsp favorite spice mix
- 1 tsp olive oil
- Sauce:
- ¼ cup olive oil
- 1 tsp red pepper flakes
- 2 tbsp lemon juice
- 2 tbsp fresh mint
- 3 garlic cloves, pressed
- 2 tbsp lemon zest
- ¼ cup parsley
- ½ tsp smoked paprika

Directions:
1. Rub the lamb with the oil and sprinkle with the seasoning. Preheat the grill to medium. Grill the lamb chops for about 3 minutes per side. Whisk together the sauce ingredients. Serve the lamb chops with the sauce.

Nutrition Info:
- Per Servings 1g Carbs, 29g Protein, 31g Fat, 392 Calories

Beef Stuffed Roasted Squash

Servings: 4 | Cooking Time: 1 Hour 15 Minutes

Ingredients:
- 2 lb butternut squash, pricked with a fork
- Salt and ground black pepper, to taste
- 3 garlic cloves, minced
- 1 onion, peeled and chopped
- 1 button mushroom, sliced
- 28 ounces canned diced tomatoes
- 1 tsp dried oregano
- ¼ tsp cayenne pepper
- ½ tsp dried thyme
- 1 pound ground beef
- 1 green bell pepper, chopped

Directions:
1. Lay the butternut squash on a lined baking sheet, set in the oven at 400ºF, and bake for 40 minutes. Cut in half, set aside to let cool, deseed, scoop out most of the flesh and let sit. Heat a greased pan over medium-high heat, add in the garlic, mushrooms, onion, and beef, and cook until the meat browns.
2. Stir in the green pepper, salt, thyme, tomatoes, oregano, black pepper, and cayenne, and cook for 10 minutes; stir in the flesh. Stuff the squash halves with the beef mixture, and bake in the oven for 10 minutes. Split into plates and enjoy.

Nutrition Info:
- Per Servings 12.4g Carbs, 34g Protein, 14.7g Fat, 406 Calories

Garlic Lime Marinated Pork Chops

Servings: 4 | Cooking Time: 10 Minutes

Ingredients:
- 4 6-ounce lean boneless pork chops, trimmed from fat
- 4 cloves of garlic, crushed
- 1 teaspoon cumin
- 1 teaspoon paprika
- ½ lime, juiced and zested
- 1 tsp black pepper
- ½ tsp salt
- 5 tablespoons olive oil

Directions:
1. In a bowl, season the pork with the rest of the ingredients.
2. Allow marinating inside the fridge for at least 2 hours.
3. Place the pork chops in a baking dish or broiler pan and grill for 5 minutes on each side until golden brown.
4. Serve with salad if desired.

Nutrition Info:
- Per Servings 2.4g Carbs, 38.5g Protein, 22.9g Fat, 376 Calories

Pork Lettuce Cups

Servings: 6 | Cooking Time: 20 Minutes

Ingredients:
- 2 lb ground pork
- 1 tbsp ginger- garlic paste
- Pink salt and chili pepper to taste
- 1 tsp ghee
- 1 head Iceberg lettuce
- 2 sprigs green onion, chopped
- 1 red bell pepper, seeded and chopped
- ½ cucumber, finely chopped

Directions:
1. Put the pork with ginger-garlic paste, salt, and chili pepper seasoning in a saucepan. Cook for 10 minutes over medium heat while breaking any lumps until the pork is no longer pink. Drain liquid and add the ghee, melt and brown the meat for 4 minutes, continuously stirring. Turn the heat off.
2. Pat the lettuce dry with paper towel and in each leaf, spoon two to three tablespoons of pork, top with green onions, bell pepper, and cucumber. Serve with soy drizzling sauce.

Nutrition Info:
- Per Servings 1g Carbs, 19g Protein, 24.3g Fat, 311 Calories

Beef Meatballs With Onion Sauce

Servings: 5 | Cooking Time: 35 Minutes

Ingredients:

- 2 pounds ground beef
- Salt and black pepper, to taste
- ½ tsp garlic powder
- 1 ¼ tbsp coconut aminos
- 1 cup beef stock
- ¾ cup almond flour
- 1 tbsp fresh parsley, chopped
- 1 tbsp dried onion flakes
- 1 onion, sliced
- 2 tbsp butter
- ¼ cup sour cream

Directions:

1. Using a bowl, combine the beef with salt, garlic powder, almond flour, onion flakes, parsley, 1 tablespoon coconut aminos, black pepper, ¼ cup of beef stock. Form 6 patties, place them on a baking sheet, put in the oven at 370ºF, and bake for 18 minutes.
2. Set a pan with the butter over medium heat, stir in the onion, and cook for 3 minutes. Stir in the remaining beef stock, sour cream, and remaining coconut aminos, and bring to a simmer.
3. Remove from heat, adjust the seasoning with black pepper and salt. Serve the meatballs topped with onion sauce.

Nutrition Info:

- Per Servings 6g Carbs, 32g Protein, 23g Fat, 435 Calories

Pizzaiola Steak Stew

Servings: 4 | Cooking Time: 40 Minutes

Ingredients:

- ¼ cup water
- 2-pounds London broil
- 1 medium sliced onion
- 1 yellow sweet sliced bell pepper
- Half a jar of pasta sauce
- Pepper and salt to taste

Directions:

1. Add all ingredients in a pot on high fire and bring to a boil.
2. Once boiling, lower fire to a simmer and cook for 35 minutes.
3. Adjust seasoning to taste.
4. Serve and enjoy.

Nutrition Info:

- Per Servings 5.9g Carbs, 70.7g Protein, 20.6g Fat, 488 Calories

Soy-glazed Meatloaf

Servings: 6 | Cooking Time: 60 Minutes

Ingredients:

- 1 cup white mushrooms, chopped
- 2 pounds ground beef
- 2 tbsp fresh parsley, chopped
- 2 garlic cloves, minced
- 1 onion, chopped
- 1 red bell pepper, seeded and chopped
- ½ cup almond flour
- ⅓ cup Parmesan cheese, grated
- 2 eggs
- Salt and black pepper, to taste
- 1 tsp balsamic vinegar
- 1 tbsp swerve
- 1 tbsp soy sauce
- 2 tbsp sugar-free ketchup
- 2 cups balsamic vinegar

Directions:

1. Using a bowl, combine the beef with salt, mushrooms, bell pepper, Parmesan cheese, 1 teaspoon vinegar, parsley, garlic, pepper, onion, almond flour, salt, and eggs. Set this into a loaf pan, and bake for 30 minutes in the oven at 370ºF.
2. Meanwhile, heat a small pan over medium heat, add in the 2 cups vinegar, swerve, soy sauce, and ketchup, and cook for 20 minutes. Remove the meatloaf from the oven, spread the glaze over the meatloaf, and bake in the oven for 20 more minutes. Allow the meatloaf to cool, slice, and enjoy.

Nutrition Info:

- Per Servings 7.5g Carbs, 46g Protein, 21.4g Fat, 474 Calories

Beef Stew With Bacon

Servings: 6 | Cooking Time: 1 Hour 15 Minutes

Ingredients:

- 8 ounces bacon, chopped
- 4 lb beef meat for stew, cubed
- 4 garlic cloves, minced
- 2 brown onions, chopped
- 2 tbsp olive oil
- 4 tbsp red vinegar
- 4 cups beef stock
- 2 tbsp tomato puree
- 2 cinnamon sticks
- 3 lemon peel strips
- ½ cup fresh parsley, chopped
- 4 thyme sprigs
- 2 tbsp butter
- Salt and black pepper, to taste

Directions:

1. Set a saucepan over medium-high heat and warm oil, add in the garlic, bacon, and onion, and cook for 5 minutes. Stir in the beef, and cook until slightly brown. Pour in the vinegar, pepper, butter, lemon peel strips, stock, salt, tomato puree, cin-

namon sticks and thyme; stir for 3 minutes.

2. Cook for 1 hour while covered. Get rid of the thyme, lemon peel, and cinnamon sticks. Split into serving bowls and sprinkle with parsley to serve.

Nutrition Info:
- Per Servings 5.7g Carbs, 63g Protein, 36g Fat, 592 Calories

Warm Rump Steak Salad

Servings: 4 | Cooking Time: 40 Minutes

Ingredients:
- ½ lb rump steak, excess fat trimmed
- 3 green onions, sliced
- 3 tomatoes, sliced
- 1 cup green beans, steamed and sliced
- 2 kohlrabi, peeled and chopped
- ½ cup water
- 2 cups mixed salad greens
- Salt and black pepper to season
- Salad Dressing
- 2 tsp Dijon mustard
- 1 tsp erythritol
- Salt and black pepper to taste
- 3 tbsp olive oil + extra for drizzling
- 1 tbsp red wine vinegar

Directions:
1. Preheat the oven to 400ºF. Place the kohlrabi on a baking sheet, drizzle with olive oil and bake in the oven for 25 minutes. After cooking, remove, and set aside to cool.
2. In a bowl, mix the Dijon mustard, erythritol, salt, pepper, vinegar, and olive oil. Set aside.
3. Then, preheat a grill pan over high heat while you season the meat with salt and pepper. Place the steak in the pan and brown on both sides for 4 minutes each. Remove to rest on a chopping board for 4 more minutes before slicing thinly.
4. In a shallow salad bowl, add the green onions, tomatoes, green beans, kohlrabi, salad greens, and steak slices. Drizzle the dressing over and toss with two spoons. Serve the rump steak salad warm with chunks of low carb bread.

Nutrition Info:
- Per Servings 4g Carbs, 28g Protein, 19g Fat, 325 Calories

Cajun Pork

Servings: 8 | Cooking Time: 40 Minutes

Ingredients:
- 5 lb. pork shoulder, cut into 4 to 6 chunks
- 4 tbsp organic Cajun spice mix
- 1 bay leaf
- 2 cups water
- Salt and pepper to taste

Directions:
1. In a heavy-bottomed pot, add all ingredients, including bone and mix well.
2. Cover and cook on medium-high fire until boiling. Lower

fire to a simmer and cook for 30 minutes undisturbed.
3. Remove meat, transfer to a bowl, and shred with two forks. Return to pot, bring to a boil, and boil uncovered for 10 minutes until sauce is rendered.
4. Discard bay leaf, serve and enjoy.

Nutrition Info:
- Per Servings 2.6g Carbs, 71.5g Protein, 50.2g Fat, 768 Calories

Grilled Flank Steak With Lime Vinaigrette

Servings: 6 | Cooking Time: 10 Minutes

Ingredients:
- 2 tablespoons lime juice, freshly squeezed
- ¼ cup chopped fresh cilantro
- 1 tablespoon ground cumin
- ¼ teaspoon red pepper flakes
- ¾ pound flank steak
- 2 tablespoons extra virgin olive oil
- ½ teaspoon ground black pepper
- ¼ tsp salt

Directions:
1. Heat the grill to low, medium heat
2. In a food processor, place all ingredients except for the cumin, red pepper flakes, and flank steak. Pulse until smooth. This will be the vinaigrette sauce. Set aside.
3. Season the flank steak with ground cumin and red pepper flakes and allow to marinate for at least 10 minutes.
4. Place the steak on the grill rack and cook for 5 minutes on each side. Cut into the center to check the doneness of the meat. You can also insert a meat thermometer to check the internal temperature.
5. Remove from the grill and allow to stand for 5 minutes.
6. Slice the steak to 2 inches long and toss the vinaigrette to flavor the meat.
7. Serve with salad if desired.

Nutrition Info:
- Per Servings 1.0g Carbs, 13.0g Protein, 1.0g Fat, 65 Calories

Beef Sausage Casserole

Servings: 8 | Cooking Time: 60 Minutes

Ingredients:
- ⅓ cup almond flour
- 2 eggs
- 2 pounds beef sausage, chopped
- Salt and black pepper, to taste
- 1 tbsp dried parsley
- ¼ tsp red pepper flakes
- ¼ cup Parmesan cheese, grated
- ¼ tsp onion powder
- ½ tsp garlic powder
- ¼ tsp dried oregano
- 1 cup ricotta cheese

- 1 cup sugar-free marinara sauce
- 1½ cups cheddar cheese, shredded

Directions:

1. Using a bowl, combine the sausage, pepper, pepper flakes, oregano, eggs, Parmesan cheese, onion powder, almond flour, salt, parsley, and garlic powder. Form balls, lay them on a lined baking sheet, place in the oven at 370ºF, and bake for 15 minutes.

2. Remove the balls from the oven and cover with half of the marinara sauce. Pour ricotta cheese all over followed by the rest of the marinara sauce. Scatter the cheddar cheese and bake in the oven for 10 minutes. Allow the meatballs casserole to cool before serving.

Nutrition Info:

- Per Servings 4g Carbs, 32g Protein, 35g Fat, 456 Calories

Pulled Pork With Avocado

Servings: 12 | Cooking Time: 2 Hours 55 Minutes

Ingredients:

- 4 pounds pork shoulder
- 1 tbsp avocado oil
- ½ cup beef stock
- ¼ cup jerk seasoning
- 6 avocado, sliced

Directions:

1. Rub the pork shoulder with jerk seasoning, and set in a greased baking dish. Pour in the stock, and cook for 1 hour 45 minutes in your oven at 350ºF covered with aluminium foil.

2. Discard the foil and cook for another 20 minutes. Leave to rest for 30 minutes, and shred it with 2 forks. Serve topped with avocado slices.

Nutrition Info:

- Per Servings 4.1g Carbs, 42g Protein, 42.6g Fat, 567 Calories

Beef And Egg Rice Bowls

Servings: 4 | Cooking Time: 22 Minutes

Ingredients:

- 2 cups cauli rice
- 3 cups frozen mixed vegetables
- 3 tbsp ghee
- 1 lb skirt steak
- Salt and black pepper to taste
- 4 fresh eggs
- Hot sauce (sugar-free) for topping

Directions:

1. Mix the cauli rice and mixed vegetables in a bowl, sprinkle with a little water, and steam in the microwave for 1 minute to be tender. Share into 4 serving bowls.

2. Melt the ghee in a skillet, season the beef with salt and pepper, and brown for 5 minutes on each side. Use a perforated spoon to ladle the meat onto the vegetables.

3. Wipe out the skillet and return to medium heat, crack in an

egg, season with salt and pepper and cook until the egg white has set, but the yolk is still runny 3 minutes. Remove egg onto the vegetable bowl and fry the remaining 3 eggs. Add to the other bowls.

4. Drizzle the beef bowls with hot sauce and serve.

Nutrition Info:

- Per Servings 4g Carbs, 15g Protein, 26g Fat, 320 Calories

Simple Pulled Pork

Servings: 4 | Cooking Time: 25 Minutes

Ingredients:

- 4 pork chops, deboned
- 1 onion, sliced
- 5 cloves of garlic, minced
- 1 tbsp soy sauce
- 1 ½ cups water
- Salt and pepper to taste

Directions:

1. In a heavy-bottomed pot, add all ingredients and mix well.

2. Cover and cook on medium-high fire until boiling. Lower fire to a simmer and cook for 25 minutes undisturbed.

3. Turn off fire and let it cool a bit.

4. With two forks, shred meat.

5. Serve and enjoy.

Nutrition Info:

- Per Servings 2.4g Carbs, 40.7g Protein, 17.4g Fat, 339 Calories

Bacon Smothered Pork Chops

Servings: 6 | Cooking Time: 25 Minutes

Ingredients:

- 7 strips bacon, chopped
- 6 pork chops
- Pink salt and black pepper to taste
- 5 sprigs fresh thyme + extra to garnish
- ¼ cup chicken broth
- ½ cup heavy cream

Directions:

1. Cook bacon in a large skillet on medium heat for 5 minutes to be crispy. Remove with a slotted spoon onto a paper towel-lined plate to soak up excess fat.

2. Season pork chops with salt and black pepper, and brown in the bacon fat for 4 minutes on each side. Remove to the bacon plate. Stir in the thyme, chicken broth, and heavy cream and simmer for 5 minutes. Season with salt and black pepper.

3. Return the chops and bacon, and cook further for another 2 minutes. Serve chops and a generous ladle of sauce with cauli mash. Garnish with thyme leaves.

Nutrition Info:

- Per Servings 3g Carbs, 22g Protein, 37g Fat, 435 Calories

Mushroom Beef Stew

Servings: 5 | Cooking Time: 1h 30mins

Ingredients:

- 2 pounds beef chuck roast, cut into 1/2-inch thick strips
- 1/2 medium onion, sliced or diced
- 8 ounces sliced mushrooms
- 2 cups beef broth, divided
- Salt and pepper to taste
- 1 tablespoon butter
- 2 cloves garlic, minced
- 1 tablespoon fresh chopped chives
- 1 tablespoon olive oil

Directions:

1. Heat olive oil in a large skillet over high heat. Stir in beef with salt and pepper; cook, stirring constantly, for 6-7 minutes. Remove beef from the pan and set aside.
2. Add butter, mushrooms and onions into the pan; cook and stir over medium heat.
3. Add garlic and stir for 30 seconds. Stir in 1 cup. broth and simmer 3-4 minutes.
4. Return beef to the pan. Stir in remaining broth and chives; bring to a simmer and cook on low heat for about 1 hour, covered, stirring every 20 minutes.
5. Season with salt and pepper to taste. Serve.

Nutrition Info:

- Per Servings 4.1g Carbs, 15.8g Protein, 24.5g Fat, 307 Calories

Swiss-style Italian Sausage

Servings: 6 | Cooking Time: 25 Minutes

Ingredients:

- ¼ cup olive oil
- 2 pounds Italian pork sausage, chopped
- 1 onion, sliced
- 4 sun-dried tomatoes, sliced thin
- Salt and black pepper, to taste
- ½ pound gruyere cheese, grated
- 3 yellow bell peppers, seeded and chopped
- 3 orange bell peppers, seeded and chopped
- A pinch of red pepper flakes
- ½ cup fresh parsley, chopped

Directions:

1. Set a pan over medium-high heat and warm oil, place in the sausage slices, cook each side for 3 minutes, remove to a bowl, and set aside.
2. Stir in the tomatoes, bell peppers, and onion, and cook for 5 minutes. Season with black pepper, pepper flakes, and salt and mix well. Cook for 1 minute, and remove from heat.
3. Lay the sausage slices into a baking dish, place the bell peppers mixture on top, scatter with the gruyere cheese, set in the oven at 340º F, and bake for 10 minutes until the cheese melts. Serve topped with fresh parsley.

Nutrition Info:

- Per Servings 7.6g Carbs, 34g Protein, 45g Fat, 567 Calories

Beefy Scotch Eggs

Servings: 7 | Cooking Time: 25 Minutes

Ingredients:

- 2 eggs, beaten
- 1-pound ground beef
- 2 tablespoons butter, melted
- ¼ cup coconut flour
- 7 large eggs, boiled and peeled
- Cooking spray
- Salt and pepper to taste

Directions:

1. Preheat the oven to 350oF.
2. Place the beaten eggs, ground beef, butter, and coconut flour in a mixing bowl. Season with salt and pepper to taste.
3. Coat the boiled eggs with the meat mixture and place them on a baking sheet.
4. Bake for 25 minutes.

Nutrition Info:

- Per Servings 1.8g Carbs, 21.4g Protein, 25.8g Fat, 312 Calories

Spicy Mesquite Ribs

Servings: 6 | Cooking Time: 8 Hours 45 Minutes

Ingredients:

- 3 racks pork ribs, silver lining removed
- 2 cups sugar-free BBQ sauce
- 2 tbsp erythritol
- 2 tsp chili powder
- 2 tsp cumin powder
- 2 tsp onion powder
- 2 tsp smoked paprika
- 2 tsp garlic powder
- Salt and black pepper to taste
- 1 tsp mustard powder

Directions:

1. Preheat a smoker to 400ºF using mesquite wood to create flavor in the smoker.
2. In a bowl, mix the erythritol, chili powder, cumin powder, black pepper, onion powder, smoked paprika, garlic powder, salt, and mustard powder. Rub the ribs and let marinate for 30 minutes.
3. Place on the grill grate, and cook at reduced heat of 225ºF for 4 hours. Flip the ribs after and continue cooking for 4 hours. Brush the ribs with bbq sauce on both sides and sear them in increased heat for 3 minutes per side. Remove the ribs and let sit for 4 minutes before slicing. Serve with red cabbage coleslaw.

Nutrition Info:

- Per Servings 0g Carbs, 44.5g Protein, 36.6g Fat, 580 Calories

Bbq Pork Pizza With Goat Cheese

Servings: 4 | Cooking Time: 30 Minutes

Ingredients:

• 1 low carb pizza bread
• Olive oil for brushing
• 1 cup grated manchego cheese
• 2 cups leftover pulled pork
• ½ cup sugar-free BBQ sauce
• 1 cup crumbled goat cheese

Directions:

1. Preheat oven to 400ºF and put pizza bread on a pizza pan. Brush with olive oil and sprinkle the manchego cheese all over. Mix the pork with BBQ sauce and spread over the cheese. Drop goat cheese on top and bake for 25 minutes until the cheese has melted and golden brown on top. Slice the pizza with a cutter and serve warm.

Nutrition Info:

• Per Servings 6g Carbs, 5g Protein, 24g Fat, 344 Calories

Roasted Pork Loin With Sauce

Servings: 8 | Cooking Time: 3 H

Ingredients:

• 1 teaspoon. rubbed sage
• 1 clove garlic, crushed
• 1 boneless pork loin
• 1 tablespoon almond flour
• 1/4 cup. water
• 1/2 teaspoon salt
• 1/4 cup vinegar
• 2 tablespoons soy sauce, low-carb
• 1/4 teaspoon pepper

Directions:

1. Preheat oven to 325 degrees F.
2. In a bowl, combine sage, salt, pepper, and garlic. Rub thoroughly all over pork and place it in an uncovered roasting pan on the middle oven rack.
3. Bake in the preheated oven approximately 3 hours at least 145 degrees F.
4. Meanwhile, place flour, vinegar, water, and soy sauce in a small saucepan. Heat, stirring occasionally, until mixture thicken slightly.
5. Brush roast with glaze 3 or 4 times during the last 1/2 hour of cooking. Pour remaining glaze over roast, and serve.

Nutrition Info:

• Per Servings 13.9g Carbs, 45.8g Protein, 24.6g Fat, 472 Calories

Beefy Bbq Ranch

Servings: 4 | Cooking Time: 40 Minutes

Ingredients:

• 2-lbs London broil roast, sliced into 2-inch cubes
• 1 Hidden Valley Ranch seasoning mix packet
• 1-pound bacon
• 1 tablespoon barbecue powder
• 1 cup water
• Pepper and salt to taste

Directions:

1. Add all ingredients in a pot on high fire and bring to a boil.
2. Once boiling, lower fire to a simmer and cook for 35 minutes.
3. Adjust seasoning to taste.
4. Serve and enjoy.

Nutrition Info:

• Per Servings 8.4g Carbs, 65.3g Protein, 39.7g Fat, 642 Calories

Pork Nachos

Servings: 4 | Cooking Time: 15 Minutes

Ingredients:

• 1 bag low carb tortilla chips
• 2 cups leftover pulled pork
• 1 red bell pepper, seeded and chopped
• 1 red onion, diced
• 2 cups shredded Monterey Jack cheese

Directions:

1. Preheat oven to 350ºF. Arrange the chips in a medium cast iron pan, scatter pork over, followed by red bell pepper, and onion, and sprinkle with cheese. Place the pan in the oven and cook for 10 minutes until the cheese has melted. Allow cooling for 3 minutes and serve.

Nutrition Info:

• Per Servings 9.3g Carbs, 22g Protein, 25g Fat, 452 Calories

Charred Tenderloin With Lemon Chimichurri

Servings: 4 | Cooking Time: 64 Minutes

Ingredients:

• Lemon Chimichurri
• 1 lemon, juiced
• ¼ cup chopped mint leaves
• ¼ cup chopped oregano leaves
• 2 cloves garlic, minced
• ¼ cup olive oil
• Salt to taste
• Pork
• 1 pork tenderloin
• Salt and black pepper to season
• Olive oil for rubbing

Directions:

1. Make the lemon chimichurri to have the flavors incorporate while the pork cooks.

2. In a bowl, mix the mint, oregano, and garlic. Then, add the lemon juice, olive oil, and salt, and combine well. Set the sauce aside at room temperature.

3. Preheat the charcoal grill to 450ºF in medium-high heat creating a direct heat area and indirect heat area. Rub the pork with olive oil, season with salt and pepper. Place the meat over direct heat and sear for 3 minutes on each side, after which, move to the indirect heat area.

4. Close the lid and cook for 25 minutes on one side, then open, turn the meat, and grill closed for 20 minutes on the other side. Remove the pork from the grill and let it sit for 5 minutes before slicing. Spoon lemon chimichurri over the pork and serve with a fresh salad.

Nutrition Info:

- Per Servings 2.1g Carbs, 28g Protein, 18g Fat, 388 Calories

Hot Pork With Dill Pickles

Servings: 4 | Cooking Time: 20 Minutes

Ingredients:

- ¼ cup lime juice
- 4 pork chops
- 1 tbsp coconut oil, melted
- 2 garlic cloves, minced
- 1 tbsp chili powder
- 1 tsp ground cinnamon
- 2 tsp cumin
- Salt and black pepper, to taste
- ½ tsp hot pepper sauce
- 4 dill pickles, cut into spears and squeezed

Directions:

1. Using a bowl, combine the lime juice with oil, cumin, salt, hot pepper sauce, pepper, cinnamon, garlic, and chili powder. Place in the pork chops, toss to coat, and refrigerate for 4 hours.

2. Arrange the pork on a preheated grill over medium heat, cook for 7 minutes, turn, add in the dill pickles, and cook for another 7 minutes. Split among serving plates and enjoy.

Nutrition Info:

- Per Servings 2.3g Carbs, 36g Protein, 18g Fat, 315 Calories

Filling Beefy Soup

Servings: 4 | Cooking Time: 15 Minutes

Ingredients:

- 1 small onion, diced
- 3 cloves of garlic, minced
- 1-pound lean ground sirloin
- 3 cups low-sodium beef broth
- 1 bag frozen vegetables of your choice
- 5 tablespoons oil
- Black pepper and salt to taste

Directions:

1. In a large saucepan, heat the oil over medium heat and sauté the onion and garlic until fragrant.

2. Stir in the lean ground sirloin and cook for 3 minutes until lightly golden.

3. Add in the rest of the ingredients and bring the broth to a boil for 10 minutes.

4. Serve warm.

Nutrition Info:

- Per Servings 5.0g Carbs, 29.0g Protein, 34.0g Fat, 334 Calories

Stuffed Pork With Red Cabbage Salad

Servings: 4 | Cooking Time: 40 Minutes

Ingredients:

- Zest and juice from 2 limes
- 2 garlic cloves, minced
- ¾ cup olive oil
- 1 cup fresh cilantro, chopped
- 1 cup fresh mint, chopped
- 1 tsp dried oregano
- Salt and black pepper, to taste
- 2 tsp cumin
- 4 pork loin steaks
- 2 pickles, chopped
- 4 ham slices
- 6 Swiss cheese slices
- 2 tbsp mustard
- For the Salad
- 1 head red cabbage, shredded
- 2 tbsp vinegar
- 3 tbsp olive oil
- Salt to taste

Directions:

1. In a food processor, combine the lime zest, oil, oregano, pepper, cumin, cilantro, lime juice, garlic, mint, and salt. Season the steaks with pepper and salt, set them into a bowl, place in the marinade, and toss well to coat; set aside for some hours in the fridge.

2. Arrange the steaks on a working surface, split the pickles, mustard, cheese, and ham on them, roll, and secure with toothpicks. Heat a pan over medium heat, add in the pork rolls, cook each side for 2 minutes and remove to a baking sheet. Bake in the oven at 350ºF for 25 minutes. Meanwhile, prepare the red cabbage salad by mixing all salad ingredients and serve with the meat.

Nutrition Info:

- Per Servings 3g Carbs, 26g Protein, 37g Fat, 413 Calories

Broccoli & Ground Beef Casserole

Servings: 6 | Cooking Time: 4 Hours 15 Minutes

Ingredients:

- 1 tbsp olive oil
- 2 pounds ground beef
- 1 head broccoli, cut into florets
- Salt and black pepper, to taste
- 2 tsp mustard
- 2 tsp Worcestershire sauce
- 28 ounces canned diced tomatoes
- 2 cups mozzarella cheese, grated
- 16 ounces tomato sauce
- 2 tbsp fresh parsley, chopped
- 1 tsp dried oregano

Directions:

1. Apply pepper and salt to the broccoli florets, set them into a bowl, drizzle over the olive oil, and toss well to coat completely. In a separate bowl, combine the beef with Worcestershire sauce, salt, mustard, and pepper, and stir well. Press on the slow cooker's bottom.
2. Scatter in the broccoli, add the tomatoes, parsley, mozzarella, oregano, and tomato sauce. Cook for 4 hours on low; covered. Split the casserole among bowls and enjoy while hot.

Nutrition Info:

- Per Servings 5.6g Carbs, 51g Protein, 21g Fat, 434 Calories

Garlic Pork Chops

Servings: 4 | Cooking Time: 30 Minutes

Ingredients:

- 1 ½ cups chicken broth
- 1 tablespoon butter
- 2 lemons, juiced
- 4 ¾ inch boneless pork chops
- 6 cloves garlic, minced
- Salt and pepper to taste
- 1 tablespoon olive oil

Directions:

1. Heat the olive oil in a large pot on medium-high fire.
2. Season the pork with salt, pepper, and garlic powder.
3. Place the pork in the Instant Pot and brown the sides. Set aside.
4. Add the garlic and sauté for a minute. Add the lemon juice and chicken broth. Stir in the butter.
5. Add the pork chops back to the pan. Cover the lid and simmer for 20 minutes.
6. Serve and enjoy.

Nutrition Info:

- Per Servings 4.8g Carbs, 50.2g Protein, 14.0g Fat, 355 Calories

Keto Ground Beef Stroganoff

Servings: 4 | Cooking Time: 20 Minutes

Ingredients:

- 1 pound ground beef, lean
- 4 oz mushrooms, sliced
- 1/4 cup onions, chopped or sliced
- 1 tsp beef bouillon
- 1 cup sour cream
- 1 tbsp Worcestershire sauce
- 3 tbsp butter, divided
- 1-2 pinches grated nutmeg
- 1 tbsp chopped parsley
- salt and pepper to taste

Directions:

1. In a large pan over medium heat, melt butter and add the mushrooms to spread evenly in the pan. Cook for 2 minutes, turning over for more 2 minutes' cooking.
2. Add remaining butter and onions to cook until tender. Remove the mushrooms and onions from the pan.
3. Cook the ground beef in the pan, breaking it up into small pieces, until just cooked through. Add the beef bouillon and Worcestershire sauce, stirring well.
4. Mix in the mushroom mixture and ground beef back into the pan, sprinkle the nutmeg over the top. Whisk in the sour cream and simmer gently until thickened. Add the parsley, season with salt and pepper to taste.
5. Serve with cooked cauliflower rice if desired.

Nutrition Info:

- Per Servings 5.86g Carbs, 23g Protein, 31.7g Fat, 468 Calories

Poultry Recipes

Sweet Garlic Chicken Skewers

Servings: 4 | Cooking Time: 17 Minutes + Time Refrigeration

Ingredients:
- For the Skewers
- 3 tbsp soy sauce
- 1 tbsp ginger-garlic paste
- 2 tbsp swerve brown sugar
- Chili pepper to taste
- 2 tbsp olive oil
- 3 chicken breasts, cut into cubes
- For the Dressing
- ½ cup tahini
- ½ tsp garlic powder
- Pink salt to taste
- ¼ cup warm water

Directions:

1. In a small bowl, whisk the soy sauce, ginger-garlic paste, brown sugar, chili pepper, and olive oil.

2. Put the chicken in a zipper bag, pour the marinade over, seal and shake for an even coat. Marinate in the fridge for 2 hours.

3. Preheat a grill to 400ºF and thread the chicken on skewers. Cook for 10 minutes in total with three to four turnings to be golden brown. Plate them. Mix the tahini, garlic powder, salt, and warm water in a bowl. Pour into serving jars.

4. Serve the chicken skewers and tahini dressing with cauli fried rice.

Nutrition Info:
- Per Servings 2g Carbs, 15g Protein, 17.4g Fat, 225 Calories

Thyme Chicken Thighs

Servings: 4 | Cooking Time: 30 Minutes

Ingredients:
- ½ cup chicken stock
- 1 tbsp olive oil
- ½ cup chopped onion
- 4 chicken thighs
- ¼ cup heavy cream
- 2 tbsp Dijon mustard
- 1 tsp thyme
- 1 tsp garlic powder

Directions:

1. Heat the olive oil in a pan. Cook the chicken for about 4 minutes per side. Set aside. Sauté the onion in the same pan for 3 minutes, add the stock, and simmer for 5 minutes. Stir in mustard and heavy cream, along with thyme and garlic powder. Pour the sauce over the chicken and serve.

Nutrition Info:
- Per Servings 4g Carbs, 33g Protein, 42g Fat, 528 Calories

Turkey Burgers With Fried Brussels Sprouts

Servings: 4 | Cooking Time: 30 Minutes

Ingredients:
- For the burgers
- 1 pound ground turkey
- 1 free-range egg
- ½ onion, chopped
- 1 tsp salt
- ½ tsp ground black pepper
- 1 tsp dried thyme
- 2 oz butter
- For the fried Brussels sprouts
- 1 ½ lb Brussels sprouts, halved
- 3 oz butter
- 1 tsp salt
- ½ tsp ground black pepper

Directions:

1. Combine the burger ingredients in a mixing bowl. Create patties from the mixture. Set a large pan over medium-high heat, warm butter, and fry the patties until cooked completely.

2. Place on a plate and cover with aluminium foil to keep warm. Fry brussels sprouts in butter, season to your preference, then set to a bowl. Plate the burgers and brussels sprouts and serve.

Nutrition Info:
- Per Servings 5.8g Carbs, 31g Protein, 25g Fat, 443 Calories

Oregano & Chili Flattened Chicken

Servings: 6 | Cooking Time: 5 Minutes

Ingredients:
- 6 chicken breasts
- 4 cloves garlic, minced
- ½ cup oregano leaves, chopped
- ½ cup lemon juice
- 2/3 cup olive oil
- ¼ cup erythritol
- Salt and black pepper to taste
- 3 small chilies, minced

Directions:

1. Preheat a grill to 350ºF.

2. In a bowl, mix the garlic, oregano, lemon Juice, olive oil, and erythritol. Set aside.

3. While the spices incorporate in flavor, cover the chicken with plastic wraps, and use the rolling pin to pound to ½ -inch thickness. Remove the wrap afterward, and brush the mixture on the chicken on both sides. Place on the grill, cover the lid and cook for 15 minutes.

4. Then, baste the chicken with more of the spice mixture, and continue cooking for 15 more minutes.

Nutrition Info:
- Per Servings 3g Carbs, 26g Protein, 9g Fat, 265 Calories

Chicken Breasts With Spinach & Artichoke

Servings: 4 | Cooking Time: 60 Minutes

Ingredients:
- 4 ounces cream cheese
- 4 chicken breasts
- 8 oz canned artichoke hearts, chopped
- 1 cup spinach
- ½ cup Pecorino cheese, grated
- 1 tbsp onion powder
- 1 tbsp garlic powder
- Salt and ground black pepper, to taste
- 4 ounces Monterrey Jack cheese, shredded

Directions:
1. Lay the chicken breasts on a lined baking sheet, season with pepper and salt, set in the oven at 350ºF, and bake for 35 minutes. In a bowl, combine the artichokes with onion powder, Pecorino cheese, salt, spinach, cream cheese, garlic powder, and pepper.
2. Remove the chicken from the oven, cut each piece in half, divide artichokes mixture on top, spread with Monterrey cheese, set in the oven at 350ºF, and bake for 20 minutes.

Nutrition Info:
- Per Servings 3.5g Carbs, 36g Protein, 21g Fat, 431 Calories

Cheese Stuffed Chicken Breasts With Spinach

Servings: 4 | Cooking Time: 50 Minutes

Ingredients:
- 4 chicken breasts, boneless and skinless
- ½ cup mozzarella cheese
- ⅓ cup Parmesan cheese
- 6 ounces cream cheese
- 2 cups spinach, chopped
- A pinch of nutmeg
- ½ tsp minced garlic
- Breading:
- 2 eggs
- ⅓ cup almond flour
- 2 tbsp olive oil
- ½ tsp parsley
- ⅓ cup Parmesan cheese
- A pinch of onion powder

Directions:
1. Pound the chicken until it doubles in size. Mix the cream cheese, spinach, mozzarella, nutmeg, salt, pepper, and parmesan in a bowl. Divide the mixture between the chicken breasts

and spread it out evenly. Wrap the chicken in a plastic wrap. Refrigerate for 15 minutes.
2. Heat the oil in a pan and preheat the oven to 370ºF. Beat the eggs and combine all other breading ingredients in a bowl. Dip the chicken in egg first, then in the breading mixture. Cook in the pan until browned. Place on a lined baking sheet and bake for 20 minutes.

Nutrition Info:
- Per Servings 3.5g Carbs, 38g Protein, 36g Fat, 491 Calories

Coconut Aminos Chicken Bake

Servings: 4 | Cooking Time: 20 Minutes

Ingredients:
- 3 green onions, chopped
- 4 chicken breasts
- 4 oz. cheddar cheese, shredded
- 4 bacon strips
- 1 oz. coconut aminos
- 2 tbsp. coconut oil

Directions:
1. Heat oil in a skillet over high heat. Add chicken breasts and cook for 7 minutes both sides.
2. In another pan over medium-high heat, sauté bacon and place to a plate lined with a paper towel and crumble it.
3. Lay the chicken in a baking dish, sprinkle with coconut aminos, bacon, shredded cheese and chopped green onions.
4. Place the baking dish in the broiler and cook on High for 5 minutes. Serve and enjoy.

Nutrition Info:
- Per Servings 2g Carbs, 18g Protein, 49g Fat, 570 Calories

Creamy Stuffed Chicken With Parma Ham

Servings: 4 | Cooking Time: 40 Minutes

Ingredients:
- 4 chicken breasts
- 2 tbsp olive oil
- 3 cloves garlic, minced
- 3 shallots, finely chopped
- 4 tbsp dried mixed herbs
- 8 slices Parma ham
- 8 oz cream cheese
- 2 lemons, zested
- Salt and black pepper to taste

Directions:
1. Preheat the oven to 350ºF.
2. Heat the oil in a small skillet and sauté the garlic and shallots with a pinch of salt and lemon zest for 3 minutes. Turn the heat off and let it cool. After, stir the cream cheese and mixed herbs into the shallot mixture.
3. Score a pocket in each chicken breast, fill the holes with the cream cheese mixture and cover with the cut-out chicken. Wrap each breast with two Parma ham and secure the ends

with a toothpick.

4. Lay the chicken parcels on a greased baking sheet and cook in the oven for 20 minutes. After cooking, remove to rest for 4 minutes before serving with a green salad and roasted tomatoes.

Nutrition Info:

• Per Servings 2g Carbs, 26g Protein, 35g Fat, 485 Calories

Eggplant & Tomato Braised Chicken Thighs

Servings: 4 | Cooking Time: 45 Minutes

Ingredients:

• 2 tbsp ghee
• 1 lb chicken thighs
• Pink salt and black pepper to taste
• 2 cloves garlic, minced
• 1 can whole tomatoes
• 1 eggplant, diced
• 10 fresh basil leaves, chopped + extra to garnish

Directions:

1. Melt ghee in a saucepan over medium heat, season the chicken with salt and black pepper, and fry for 4 minutes on each side until golden brown. Remove chicken onto a plate.

2. Sauté the garlic in the ghee for 2 minutes, pour in the tomatoes, and cook covered for 8 minutes.

3. Add in the eggplant and basil. Cook for 4 minutes. Season the sauce with salt and black pepper, stir and add the chicken. Coat with sauce and simmer for 3 minutes.

4. Serve chicken with sauce on a bed of squash pasta. Garnish with extra basil.

Nutrition Info:

• Per Servings 2g Carbs, 26g Protein, 39.5g Fat, 468 Calories

Chicken & Squash Traybake

Servings: 4 | Cooking Time: 60 Minutes

Ingredients:

• 2 lb chicken thighs
• 1 pound butternut squash, cubed
• ½ cup black olives, pitted
• ¼ cup olive oil
• 5 garlic cloves, sliced
• 1 tbsp dried oregano
• Salt and black pepper, to taste

Directions:

1. Set oven to 400ºF and grease a baking dish. Place in the chicken with the skin down. Set the garlic, olives and butternut squash around the chicken then drizzle with oil.

2. Spread pepper, salt, and oregano over the mixture then add into the oven. Cook for 45 minutes.

Nutrition Info:

• Per Servings 5.5g Carbs, 31g Protein, 15g Fat, 411 Calories

Chicken And Mushrooms

Servings: 6 | Cooking Time: 30 Minutes

Ingredients:

• 6 boneless chicken breasts, halved
• 1 onion, chopped
• 4 cloves of garlic, minced
• ½ cup coconut milk
• 1 cup mushrooms, sliced
• Pepper and salt to taste
• ½ cup water

Directions:

1. On high fire, heat a saucepan for 2 minutes. Add oil to the pan and swirl to coat bottom and sides. Heat oil for a minute.

2. Add chicken and sear for 4 minutes per side. Transfer chicken to a chopping board and chop into bite-sized chunks.

3. In the same pan, lower fire to medium and sauté garlic for a minute. Add onion and sauté for 3 minutes. Stir in mushrooms and water. Deglaze pot.

4. Return chicken to the pot and mix well. Season with pepper and salt.

5. Cover and lower fire to simmer and cook for 15 minutes.

Nutrition Info:

• Per Servings 3.5g Carbs, 62.2g Protein, 11.9g Fat, 383 Calories

Chicken And Bacon Rolls

Servings: 4 | Cooking Time: 45 Minutes

Ingredients:

• 1 tbsp fresh chives, chopped
• 8 ounces blue cheese
• 2 pounds chicken breasts, skinless, boneless, halved
• 12 bacon slices
• 2 tomatoes, chopped
• Salt and ground black pepper, to taste

Directions:

1. Set a pan over medium heat, place in the bacon, cook until halfway done, remove to paper towels, and drain the grease. Using a bowl, stir together the blue cheese, chives, tomatoes, pepper, and salt.

2. Use a meat tenderizer to flatten the chicken breasts well, season and lay the cream cheese mixture on top. Roll them up, and wrap each in a bacon slice. Place the wrapped chicken breasts in a greased baking dish, and roast in the oven at 370ºF for 30 minutes. Serve on top of wilted kale.

Nutrition Info:

• Per Servings 5g Carbs, 38g Protein, 48g Fat, 623 Calories

Stewed Italian Chicken

Servings: 4 | Cooking Time: 25 Minutes

Ingredients:
- 3 ounces Italian dressing
- 4 boneless skinless chicken breasts thawed
- 5 tablespoons olive oil
- ½ cup water
- Salt and pepper to taste

Directions:
1. Add all ingredients in a pot on high fire and bring it to a boil.
2. Once boiling, lower fire to a simmer and cook for 20 minutes.
3. Adjust seasoning to taste.
4. Serve and enjoy.

Nutrition Info:
- Per Servings 3.6g Carbs, 53.6g Protein, 31.0g Fat, 545 Calories

Fennel Shredded Chicken

Servings: 8 | Cooking Time: 30 Minutes

Ingredients:
- 2 lb. chicken thighs, bone-in, and skin removed
- ¼ cup fennel bulb
- 4 cloves of garlic, minced
- 3 tbsp. lemon juice, freshly squeezed
- 1 tsp. cinnamon
- Salt and pepper to taste
- ½ cup water

Directions:
1. Place all ingredients in a heavy-bottomed pot and give a good stir.
2. Place on high fire and bring it to a boil for 5 minutes. Cover, lower fire to a simmer, and cook for 20 minutes.
3. Remove chicken and place in a bowl. Shred using two forks. Discard bones and return shredded chicken to the pot.
4. Boil for 5 minutes or until sauce is rendered.
5. Serve and enjoy.

Nutrition Info:
- Per Servings 1.9g Carbs, 18.7g Protein, 18.8g Fat, 257 Calories

Simple Chicken Garlic-tomato Stew

Servings: 4 | Cooking Time: 45 Minutes

Ingredients:
- 3 tbsp. coconut oil
- 5 cloves of garlic, minced
- 4 chicken breasts halves
- 3 roma tomatoes chopped
- 1 small onion chopped
- Salt and pepper to taste
- 1 ½ cups water

Directions:
1. Place a large saucepan on medium-high fire and heat for 2 minutes.
2. Add 1 tbsp oil and heat for a minute.
3. Season chicken breasts generously with pepper and salt.
4. Sear for 5 minutes per side of the chicken breast. Transfer to a plate and let it rest.
5. In the same pan, add remaining oil and sauté garlic for a minute. Stir in onions and tomatoes. Sauté for 7 minutes.
6. Meanwhile, chop chicken into bite-sized pieces.
7. Deglaze pan with water and add chopped chicken. Cover and simmer for 15 minutes.
8. Adjust seasoning if needed.
9. Serve and enjoy.

Nutrition Info:
- Per Servings 1.1g Carbs, 60.8g Protein, 37.5g Fat, 591 Calories

Easy Asian Chicken

Servings: 5 | Cooking Time: 16 Minutes

Ingredients:
- 1 ½ lb. boneless chicken breasts, sliced into strips
- 1 tbsp ginger slices
- 3 tbsp coconut aminos
- ¼ cup organic chicken broth
- 3 cloves of garlic, minced
- 5 tablespoons sesame oil

Directions:
1. On high fire, heat a heavy-bottomed pot for 2 minutes. Add oil to a pan and swirl to coat bottom and sides. Heat oil for a minute.
2. Add garlic and ginger sauté for a minute.
3. Stir in chicken breast and sauté for 5 minutes. Season with coconut aminos and sauté for another 2 minutes.
4. Add remaining ingredients and bring to a boil.
5. Let it boil for 5 minutes.
6. Serve and enjoy.

Nutrition Info:
- Per Servings 1.2g Carbs, 30.9g Protein, 17.6g Fat, 299 Calories

Pancetta & Chicken Casserole

Servings: 3 | Cooking Time: 40 Minutes

Ingredients:
- 8 pancetta strips, chopped
- ⅓ cup Dijon mustard
- Salt and black pepper, to taste
- 1 onion, chopped
- 1 tbsp olive oil
- 1½ cups chicken stock
- 3 chicken breasts, skinless and boneless
- ¼ tsp sweet paprika

Directions:

1. Using a bowl, combine the paprika, pepper, salt, and mustard. Sprinkle this on chicken breasts and massage. Set a pan over medium-high heat, stir in the pancetta, cook until it browns, and remove to a plate. Place oil in the same pan and heat over medium-high heat, add in the chicken breasts, cook for each side for 2 minutes and set aside.

2. Place in the stock, and bring to a simmer. Stir in pepper, pancetta, salt, and onion. Return the chicken to the pan as well, stir gently, and simmer for 20 minutes over medium heat, turning the meat halfway through. Split the chicken on serving plates, sprinkle the sauce over it to serve.

Nutrition Info:

• Per Servings 3g Carbs, 26g Protein, 18g Fat, 313 Calories

Stewed Chicken Salsa

Servings: 4 | Cooking Time: 25 Minutes

Ingredients:

• 1 cup shredded cheddar cheese
• 8-ounces cream cheese
• 16-ounces salsa
• 4 skinless and boneless thawed chicken breasts
• 4 tablespoons butter
• 1 cup water

Directions:

1. Add all ingredients in a pot, except for sour cream, on high fire, and bring to a boil.
2. Once boiling, lower fire to a simmer and cook for 20 minutes.
3. Adjust seasoning to taste and stir in sour cream.
4. Serve and enjoy.

Nutrition Info:

• Per Servings 9.6g Carbs, 67.8g Protein, 32.6g Fat, 658 Calories

Chicken Cacciatore

Servings: 6 | Cooking Time: 35 Minutes

Ingredients:

• 6 chicken drumsticks, bone-in
• 1 bay leaf
• 4 roma tomatoes, chopped
• ½ cup black olives, pitted
• 3 cloves garlic, minced
• Salt and pepper to taste
• 1 cup water
• 1 tsp oil

Directions:

1. On high fire, heat a saucepan for 2 minutes. Add oil to the pan and swirl to coat bottom and sides. Heat oil for a minute.
2. Add garlic and sauté for a minute. Stir in tomatoes and bay leaf. Crumble and wilt tomatoes for 5 minutes.
3. Add chicken and continue sautéing for 7 minutes.
4. Deglaze the pot with ½ cup water.
5. Add remaining ingredients. Season generously with salt and pepper.
6. Lower fire to low, cover, and simmer for 20 minutes.
7. Serve and enjoy.

Nutrition Info:

• Per Servings 9.5g Carbs, 25.3g Protein, 13.2g Fat, 256 Calories

Lemon Chicken Bake

Servings: 6 | Cooking Time: 55 Minutes

Ingredients:

• 6 skinless chicken breasts
• 1 parsnip, cut into wedges
• Salt and ground black pepper, to taste
• Juice from 2 lemons
• Zest from 2 lemons
• Lemon rinds from 2 lemons

Directions:

1. In a baking dish, add the chicken alongside pepper and salt. Sprinkle with lemon juice. Toss well to coat, place in parsnip, lemon rinds and lemon zest, set in an oven at 370ºF, and bake for 45 minutes.
2. Get rid of the lemon rinds, split the chicken onto plates, sprinkle sauce from the baking dish over.

Nutrition Info:

• Per Servings 4.5g Carbs, 25g Protein, 9g Fat, 274 Calories

Coconut Chicken Soup

Servings: 4 | Cooking Time: 30 Minutes

Ingredients:

• 3 tbsp butter
• 4 ounces cream cheese
• 2 chicken breasts, diced
• 4 cups chicken stock
• Salt and black pepper, to taste
• ½ cup coconut cream
• ¼ cup celery, chopped

Directions:

1. In the blender, combine stock, butter, coconut cream, salt, cream cheese, and pepper. Remove to a pot, heat over medium heat, and stir in the chicken and celery. Simmer for 15 minutes, separate into bowls, and enjoy.

Nutrition Info:

• Per Servings 5g Carbs, 31g Protein, 23g Fat, 387 Calories

Spicy Chicken Kabobs

Servings: 6 | Cooking Time: 1 Hour And 20 Minutes

Ingredients:

- 2 pounds chicken breasts, cubed
- 1 tsp sesame oil
- 1 tbsp olive oil
- 1 cup red bell pepper pieces
- 2 tbsp five spice powder
- 2 tbsp granulated sweetener
- 1 tbsp fish sauce

Directions:

1. Combine the sauces and seasonings in a bowl. Add the chicken, and let marinate for 1 hour in the fridge. Preheat the grill. Take 12 skewers and thread the chicken and bell peppers. Grill for 3 minutes per side.

Nutrition Info:

- Per Servings 3.1g Carbs, 17.5g Protein, 13.5g Fat, 198 Calories

Bacon Chicken Alfredo

Servings: 4 | Cooking Time: 35 Minutes

Ingredients:

- 4-ounces mushrooms drained and sliced
- 1 cup shredded mozzarella cheese
- 1 jar Classico creamy alfredo sauce
- 6 slices chopped hickory bacon
- 4 boneless skinless chicken breasts thawed or fresh
- Pepper and salt to taste
- ½ cup water

Directions:

1. Add all ingredients in a pot on high fire and bring it to a boil.
2. Once boiling, lower fire to a simmer and cook for 30 minutes, stirring every now and then.
3. Adjust seasoning to taste.
4. Serve and enjoy.

Nutrition Info:

- Per Servings 7.7g Carbs, 75.8g Protein, 70.8g Fat, 976 Calories

Stuffed Avocados With Chicken

Servings: 2 | Cooking Time: 10 Minutes

Ingredients:

- 2 avocados, cut in half and pitted
- ¼ cup pesto
- 1 tsp dried thyme
- 2 tbsp cream cheese
- 1½ cups chicken, cooked and shredded
- Salt and ground black pepper, to taste
- ¼ tsp cayenne pepper
- ½ tsp onion powder
- ½ tsp garlic powder

- 1 tsp paprika
- Salt and black pepper, to taste
- 2 tbsp lemon juice

Directions:

1. Scoop the insides of the avocado halves, and place the flesh in a bowl. Add in the chicken. Stir in the remaining ingredients. Stuff the avocado cups with chicken mixture and enjoy.

Nutrition Info:

- Per Servings 5g Carbs, 24g Protein, 40g Fat, 511 Calories

Lemon Chicken Wings

Servings: 4 | Cooking Time: 30 Minutes

Ingredients:

- 1 cup omission ipa
- A pinch of garlic powder
- 1 tsp lemon zest
- 3 tbsp lemon juice
- ½ tsp ground cilantro
- 1 tbsp fish sauce
- 2 tbsp butter
- ¼ tsp xanthan gum
- 3 tbsp swerve sweetener
- 20 chicken wings
- Salt and black pepper, to taste

Directions:

1. Combine lemon juice and zest, fish sauce, cilantro, omission ipa, sweetener, and garlic powder in a saucepan. Bring to a boil, cover, lower the heat, and let simmer for 10 minutes. Stir in the butter and xanthan gum. Set aside. Season the wings with some salt and pepper.
2. Preheat the grill and cook for 5 minutes per side. Serve topped with the sauce.

Nutrition Info:

- Per Servings 4g Carbs, 21g Protein, 25g Fat, 365 Calories

Chicken Country Style

Servings: 4 | Cooking Time: 25 Minutes

Ingredients:

- 3 tablespoons butter
- 1 packet dry Lipton's onion soup mix
- 1 can Campbell's chicken gravy
- 4 skinless and boneless chicken breasts
- 1/3 teaspoon pepper
- 1 cup water

Directions:

1. Add all ingredients in a pot on high fire and bring it to a boil.
2. Once boiling, lower fire to a simmer and cook for 25 minutes.
3. Adjust seasoning to taste.
4. Serve and enjoy.

Nutrition Info:

- Per Servings 6.8g Carbs, 53.7g Protein, 16.9g Fat, 380 Calories

Spinach Chicken Cheesy Bake

Servings: 6 | Cooking Time: 45 Minutes

Ingredients:

- 6 chicken breasts, skinless and boneless
- 1 tsp mixed spice seasoning
- Pink salt and black pepper to season
- 2 loose cups baby spinach
- 3 tsp olive oil
- 4 oz cream cheese, cubed
- 1 ¼ cups shredded mozzarella cheese
- 4 tbsp water

Directions:

1. Preheat oven to 370ºF.
2. Season chicken with spice mix, salt, and black pepper. Pat with your hands to have the seasoning stick on the chicken. Put in the casserole dish and layer spinach over the chicken. Mix the oil with cream cheese, mozzarella, salt, and black pepper and stir in water a tablespoon at a time. Pour the mixture over the chicken and cover the pot with aluminium foil.
3. Bake for 20 minutes, remove foil and continue cooking for 15 minutes until a nice golden brown color is formed on top. Take out and allow sitting for 5 minutes.
4. Serve warm with braised asparagus.

Nutrition Info:

- Per Servings 3.1g Carbs, 15g Protein, 30.2g Fat, 340 Calories

Chicken With Asparagus & Root Vegetables

Servings: 4 | Cooking Time: 35 Minutes

Ingredients:

- 2 cups whipping cream
- 3 chicken breasts, boneless, skinless, chopped
- 3 tbsp butter
- ½ cup onion, chopped
- ¾ cup carrot, chopped
- 5 cups chicken stock
- Salt and black pepper, to taste
- 1 bay leaf
- 1 turnip, chopped
- 1 parsnip, chopped
- 17 ounces asparagus, trimmed
- 3 tsp fresh thyme, chopped

Directions:

1. Set a pan over medium heat and add whipping cream, allow simmering, and cook until it's reduced by half for about 7 minutes. Set another pan over medium heat and warm butter, sauté the onion for 3 minutes. Pour in the chicken stock, carrots, turnip, and parsnip, chicken, and bay leaf, bring to a boil, and simmer for 20 minutes.
2. Add in the asparagus and cook for 7 minutes. Discard the bay leaf, stir in the reduced whipping cream, adjust the seasoning and ladle the stew into serving bowls. Scatter with fresh thyme.

Nutrition Info:

- Per Servings 7.4g Carbs, 37g Protein, 31g Fat, 497 Calories

Chicken In Creamy Spinach Sauce

Servings: 4 | Cooking Time: 20 Minutes

Ingredients:

- 1 pound chicken thighs
- 2 tbsp coconut oil
- 2 tbsp coconut flour
- 2 cups spinach, chopped
- 1 tsp oregano
- 1 cup heavy cream
- 1 cup chicken broth
- 2 tbsp butter

Directions:

1. Warm the coconut oil in a skillet and brown the chicken on all sides, about 6-8 minutes. Set aside.
2. Melt the butter and whisk in the flour over medium heat. Whisk in the heavy cream and chicken broth and bring to a boil. Stir in oregano. Add the spinach to the skillet and cook until wilted.
3. Add the thighs in the skillet and cook for an additional 5 minutes.

Nutrition Info:

- Per Servings 2.6g Carbs, 18g Protein, 38g Fat, 446 Calories

Baked Chicken With Acorn Squash And Goat's Cheese

Servings: 6 | Cooking Time: 1 Hour 15 Minutes

Ingredients:

- 6 chicken breasts, skinless and boneless
- 1 lb acorn squash, peeled and sliced
- Salt and ground black pepper, to taste
- 1 cup goat's cheese, shredded
- Cooking spray

Directions:

1. Take cooking oil and spray on a baking dish, add in chicken breasts, pepper, squash, and salt and drizzle with olive. Transfer in the oven set at 420ºF, and bake for 1 hour. Scatter goat's cheese, and bake for 15 minutes. Remove to a serving plate and enjoy.

Nutrition Info:

- Per Servings 5g Carbs, 12g Protein, 16g Fat, 235 Calories

Chicken With Anchovy Tapenade

Servings: 2 | Cooking Time: 30 Minutes

Ingredients:
- 1 chicken breast, cut into 4 pieces
- 2 tbsp coconut oil
- 3 garlic cloves, and crushed
- For the tapenade
- 1 cup black olives, pitted
- 1 oz anchovy fillets, rinsed
- 1 garlic clove, crushed
- Salt and ground black pepper, to taste
- 2 tbsp olive oil
- ¼ cup fresh basil, chopped
- 1 tbsp lemon juice

Directions:
1. Using a food processor, combine the olives, salt, olive oil, basil, lemon juice, anchovy fillets, and pepper, blend well. Set a pan over medium-high heat and warm coconut oil, stir in the garlic, and cook for 2 minutes.
2. Place in the chicken pieces and cook each side for 4 minutes. Split the chicken among plates and apply a topping of the anchovy tapenade.

Nutrition Info:
- Per Servings 3g Carbs, 25g Protein, 13g Fat, 155 Calories

Greek Chicken Stew

Servings: 4 | Cooking Time: 30 Minutes

Ingredients:
- ¼ cup feta cheese
- Sliced and pitted Kalamata olives
- 1 bottle ken's steak house Greek dressing with Feta cheese, olive oil, and black olives
- 4 boneless and skinless thawed chicken breasts
- 1 cup water

Directions:
1. Add all ingredients in a pot, except for feta, on high fire, and bring to a boil.
2. Once boiling, lower fire to a simmer and cook for 25 minutes.
3. Adjust seasoning to taste and stir in feta.
4. Serve and enjoy.

Nutrition Info:
- Per Servings 3.2g Carbs, 54.4g Protein, 65.1g Fat, 818 Calories

Easy Creamy Chicken

Servings: 8 | Cooking Time: 15 Minutes

Ingredients:
- 5 tablespoons butter
- 2 cans crushed tomatoes
- 4 cooked chicken breasts, shredded
- 1 teaspoon herb seasoning mix of your choice
- ¼ cup parmesan cheese, grated
- Pepper and salt to taste

Directions:
1. Place a heavy-bottomed pot on medium-high fire and melt butter. Add tomatoes.
2. Sauté for 5 minutes, season with pepper, salt, and seasoning mix.
3. Stir in chicken. Mix well.
4. Cook until heated through, around 5 minutes.
5. Serve with a sprinkle of parmesan cheese.

Nutrition Info:
- Per Servings 2.3g Carbs, 29.5g Protein, 11.3g Fat, 235 Calories

Lemon & Rosemary Chicken In A Skillet

Servings: 4 | Cooking Time: 1 Hour And 20 Minutes

Ingredients:
- 8 chicken thighs
- 1 tsp salt
- 2 tbsp lemon juice
- 1 tsp lemon zest
- 2 tbsp olive oil
- 1 tbsp chopped rosemary
- ¼ tsp black pepper
- 1 garlic clove, minced

Directions:
1. Combine all ingredients in a bowl. Place in the fridge for one hour.
2. Heat a skillet over medium heat. Add the chicken along with the juices and cook until crispy, about 7 minutes per side.

Nutrition Info:
- Per Servings 2.5g Carbs, 31g Protein, 31g Fat, 477 Calories

Turkey Stew With Salsa Verde

Servings: 6 | Cooking Time: 30 Minutes

Ingredients:
- 4 cups leftover turkey meat, chopped
- 2 cups green beans
- 6 cups chicken stock
- Salt and ground black pepper, to taste
- 1 tbsp canned chipotle peppers, chopped
- ½ tsp garlic powder
- ½ cup salsa verde
- 1 tsp ground coriander
- 2 tsp cumin

- ¼ cup sour cream
- 1 tbsp fresh cilantro, chopped

Directions:

1. Set a pan over medium heat. Add in the stock and heat. Stir in the green beans, and cook for 10 minutes. Place in the turkey, garlic powder, ground coriander, salt, salsa verde, chipotles, cumin, and pepper, and cook for 10 minutes.
2. Stir in the sour cream, kill the heat, and separate into bowls. Top with chopped cilantro and enjoy.

Nutrition Info:

- Per Servings 2g Carbs, 27g Protein, 11g Fat, 193 Calories

Easy Bbq Chicken And Cheese

Servings: 4 | Cooking Time: 40 Minutes

Ingredients:

- 1-pound chicken tenders, boneless
- ½ cup commercial BBQ sauce, keto-friendly
- 1 teaspoon liquid smoke
- 1 cup mozzarella cheese, grated
- ½ pound bacon, fried and crumbled
- Pepper and salt to taste

Directions:

1. With paper towels, dry chicken tenders. Season with pepper and salt.
2. Place chicken tenders on an oven-safe dish.
3. Whisk well BBQ sauce and liquid smoke in a bowl and pour over chicken tenders. Coat well in the sauce.
4. Bake in a preheated 400oF oven for 30 minutes.
5. Remove from oven, turnover chicken tenders, sprinkle cheese on top.
6. Return to the oven and continue baking for 10 minutes more.
7. Serve and enjoy with a sprinkle of bacon bits.

Nutrition Info:

- Per Servings 6.7g Carbs, 34.6g Protein, 31.5g Fat, 351 Calories

Turkey & Cheese Stuffed Mushrooms

Servings: 5 | Cooking Time: 20 Minutes

Ingredients:

- 12 ounces button mushroom caps
- 3 ounces cream cheese
- ¼ cup carrot, chopped
- 1 tsp ranch seasoning mix
- 4 tbsp hot sauce
- ¾ cup blue cheese, crumbled
- ¼ cup onion, chopped
- ½ cup turkey breasts, cooked, chopped
- Salt and black pepper, to taste
- Cooking spray

Directions:

1. Using a bowl, combine the cream cheese with the blue cheese, ranch seasoning, turkey, onion, carrot, salt, hot sauce,

and pepper. Stuff each mushroom cap with this mixture, set on a lined baking sheet, spray with cooking spray, place in the oven at 425ºF, and bake for 10 minutes.

Nutrition Info:

- Per Servings 8.6g Carbs, 51g Protein, 17g Fat, 486 Calories

Turkey Breast Salad

Servings: 4 | Cooking Time: 25 Minutes

Ingredients:

- 1 tbsp swerve
- 1 red onion, chopped
- ¼ cup vinegar
- ¼ cup olive oil
- ¼ cup water
- 1¾ cups raspberries
- 1 tbsp Dijon mustard
- Salt and ground black pepper, to taste
- 10 ounces baby spinach
- 2 medium turkey breasts, boneless
- 4 ounces goat cheese, crumbled
- ½ cup pecans halves

Directions:

1. Using a blender, combine swerve, vinegar, 1 cup raspberries, pepper, mustard, water, onion, oil, and salt, and ensure well blended. Strain this into a bowl, and set aside. Cut the turkey breast in half, add a seasoning of pepper and salt, and place skin side down into a pan.
2. Cook for 8 minutes flipping to the other side and cooking for 5 minutes. Split the spinach among plates, spread with the remaining raspberries, pecan halves, and goat cheese. Slice the turkey breasts, put over the salad and top with raspberries vinaigrette and enjoy.

Nutrition Info:

- Per Servings 6g Carbs, 28g Protein, 33g Fat, 451 Calories

Creamy Stewed Chicken

Servings: 6 | Cooking Time: 30 Minutes

Ingredients:

- 10.5-ounce can cream of chicken soup
- 12-ounce package frozen broccoli
- 0.6-ounce package Italian dry mix dressing
- 8-ounces cream cheese
- 1 ½-pounds skinless, boneless chicken breasts
- 5 tablespoons olive oil
- ½ cup water
- Pepper and salt to taste

Directions:

1. Add all ingredients in a pot on high fire and bring to a boil.
2. Once boiling, lower fire to a simmer and cook for 25 minutes, stirring every now and then.
3. Adjust seasoning to taste.
4. Serve and enjoy.

Nutrition Info:

- Per Servings 7.0g Carbs, 31.0g Protein, 21.5g Fat, 350 Calories

Parmesan Wings With Yogurt Sauce

Servings: 6 | Cooking Time: 25 Minutes

Ingredients:
- For the Dipping Sauce
- 1 cup plain yogurt
- 1 tsp fresh lemon juice
- Salt and black pepper to taste
- For the Wings
- 2 lb chicken wings
- Salt and black pepper to taste
- Cooking spray
- ½ cup melted butter
- ½ cup Hot sauce
- ¼ cup grated Parmesan cheese

Directions:

1. Mix the yogurt, lemon juice, salt, and black pepper in a bowl. Chill while making the chicken.
2. Preheat oven to 400°F and season wings with salt and black pepper. Line them on a baking sheet and grease lightly with cooking spray. Bake for 20 minutes until golden brown. Mix butter, hot sauce, and parmesan in a bowl. Toss chicken in the sauce to evenly coat and plate. Serve with yogurt dipping sauce and celery strips.

Nutrition Info:
- Per Servings 4g Carbs, 24g Protein, 36.4g Fat, 452 Calories

Chicken Thighs With Broccoli & Green Onions

Servings: 2 | Cooking Time: 25 Minutes

Ingredients:
- 2 chicken thighs, skinless, boneless, cut into strips
- 1 tbsp olive oil
- 1 tsp red pepper flakes
- 1 tsp onion powder
- 1 tbsp fresh ginger, grated
- ¼ cup tamari sauce
- ½ tsp garlic powder
- ½ cup water
- ½ cup erythritol
- ½ tsp xanthan gum
- ½ cup green onions, chopped
- 1 small head broccoli, cut into florets

Directions:

1. Set a pan over medium heat and warm oil, cook in the chicken and ginger for 4 minutes. Stir in the water, onion powder, pepper flakes, garlic powder, tamari sauce, xanthan gum, and erythritol, and cook for 15 minutes. Add in the green onions and broccoli, cook for 6 minutes. Serve hot.

Nutrition Info:
- Per Servings 5g Carbs, 27g Protein, 23g Fat, 387 Calories

Chicken Wings With Thyme Chutney

Servings: 4 | Cooking Time: 45 Minutes

Ingredients:
- 12 chicken wings, cut in half
- 1 tbsp turmeric
- 1 tbsp cumin
- 3 tbsp fresh ginger, grated
- 1 tbsp cilantro, chopped
- 2 tbsp paprika
- Salt and ground black pepper, to taste
- 3 tbsp olive oil
- Juice of ½ lime
- 1 cup thyme leaves
- ¾ cup cilantro, chopped
- 1 tbsp water
- 1 jalapeño pepper

Directions:

1. Using a bowl, stir together 1 tbsp ginger, cumin, paprika, salt, 2 tbsp olive oil, pepper, turmeric, and cilantro. Place in the chicken wings pieces, toss to coat, and refrigerate for 20 minutes. Heat the grill, place in the marinated wings, cook for 25 minutes, turning from time to time, remove and set to a bowl.
2. Using a blender, combine thyme, remaining ginger, salt, jalapeno pepper, black pepper, lime juice, cilantro, remaining olive oil, and water, and blend well. Set the chicken wings on serving plate and top with the sauce.

Nutrition Info:
- Per Servings 3.5g Carbs, 22g Protein, 15g Fat, 243 Calories

Oven-baked Skillet Lemon Chicken

Servings: 4 | Cooking Time: 60 Minutes

Ingredients:
- 6 small chicken thighs
- 1 medium onion
- 1 lemon
- ¼ cup lemon juice, freshly squeezed
- Salt and pepper to taste

Directions:

1. Place all ingredients in a Ziploc bag and allow to marinate for at least 6 hours in the fridge.
2. Preheat the oven to 350F.
3. Place the chicken–sauce and all–into a skillet.
4. Put the skillet in the oven and bake for 1 hour or until the chicken is tender.

Nutrition Info:
- Per Servings 6.2g Carbs, 48.2g Protein, 42.4g Fat, 610 Calories

Chicken In Creamy Mushroom Sauce

Servings: 4 | Cooking Time: 36 Minutes

Ingredients:
- 1 tbsp ghee
- 4 chicken breasts, cut into chunks
- Salt and black pepper to taste
- 1 packet white onion soup mix
- 2 cups chicken broth
- 15 baby bella mushrooms, sliced
- 1 cup heavy cream
- 1 small bunch parsley, chopped

Directions:
1. Melt ghee in a saucepan over medium heat, season the chicken with salt and black pepper, and brown on all sides for 6 minutes in total. Put in a plate.
2. In a bowl, stir the onion soup mix with chicken broth and add to the saucepan. Simmer for 3 minutes and add the mushrooms and chicken. Cover and simmer for another 20 minutes.
3. Stir in heavy cream and parsley, cook on low heat for 3 minutes, and season with salt and pepper.
4. Ladle the chicken with creamy sauce and mushrooms over beds of cauli mash. Garnish with parsley.

Nutrition Info:
- Per Servings 2g Carbs, 22g Protein, 38.2g Fat, 448 Calories

Cilantro Chicken Breasts With Mayo-avocado Sauce

Servings: 4 | Cooking Time: 22 Minutes

Ingredients:
- For the Sauce
- 1 avocado, pitted
- ½ cup mayonnaise
- Salt to taste
- For the Chicken
- 3 tbsp ghee
- 4 chicken breasts
- Pink salt and black pepper to taste
- 1 cup chopped cilantro leaves
- ½ cup chicken broth

Directions:
1. Spoon the avocado, mayonnaise, and salt into a small food processor and puree until smooth sauce is derived. Adjust taste with salt as desired.
2. Pour sauce into a jar and refrigerate while you make the chicken.
3. Melt ghee in a large skillet, season chicken with salt and black pepper and fry for 4 minutes on each side to golden brown. Remove chicken to a plate.
4. Pour the broth in the same skillet and add the cilantro. Bring to simmer covered for 3 minutes and add the chicken. Cover and cook on low heat for 5 minutes until liquid has reduced and chicken is fragrant. Dish chicken only into serving plates and spoon the mayo-avocado sauce over.

Nutrition Info:
- Per Servings 4g Carbs, 24g Protein, 32g Fat, 398 Calories

Grilled Chicken Wings

Servings: 4 | Cooking Time: 2 Hours 25 Minutes

Ingredients:
- 2 pounds wings
- Juice from 1 lemon
- ½ cup fresh parsley, chopped
- 2 garlic cloves, peeled and minced
- 1 Serrano pepper, chopped
- 3 tbsp olive oil
- ½ tsp cilantro
- Salt and ground black pepper, to taste
- Lemon wedges, for serving
- Ranch dip, for serving

Directions:
1. Using a bowl, stir together lemon juice, garlic, salt, serrano pepper, cilantro, olive oil, and pepper. Place in the chicken wings and toss well to coat. Refrigerate for 2 hours. Set a grill over high heat and add on the chicken wings; cook each side for 6 minutes. Set the chicken wings on a plate and serve alongside lemon wedges and ranch dip.

Nutrition Info:
- Per Servings 4.3g Carbs, 18.5g Protein, 11.5g Fat, 216 Calories

Chicken, Broccoli & Cashew Stir-fry

Servings: 4 | Cooking Time: 30 Minutes

Ingredients:
- 2 chicken breasts, cut into strips
- 3 tbsp olive oil
- 2 tbsp soy sauce
- 2 tsp white wine vinegar
- 1 tsp erythritol
- 2 tsp xanthan gum
- 1 lemon, juiced
- 1 cup unsalted cashew nuts
- 2 cups broccoli florets
- 1 white onion, thinly sliced
- Pepper to taste

Directions:
1. In a bowl, mix the soy sauce, vinegar, lemon juice, erythritol, and xanthan gum. Set aside.
2. Heat the oil in a wok and fry the cashew for 4 minutes until golden-brown. Remove the cashews into a paper towel lined plate and set aside. Sauté the onion in the same oil for 4 minutes until soft and browned; add to the cashew nuts.
3. Add the chicken to the wok and cook for 4 minutes; include the broccoli and pepper. Stir-fry and pour the soy sauce mixture in. Stir and cook the sauce for 4 minutes and pour in the cashews and onion. Stir once more, cook for 1 minute, and turn the heat off.
4. Serve the chicken stir-fry with some steamed cauli rice.

Nutrition Info:
- Per Servings 3.4g Carbs, 17.3g Protein, 10.1g Fat, 286 Calories

Smoky Paprika Chicken

Servings: 8 | Cooking Time: 10 Minutes

Ingredients:
- 2 lb. chicken breasts, sliced into strips
- 2 tbsp. smoked paprika
- 1 tsp Cajun seasoning
- 1 tbsp minced garlic
- 1 large onion, sliced thinly
- Salt and pepper to taste
- 1 tbsp. olive oil

Directions:

1. In a large bowl, marinate chicken strips in paprika, Cajun, pepper, salt, and minced garlic for at least 30 minutes.
2. On high fire, heat a saucepan for 2 minutes. Add oil to the pan and swirl to coat bottom and sides. Heat oil for a minute.
3. Stir fry chicken and onion for 7 minutes or until chicken is cooked.
4. Serve and enjoy.

Nutrition Info:
- Per Servings 1.5g Carbs, 34g Protein, 12.4g Fat, 217 Calories

Lemon Threaded Chicken Skewers

Servings: 4 | Cooking Time: 2 Hours 17 Minutes

Ingredients:
- 3 chicken breasts, cut into cubes
- 2 tbsp olive oil, divided
- 2/3 jar preserved lemon, flesh removed, drained
- 2 cloves garlic, minced
- ½ cup lemon juice
- Salt and black pepper to taste
- 1 tsp rosemary leaves to garnish
- 2 to 4 lemon wedges to garnish

Directions:

1. First, thread the chicken onto skewers and set aside.
2. In a wide bowl, mix half of the oil, garlic, salt, pepper, and lemon juice, and add the chicken skewers, and lemon rind. Cover the bowl and let the chicken marinate for at least 2 hours in the refrigerator.
3. When the marinating time is almost over, preheat a grill to 350ºF, and remove the chicken onto the grill. Cook for 6 minutes on each side.
4. Remove and serve warm garnished with rosemary leaves and lemons wedges.

Nutrition Info:
- Per Servings 3.5g Carbs, 34g Protein, 11g Fat, 350 Calories

Chicken Skewers With Celery Fries

Servings: 4 | Cooking Time: 60 Minutes

Ingredients:
- 2 chicken breasts
- ½ tsp salt
- ¼ tsp ground black pepper
- 2 tbsp olive oil
- 1/4 chicken broth
- For the fries
- 1 lb celery root
- 2 tbsp olive oil
- ½ tsp salt
- ¼ tsp ground black pepper

Directions:

1. Set an oven to 400ºF. Grease and line a baking sheet. In a large bowl, mix oil, spices and the chicken; set in the fridge for 10 minutes while covered. Peel and chop celery root to form fry shapes and place into a separate bowl. Apply oil to coat and add pepper and salt for seasoning. Arrange to the baking tray in an even layer and bake for 10 minutes.
2. Take the chicken from the refrigerator and thread onto the skewers. Place over the celery, pour in the chicken broth, then set in the oven for 30 minutes. Serve with lemon wedges.

Nutrition Info:
- Per Servings 6g Carbs, 39g Protein, 43g Fat, 579 Calories

Turkey & Leek Soup

Servings: 4 | Cooking Time: 45 Minutes

Ingredients:
- 3 celery stalks, chopped
- 2 leeks, chopped
- 1 tbsp butter
- 6 cups chicken stock
- Salt and ground black pepper, to taste
- ¼ cup fresh parsley, chopped
- 3 cups zoodles
- 3 cups turkey meat, cooked and chopped

Directions:

1. Set a pot over medium-high heat, stir in leeks and celery and cook for 5 minutes. Place in the parsley, turkey meat, pepper, salt, and stock, and cook for 20 minutes. Stir in the zoodles, and cook turkey soup for 5 minutes. Serve in bowls and enjoy.

Nutrition Info:
- Per Servings 3g Carbs, 15g Protein, 11g Fat, 305 Calories

Broccoli Chicken Stew

Servings: 4 | Cooking Time: 30 Minutes

Ingredients:
- 1 package frozen chopped broccoli
- 1 cup shredded sharp cheddar cheese
- ½ cup sour cream
- ¾ cup Campbell's broccoli cheese soup
- 4 boneless skinless chicken breasts, thawed
- ½ cup water

Directions:

1. Add all ingredients, except for broccoli in a pot on high fire and bring to a boil.

2. Once boiling, lower fire to a simmer and cook for 20 minutes, stirring frequently.
3. Adjust seasoning to taste. Add broccoli and continue cooking and stirring for another 5 minutes.
4. Serve and enjoy.

Nutrition Info:
• Per Servings 9.7g Carbs, 63.9g Protein, 22.1g Fat, 511 Calories

Rotisserie Chicken With Garlic Paprika

Servings: 12 | Cooking Time: 1 Hour And 40 Minutes

Ingredients:
• 1 whole chicken
• 1 tbsp. thyme
• 1 tbsp. paprika
• 6 cloves garlic
• 2 bay leaves
• 1 tsp salt
• ½ tbsp pepper

Directions:
1. In a small bowl, mix well thyme, paprika, salt, and pepper.
2. Rub and massage the entire chicken and inside the cavity with the spices.
3. Smash and peel 6 garlic cloves and mince. Rub all over chicken and inside of the chicken.
4. Smash remaining garlic and place in the chicken cavity along with bay leaves.
5. Place chicken on a wire rack placed on top of a baking pan. Tent with foil.
6. Pop in a preheated 350oF oven and bake for 60 minutes.
7. Remove foil and continue baking for another 30 minutes.
8. Let chicken rest for 10 minutes before serving and enjoy.

Nutrition Info:
• Per Servings 1.4g Carbs, 21.3g Protein, 17.2g Fat, 249 Calories

Garlic & Ginger Chicken With Peanut Sauce

Servings: 6 | Cooking Time: 1 Hour And 50 Minutes

Ingredients:
• 1 tbsp wheat-free soy sauce
• 1 tbsp sugar-free fish sauce
• 1 tbsp lime juice
• 1 tsp cilantro
• 1 tsp minced garlic
• 1 tsp minced ginger
• 1 tbsp olive oil
• 1 tbsp rice wine vinegar
• 1 tsp cayenne pepper
• 1 tsp erythritol
• 6 chicken thighs
• Sauce:
• ½ cup peanut butter

• 1 tsp minced garlic
• 1 tbsp lime juice
• 2 tbsp water
• 1 tsp minced ginger
• 1 tbsp chopped jalapeño
• 2 tbsp rice wine vinegar
• 2 tbsp erythritol
• 1 tbsp fish sauce

Directions:
1. Combine all chicken ingredients in a large Ziploc bag. Seal the bag and shake to combine. Refrigerate for 1 hour. Remove from fridge about 15 minutes before cooking.
2. Preheat the grill to medium and grill the chicken for 7 minutes per side. Whisk together all sauce ingredients in a mixing bowl. Serve the chicken drizzled with peanut sauce.

Nutrition Info:
• Per Servings 3g Carbs, 35g Protein, 36g Fat, 492 Calories

Turkey Enchilada Bowl

Servings: 4 | Cooking Time: 30 Minutes

Ingredients:
• 2 tbsp coconut oil
• 1 lb boneless, skinless turkey thighs, cut into pieces
• ¾ cup red enchilada sauce (sugar-free)
• ¼ cup water
• ¼ cup chopped onion
• 3 oz canned diced green chilis
• 1 avocado, diced
• 1 cup shredded mozzarella cheese
• ¼ cup chopped pickled jalapeños
• ½ cup sour cream
• 1 tomato, diced

Directions:
1. Set a large pan over medium-high heat. Add coconut oil and warm. Place in the turkey and cook until browned on the outside. Stir in onion, chillis, water, and enchilada sauce, then close with a lid.
2. Allow simmering for 20 minutes until the turkey is cooked through. Spoon the turkey on a serving bowl and top with the sauce, cheese, sour cream, tomato, and avocado.

Nutrition Info:
• Per Servings 5.9g Carbs, 38g Protein, 40.2g Fat, 568 Calories

Soups, Stew & Salads

Soups, Stew & Salads

Creamy Soup With Greens

Servings: 6 | Cooking Time: 20 Minutes

Ingredients:
- ½-pounds collard greens, torn to bite-sized pieces
- 5 cups chicken broth
- 2 cups broccoli florets
- 1 cup diced onion
- 3 tablespoon oil
- 4 tablespoons butter
- Salt and pepper to taste

Directions:
1. Add all ingredients to the pot and bring to a boil.
2. Lower fire to a simmer and simmer for 15 minutes while covered.
3. With an immersion blender, puree soup until creamy.
4. Adjust seasoning to taste.
5. Serve and enjoy.

Nutrition Info:
- Per Servings 6.5g Carbs, 50.6g Protein, 33.5g Fat, 548 Calories

Corn And Bacon Chowder

Servings: 8 | Cooking Time: 23 Minutes

Ingredients:
- ½ cup bacon, fried and crumbled
- 1 package celery, onion, and bell pepper mix
- 2 cups full-fat milk
- ½ cup sharp cheddar cheese, grated
- 5 tablespoons butter
- Pepper and salt to taste
- 1 cup water

Directions:
1. In a heavy-bottomed pot, melt butter.
2. Saute the bacon and celery for 3 minutes.
3. Turn fire on to medium. Add remaining ingredients and cook for 20 minutes until thick.
4. Serve and enjoy with a sprinkle of crumbled bacon.

Nutrition Info:
- Per Servings 4.4g Carbs, 16.6g Protein, 13.6g Fat, 210.5 Calories

Caesar Salad With Smoked Salmon And Poached Eggs

Servings: 4 | Cooking Time: 15 Minutes

Ingredients:
- 3 cups water
- 8 eggs
- 2 cups torn romaine lettuce
- ½ cup smoked salmon, chopped
- 6 slices bacon
- 2 tbsp Heinz low carb Caesar dressing

Directions:
1. Boil the water in a pot over medium heat for 5 minutes and bring to simmer. Crack each egg into a small bowl and gently slide into the water. Poach for 2 to 3 minutes, remove with a perforated spoon, transfer to a paper towel to dry, and plate. Poach the remaining 7 eggs.
2. Put the bacon in a skillet and fry over medium heat until browned and crispy, about 6 minutes, turning once. Remove, allow cooling, and chop in small pieces.
3. Toss the lettuce, smoked salmon, bacon, and caesar dressing in a salad bowl. Divide the salad into 4 plates, top with two eggs each, and serve immediately or chilled.

Nutrition Info:
- Per Servings 5g Carbs, 8g Protein, 21g Fat, 260 Calories

Watermelon And Cucumber Salad

Servings: 10 | Cooking Time: 0 Minutes

Ingredients:
- ½ large watermelon, diced
- 1 cucumber, peeled and diced
- 1 red onion, chopped
- ¼ cup feta cheese
- ½ cup heavy cream
- Salt to taste
- 5 tbsp MCT or coconut oil

Directions:
1. Place all ingredients in a bowl.
2. Toss everything to coat.
3. Place in the fridge to cool before serving.

Nutrition Info:
- Per Servings 2.5g Carbs, 0.9g Protein, 100g Fat, 910 Calories

Pesto Tomato Cucumber Salad

Servings: 8 | Cooking Time: 0 Minutes

Ingredients:

- ½ cup Italian salad dressing
- ¼ cup prepared pesto
- 3 large tomatoes, sliced
- 2 medium cucumbers, halved and sliced
- 1 small red onion, sliced
- Salt and pepper to taste
- 3 tablespoons olive oil

Directions:

1. In a bowl, whisk the salad dressing and pesto. Season with salt and pepper to taste.
2. Toss gently to incorporate everything.
3. Refrigerate before serving.

Nutrition Info:

- Per Servings 3.7g Carbs, 1.8g Protein, 12g Fat, 128 Calories

Coconut Cauliflower Soup

Servings: 10 | Cooking Time: 26 Minutes

Ingredients:

- 1 medium onion, finely chopped
- 3 tablespoons yellow curry paste
- 2 medium heads cauliflower, broken into florets
- 1 carton vegetable broth
- 1 cup coconut milk
- 2 tablespoons olive oil

Directions:

1. In a large saucepan, heat oil over medium heat. Add onion; cook and stir until softened, 2-3 minutes.
2. Add curry paste; cook until fragrant, 1-2 minutes.
3. Add cauliflower and broth. Increase heat to high; bring to a boil. Reduce heat to medium-low; cook, covered, about 20 minutes.
4. Stir in coconut milk; cook an additional minute.
5. Remove from heat; cool slightly.
6. Puree in batches in a blender or food processor.
7. If desired, top with minced fresh cilantro.

Nutrition Info:

- Per Servings 10g Carbs, 3g Protein, 8g Fat, 111 Calories

Simplified French Onion Soup

Servings: 5 | Cooking Time: 30 Minutes

Ingredients:

- 3 large onions, sliced
- 2 bay leaves
- 5 cups Beef Bone Broth
- 1 teaspoon dried thyme
- 1-oz Gruyere cheese, sliced into 5 equal pieces
- Pepper to taste
- 4 tablespoons oil

Directions:

1. Place a heavy-bottomed pot on medium-high fire and heat pot for 3 minutes.
2. Add oil and heat for 2 minutes. Stir in onions and sauté for 5 minutes.
3. Lower fire to medium-low, continue sautéing onions for 10 minutes until soft and browned, but not burned.
4. Add remaining ingredients and mix well.
5. Bring to a boil, lower fire to a simmer, cover and cook for 5 minutes.
6. Ladle into bowls, top with cheese.
7. Let it sit for 5 minutes.
8. Serve and enjoy.

Nutrition Info:

- Per Servings 9.9g Carbs, 4.3g Protein, 16.8g Fat, 208 Calories

Easy Tomato Salad

Servings: 4 | Cooking Time: 0 Minutes

Ingredients:

- 1 ½ cups cherry tomatoes, sliced
- ¼ cup white wine vinegar
- 1/8 cup chives
- 3 tablespoons olive oil
- Salt and pepper to taste

Directions:

1. Put all ingredients in a bowl.
2. Toss to combine.
3. Serve immediately.

Nutrition Info:

- Per Servings 0.6g Carbs, 0.3g Protein, 10.1g Fat, 95 Calories

Bacon Tomato Salad

Servings: 6 | Cooking Time: 0 Minutes

Ingredients:

- 6 ounces iceberg lettuce blend
- 2 cups grape tomatoes, halved
- ¾ cup coleslaw salad dressing
- ¾ cup cheddar cheese, shredded
- 12 bacon strips, cooked and crumbled
- Salt and pepper to taste

Directions:

1. Put the lettuce and tomatoes in a salad bowl.
2. Drizzle with the dressing and sprinkle with cheese. Season with salt and pepper to taste then mix.
3. Garnish with bacon bits on top.

Nutrition Info:

- Per Servings 8g Carbs, 10g Protein, 20g Fat, 268 Calories

Rustic Beef Soup

Servings: 4 | Cooking Time: 20 Minutes

Ingredients:
- 3 cups beef broth
- 2 cups frozen mixed vegetables
- 1 teaspoon ground mustard
- Beef roast
- 1 teaspoon water
- Pinch of salt

Directions:
1. In a large saucepan, combine all the ingredients.
2. Bring to a boil.
3. Reduce heat; simmer, uncovered, for 15-20 minutes or until barley is tender.

Nutrition Info:
- Per Servings 8g Carbs, 51g Protein, 24g Fat, 450 Calories

Celery Salad

Servings: 4 | Cooking Time: 0 Minutes

Ingredients:
- 3 cups celery, thinly sliced
- ½ cup parmigiana cheese, shaved
- 1/3 cup toasted walnuts
- 4 tablespoons extra virgin olive oil
- 1 tablespoon red wine vinegar
- Salt and pepper to taste

Directions:
1. Place the celery, cheese, and walnuts in a bowl.
2. In a smaller bowl, combine the olive oil and vinegar. Season with salt and pepper to taste. Whisk to combine everything.
3. Drizzle over the celery, cheese, and walnuts. Toss to coat.

Nutrition Info:
- Per Servings 3.6g Carbs, 4.3g Protein, 14g Fat, 156 Calories

Bacon Chowder

Servings: 6 | Cooking Time: 15 Minutes

Ingredients:
- 1-pound bacon strips, chopped
- 1/4 cup chopped onion
- 1 can evaporated milk
- 1 sprig parsley, chopped
- 5 tablespoons butter
- 1/4 teaspoon salt
- 1/4 teaspoon pepper

Directions:
1. In a large skillet, cook bacon over medium heat until crisp, stirring occasionally. Remove with a slotted spoon; drain on paper towels. Discard drippings, reserving 1-1/2 teaspoons in the pan. Add onion to drippings; cook and stir over medium-high heat until tender.
2. Meanwhile, place all ingredients Bring to a boil over high heat. Reduce heat to medium; cook, uncovered, 10-15 minutes or until tender. Reserve 1 cup potato water.
3. Add milk, salt and pepper to the saucepan; heat through. Stir in bacon and onion.

Nutrition Info:
- Per Servings 5.4g Carbs, 10g Protein, 31.9g Fat, 322 Calories

Green Minestrone Soup

Servings: 4 | Cooking Time: 25 Minutes

Ingredients:
- 2 tbsp ghee
- 2 tbsp onion garlic puree
- 2 heads broccoli, cut in florets
- 2 stalks celery, chopped
- 5 cups vegetable broth
- 1 cup baby spinach
- Salt and black pepper to taste

Directions:
1. Melt the ghee in a saucepan over medium heat and sauté the garlic for 3 minutes until softened. Mix in the broccoli and celery, and cook for 4 minutes until slightly tender. Pour in the broth, bring to a boil, then reduce the heat to medium-low and simmer covered for about 5 minutes.
2. Drop in the spinach to wilt, adjust the seasonings, and cook for 4 minutes. Ladle soup into serving bowls. Serve with a sprinkle of grated Gruyere cheese and freshly baked low carb carrot bread.

Nutrition Info:
- Per Servings 2g Carbs, 8g Protein, 20.3g Fat, 227 Calories

Shrimp With Avocado & Cauliflower Salad

Servings: 6 | Cooking Time: 30 Minutes

Ingredients:
- 1 cauliflower head, florets only
- 1 pound medium shrimp
- ¼ cup + 1 tbsp olive oil
- 1 avocado, chopped
- 3 tbsp chopped dill
- ¼ cup lemon juice
- 2 tbsp lemon zest
- Salt and black pepper to taste

Directions:
1. Heat 1 tbsp olive oil in a skillet and cook the shrimp until opaque, about 8-10 minutes. Place the cauliflower florets in a microwave-safe bowl, and microwave for 5 minutes. Place the shrimp, cauliflower, and avocado in a large bowl.
2. Whisk together the remaining olive oil, lemon zest, juice, dill, and some salt and pepper, in another bowl. Pour the dressing over, toss to combine and serve immediately.

Nutrition Info:
- Per Servings 5g Carbs, 15g Protein, 17g Fat, 214 Calories

Strawberry Salad With Spinach, Cheese & Almonds

Servings: 2 | Cooking Time: 20 Minutes

Ingredients:

- 4 cups spinach
- 4 strawberries, sliced
- ½ cup flaked almonds
- 1 ½ cup grated hard goat cheese
- 4 tbsp raspberry vinaigrette
- Salt and black pepper, to taste

Directions:

1. Preheat your oven to 400ºF. Arrange the grated goat cheese in two circles on two pieces of parchment paper. Place in the oven and bake for 10 minutes.
2. Find two same bowls, place them upside down, and carefully put the parchment paper on top to give the cheese a bowl-like shape. Let cool that way for 15 minutes. Divide spinach among the bowls stir in salt, pepper and drizzle with vinaigrette. Top with almonds and strawberries.

Nutrition Info:

- Per Servings 5.3g Carbs, 33g Protein, 34.2g Fat, 445 Calories

Tuna Caprese Salad

Servings: 4 | Cooking Time: 10 Minutes

Ingredients:

- 2 cans tuna chunks in water, drained
- 2 tomatoes, sliced
- 8 oz fresh mozzarella cheese, sliced
- 6 basil leaves
- ½ cup black olives, pitted and sliced
- 2 tbsp extra virgin olive oil
- ½ lemon, juiced

Directions:

1. Place the tuna in the center of a serving platter. Arrange the cheese and tomato slices around the tuna. Alternate a slice of tomato, cheese, and a basil leaf.
2. To finish, scatter the black olives over the top, drizzle with olive oil and lemon juice, and serve with grilled chicken breasts.

Nutrition Info:

- Per Servings 1g Carbs, 21g Protein, 31g Fat, 360 Calories

Pesto Arugula Salad

Servings: 4 | Cooking Time: 10 Minutes

Ingredients:

- ¾ cup red peppers, seeded and chopped
- ¾ cup commercial basil pesto
- 1 small mozzarella cheese ball, diced
- 3 handfuls of arugulas, washed
- Salt and pepper to taste
- 5 tablespoons olive oil

Directions:

1. Mix all ingredients in a salad bowl and toss to coat.
2. Season with salt and pepper to taste.

Nutrition Info:

- Per Servings 2.8g Carbs, 6.7g Protein, 20g Fat, 214 Calories

Green Mackerel Salad

Servings: 2 | Cooking Time: 25 Minutes

Ingredients:

- 2 mackerel fillets
- 2 hard-boiled eggs, sliced
- 1 tbsp coconut oil
- 2 cups green beans
- 1 avocado, sliced
- 4 cups mixed salad greens
- 2 tbsp olive oil
- 2 tbsp lemon juice
- 1 tsp Dijon mustard
- Salt and black pepper, to taste

Directions:

1. Fill a saucepan with water and add the green beans and salt. Cook over medium heat for about 3 minutes. Drain and set aside.
2. Melt the coconut oil in a pan over medium heat. Add the mackerel fillets and cook for about 4 minutes per side, or until opaque and crispy. Divide the green beans between two salad bowls. Top with mackerel, egg, and avocado slices.
3. In a bowl, whisk together the lemon juice, olive oil, mustard, salt, and pepper, and drizzle over the salad.

Nutrition Info:

- Per Servings 7.6g Carbs, 27.3g Protein, 41.9g Fat, 525 Calories

Garlic Chicken Salad

Servings: 4 | Cooking Time: 15 Minutes

Ingredients:

- 2 chicken breasts, boneless, skinless, flattened
- Salt and black pepper to taste
- 2 tbsp garlic powder
- 1 tsp olive oil
- 1 ½ cups mixed salad greens
- 1 tbsp red wine vinegar
- 1 cup crumbled blue cheese

Directions:

1. Season the chicken with salt, black pepper, and garlic powder. Heat oil in a pan over high heat and fry the chicken for 4 minutes on both sides until golden brown. Remove chicken to a cutting board and let cool before slicing.
2. Toss salad greens with red wine vinegar and share the salads into 4 plates. Divide chicken slices on top and sprinkle with blue cheese. Serve salad with carrots fries.

Nutrition Info:

- Per Servings 4g Carbs, 14g Protein, 23g Fat, 286 Calories

Arugula Prawn Salad With Mayo Dressing

Servings: 4 | Cooking Time: 15 Minutes

Ingredients:

- 4 cups baby arugula
- ½ cup garlic mayonnaise
- 3 tbsp olive oil
- 1 lb tiger prawns, peeled and deveined
- 1 tsp Dijon mustard
- Salt and chili pepper to season
- 2 tbsp lemon juice

Directions:

1. Add the mayonnaise, lemon juice and mustard in a small bowl. Mix until smooth and creamy. Heat 2 tbps of olive oil in a skillet over medium heat, add the prawns, season with salt, and chili pepper, and fry in the oil for 3 minutes on each side until prawns are pink. Set aside to a plate.

2. Place the arugula in a serving bowl and pour half of the dressing on the salad. Toss with 2 spoons until mixed, and add the remaining dressing. Divide salad into 4 plates and serve with prawns.

Nutrition Info:

- Per Servings 2g Carbs, 8g Protein, 20.3g Fat, 215 Calories

Mediterranean Salad

Servings: 4 | Cooking Time: 10 Minutes

Ingredients:

- 3 tomatoes, sliced
- 1 large avocado, sliced
- 8 kalamata olives
- ¼ lb buffalo mozzarella cheese, sliced
- 2 tbsp pesto sauce
- 2 tbsp olive oil

Directions:

1. Arrange the tomato slices on a serving platter and place the avocado slices in the middle. Arrange the olives around the avocado slices and drop pieces of mozzarella on the platter. Drizzle the pesto sauce all over, and drizzle olive oil as well.

Nutrition Info:

- Per Servings 4.3g Carbs, 9g Protein, 25g Fat, 290 Calories

Green Salad With Bacon And Blue Cheese

Servings: 4 | Cooking Time: 15 Minutes

Ingredients:

- 2 pack mixed salad greens
- 8 strips bacon
- 1 ½ cups crumbled blue cheese
- 1 tbsp white wine vinegar
- 3 tbsp extra virgin olive oil
- Salt and black pepper to taste

Directions:

1. Pour the salad greens in a salad bowl; set aside. Fry bacon strips in a skillet over medium heat for 6 minutes, until browned and crispy. Chop the bacon and scatter over the salad. Add in half of the cheese, toss and set aside.

2. In a small bowl, whisk the white wine vinegar, olive oil, salt, and black pepper until dressing is well combined. Drizzle half of the dressing over the salad, toss, and top with remaining cheese. Divide salad into four plates and serve with crusted chicken fries along with remaining dressing.

Nutrition Info:

- Per Servings 2g Carbs, 4g Protein, 20g Fat, 205 Calories

Slow Cooker Beer Soup With Cheddar & Sausage

Servings: 8 | Cooking Time: 8 Hr

Ingredients:

- 1 cup heavy cream
- 10 ounces sausages, sliced
- 1 cup celery, chopped
- 1 cup carrots, chopped
- 4 garlic cloves, minced
- 8 ounces cream cheese
- 1 tsp red pepper flakes
- 6 ounces beer
- 16 ounces beef stock
- 1 onion, diced
- 1 cup cheddar cheese, grated
- Salt and black pepper, to taste
- Fresh cilantro, chopped, to garnish

Directions:

1. Turn on the slow cooker. Add beef stock, beer, sausages, carrots, onion, garlic, celery, salt, red pepper flakes, and black pepper, and stir to combine. Pour in enough water to cover all the ingredients by roughly 2 inches. Close the lid and cook for 6 hours on Low.

2. Open the lid and stir in the heavy cream, cheddar, and cream cheese, and cook for 2 more hours. Ladle the soup into bowls and garnish with cilantro before serving. Yummy!

Nutrition Info:

- Per Servings 4g Carbs, 5g Protein, 17g Fat, 244 Calories

Pumpkin & Meat Peanut Stew

Servings: 6 | Cooking Time: 45 Minutes

Ingredients:

- 1 cup pumpkin puree
- 2 pounds chopped pork stew meat
- 1 tbsp peanut butter
- 4 tbsp chopped peanuts
- 1 garlic clove, minced
- ½ cup chopped onion
- ½ cup white wine
- 1 tbsp olive oil

- 1 tsp lemon juice
- ¼ cup granulated sweetener
- ¼ tsp cardamom
- ¼ tsp allspice
- 2 cups water
- 2 cups chicken stock

Directions:

1. Heat the olive oil in a large pot and sauté onion for 3 minutes, until translucent. Add garlic and cook for 30 more seconds. Add the pork and cook until browned, about 5-6 minutes, stirring occasionally. Pour in the wine and cook for one minute.

2. Add in the remaining ingredients, except for the lemon juice and peanuts. Bring the mixture to a boil, and cook for 5 minutes. Reduce the heat to low, cover the pot, and let cook for about 30 minutes. Adjust seasoning and stir in the lemon juice before serving.

3. Ladle into serving bowls and serve topped with peanuts.

Nutrition Info:

- Per Servings 4g Carbs, 27.5g Protein, 33g Fat, 451 Calories

Spinach Fruit Salad With Seeds

Servings: 4 | Cooking Time: 1 Hour 10 Minutes

Ingredients:

- 2 tablespoons sesame seeds
- 1 tablespoon poppy seeds
- 1 tablespoon minced onion
- 10 ounces fresh spinach - rinsed, dried and torn into bite-size pieces
- 1 quart strawberries - cleaned, hulled and sliced
- 1/2 cup stevia
- 1/2 cup olive oil
- 1/4 cup distilled white vinegar
- 1/4 teaspoon Worcestershire sauce
- 1/4 teaspoon paprika

Directions:

1. Mix together the spinach and strawberry in a large bowl, stir in the sesame seeds, poppy seeds, stevia, olive oil, vinegar, paprika, Worcestershire sauce and onion in a medium bowl. Cover and cool for 1 hour.

2. Pour dressing over salad to combine well. Serve immediately or refrigerate for 15 minutes.

Nutrition Info:

- Per Servings 8.6g Carbs, 6g Protein, 18g Fat, 220 Calories

Broccoli Slaw Salad With Mustard-mayo Dressing

Servings: 6 | Cooking Time: 10 Minutes

Ingredients:

- 2 tbsp granulated swerve
- 1 tbsp Dijon mustard
- 1 tbsp olive oil
- 4 cups broccoli slaw

- ⅓ cup mayonnaise, sugar-free
- 1 tsp celery seeds
- 1 ½ tbsp apple cider vinegar
- Salt and black pepper, to taste

Directions:

1. Whisk together all ingredients except the broccoli slaw. Place broccoli slaw in a large salad bowl. Pour the dressing over. Mix with your hands to combine well.

Nutrition Info:

- Per Servings 2g Carbs, 3g Protein, 10g Fat, 110 Calories

Sriracha Egg Salad With Mustard Dressing

Servings: 8 | Cooking Time: 15 Minutes

Ingredients:

- 10 eggs
- ¾ cup mayonnaise
- 1 tsp sriracha
- 1 tbsp mustard
- ½ cup scallions
- ½ stalk celery, minced
- ½ tsp fresh lemon juice
- ½ tsp sea salt
- ½ tsp black pepper, to taste
- 1 head romaine lettuce, torn into pieces

Directions:

1. Add the eggs in a pan and cover with enough water and boil. Get them from the heat and allow to set for 10 minutes while covered. Chop the eggs and add to a salad bowl.

2. Stir in the remaining ingredients until everything is well combined. Refrigerate until ready to serve.

Nutrition Info:

- Per Servings 7.7g Carbs, 7.4g Protein, 13g Fat, 174 Calories

Chicken And Cauliflower Rice Soup

Servings: 8 | Cooking Time: 20 Mins

Ingredients:

- 2 cooked, boneless chicken breast halves, shredded
- 2 packages Steamed Cauliflower Rice
- 1/4 cup celery, chopped
- 1/2 cup onion, chopped
- 4 garlic cloves, minced
- Salt and ground black pepper to taste
- 2 teaspoons poultry seasoning
- 4 cups chicken broth
- ½ cup butter
- 2 cups heavy cream

Directions:

1. Heat butter in a large pot over medium heat, add onion, celery and garlic cloves to cook until tender. Meanwhile, place the riced cauliflower steam bags in the microwave following directions on the package.

2. Add the riced cauliflower, seasoning, salt and black pepper

to butter mixture, saute them for 7 minutes on medium heat, stirring constantly to well combined.

3. Bring cooked chicken breast halves, broth and heavy cream to a broil. When it starts boiling, lower the heat, cover and simmer for 15 minutes.

Nutrition Info:

• Per Servings 6g Carbs, 27g Protein, 30g Fat, 415 Calories

Citrusy Brussels Sprouts Salad

Servings: 6 | Cooking Time: 3 Minutes

Ingredients:

• 2 tablespoons olive oil
• ¾ pound Brussels sprouts
• 1 cup walnuts
• Juice from 1 lemon
• ½ cup grated parmesan cheese
• Salt and pepper to taste

Directions:

1. Heat oil in a skillet over medium flame and sauté the Brussels sprouts for 3 minutes until slightly wilted. Removed from heat and allow to cool.
2. In a bowl, toss together the cooled Brussels sprouts and the rest of the ingredients.
3. Toss to coat.

Nutrition Info:

• Per Servings 8g Carbs, 6g Protein, 23g Fat, 259 Calories

Chicken Taco Soup

Servings: 6 | Cooking Time: 45 Minutes

Ingredients:

• 1-pound boneless chicken breast
• 1 tbsp taco seasoning
• 3 medium tomato chopped
• 1 medium onion chopped
• 2 Tablespoons garlic minced
• 5 cups water
• Salt and Pepper to taste
• Sour cream or tortilla chips for topping (optional)

Directions:

1. Add all ingredients in a heavy-bottomed pot except for garnish if using.
2. Bring to a boil, lower fire to a simmer, cover and cook for 30 minutes.
3. Remove chicken and shred. Return to the pot. Adjust seasoning with pepper and salt to taste.
4. Serve and enjoy with topping.

Nutrition Info:

• Per Servings 5.0g Carbs, 15.0g Protein, 2.0g Fat, 98 Calories

Grilled Steak Salad With Pickled Peppers

Servings: 4 | Cooking Time: 15 Minutes

Ingredients:

• 1 lb skirt steak, sliced
• Salt and black pepper to season
• 1 tsp olive oil
• 1 ½ cups mixed salad greens
• 3 chopped pickled peppers
• 2 tbsp red wine vinaigrette
• ½ cup crumbled queso fresco

Directions:

1. Brush the steak slices with olive oil and season with salt and pepper on both sides.
2. Heat frying pan over high heat and cook the steaks on each side to the desired doneness, for about 5-6 minutes. Remove to a bowl, cover and leave to rest while you make the salad.
3. Mix the salad greens, pickled peppers, and vinaigrette in a salad bowl. Add the beef and sprinkle with cheese. Serve the salad with roasted parsnips.

Nutrition Info:

• Per Servings 2g Carbs, 18g Protein, 26g Fat, 315 Calories

Brazilian Moqueca (shrimp Stew)

Servings: 6 | Cooking Time: 25 Minutes

Ingredients:

• 1 cup coconut milk
• 2 tbsp lime juice
• ¼ cup diced roasted peppers
• 1 ½ pounds shrimp, peeled and deveined
• ¼ cup olive oil
• 1 garlic clove, minced
• 14 ounces diced tomatoes
• 2 tbsp sriracha sauce
• 1 chopped onion
• ¼ cup chopped cilantro
• Fresh dill, chopped to garnish
• Salt and black pepper, to taste

Directions:

1. Heat the olive oil in a pot over medium heat. Add onion and cook for 3 minutes or until translucent. Add the garlic and cook for another minute, until soft. Add tomatoes, shrimp, and cilantro. Cook until the shrimp becomes opaque, about 3-4 minutes.
2. Stir in sriracha sauce and coconut milk, and cook for 2 minutes. Do not bring to a boil. Stir in the lime juice and season with salt and pepper. Spoon the stew in bowls, garnish with fresh dill to serve.

Nutrition Info:

• Per Servings 5g Carbs, 23.1g Protein, 21g Fat, 324 Calories

Cobb Egg Salad In Lettuce Cups

Servings: 4 | Cooking Time: 20 Minutes

Ingredients:

- 2 chicken breasts, cut into pieces
- 1 tbsp olive oil
- Salt and black pepper to season
- 6 large eggs
- 1 ½ cups water
- 2 tomatoes, seeded, chopped
- 6 tbsp Greek yogurt
- 1 head green lettuce, firm leaves removed for cups

Directions:

1. Preheat oven to 400°F. Put the chicken pieces in a bowl, drizzle with olive oil, and sprinkle with salt and black pepper. Mix the ingredients until the chicken is well coated with the seasoning.
2. Put the chicken on a prepared baking sheet and spread out evenly. Slide the baking sheet in the oven and bake the chicken until cooked through and golden brown for 8 minutes, turning once.
3. Bring the eggs to boil in salted water in a pot over medium heat for 6 minutes. Run the eggs in cold water, peel, and chop into small pieces. Transfer to a salad bowl.
4. Remove the chicken from the oven when ready and add to the salad bowl. Include the tomatoes and Greek yogurt; mix evenly with a spoon. Layer two lettuce leaves each as cups and fill with two tablespoons of egg salad each. Serve with chilled blueberry juice.

Nutrition Info:

- Per Servings 4g Carbs, 21g Protein, 24.5g Fat, 325 Calories

Balsamic Cucumber Salad

Servings: 6 | Cooking Time: 0 Minutes

Ingredients:

- 1 large English cucumber, halved and sliced
- 1 cup grape tomatoes, halved
- 1 medium red onion, sliced thinly
- ¼ cup balsamic vinaigrette
- ¾ cup feta cheese
- Salt and pepper to taste
- ¼ cup olive oil

Directions:

1. Place all ingredients in a bowl.
2. Toss to coat everything with the dressing.
3. Allow chilling before serving.

Nutrition Info:

- Per Servings 9g Carbs, 4.8g Protein, 16.7g Fat, 253 Calories

Coconut, Green Beans, And Shrimp Curry Soup

Servings: 4 | Cooking Time: 20 Minutes

Ingredients:

- 2 tbsp ghee
- 1 lb jumbo shrimp, peeled and deveined
- 2 tsp ginger-garlic puree
- 2 tbsp red curry paste
- 6 oz coconut milk
- Salt and chili pepper to taste
- 1 bunch green beans, halved

Directions:

1. Melt ghee in a medium saucepan over medium heat. Add the shrimp, season with salt and pepper, and cook until they are opaque, 2 to 3 minutes. Remove shrimp to a plate. Add the ginger-garlic puree and red curry paste to the ghee and sauté for 2 minutes until fragrant.
2. Stir in the coconut milk; add the shrimp, salt, chili pepper, and green beans. Cook for 4 minutes. Reduce the heat to a simmer and cook an additional 3 minutes, occasionally stirring. Adjust taste with salt, fetch soup into serving bowls, and serve with cauli rice.

Nutrition Info:

- Per Servings 2g Carbs, 9g Protein, 35.4g Fat, 375 Calories

Chicken Cabbage Soup

Servings: 6 | Cooking Time: 30 Minutes

Ingredients:

- 1 can Italian-style tomatoes
- 3 cups chicken broth
- 1 chicken breast
- ½ head of cabbage, shredded
- 1 packet Italian seasoning mix
- Salt and pepper to taste
- 1 cup water
- 1 tsp oil

Directions:

1. Place a heavy-bottomed pot on medium fire and heat for a minute. Add oil and swirl to coat the bottom and sides of the pot.
2. Pan fry chicken breast for 4 minutes per side. Transfer to a chopping board and cut into ½-inch cubes.
3. Add all ingredients to the pot and stir well.
4. Cover and bring to a boil, lower fire to a simmer, and cook for 20 minutes.
5. Adjust seasoning to taste, serve, and enjoy.

Nutrition Info:

- Per Servings 5.6g Carbs, 34.1g Protein, 9.3g Fat, 248 Calories

Clam Chowder

Servings: 5 | Cooking Time: 10 Minutes

Ingredients:
- 1 can condensed cream of celery soup, undiluted
- 2 cups half-and-half cream
- 2 cans minced/chopped clams, drained
- 1/4 teaspoon ground nutmeg
- 5 tablespoons butter
- Pepper to taste

Directions:
1. In a large saucepan, combine all ingredients. Cook and stir over medium heat until heated through.

Nutrition Info:
- Per Servings 3.8g Carbs, 10g Protein, 14g Fat, 251 Calories

Fruit Salad With Poppy Seeds

Servings: 5 | Cooking Time: 25 Mins

Ingredients:
- 1 tablespoon poppy seeds
- 1 head romaine lettuce, torn into bite-size pieces
- 4 ounces shredded Swiss cheese
- 1 avocado- peeled, cored and diced
- 2 teaspoons diced onion
- 1/2 cup lemon juice
- 1/2 cup stevia
- 1/2 teaspoon salt
- 2/3 cup olive oil
- 1 teaspoon Dijon style prepared mustard

Directions:
1. Combine stevia, lemon juice, onion, mustard, and salt in a blender. Process until well blended.
2. Add oil until mixture is thick and smooth. Add poppy seeds, stir just a few seconds or more to mix.
3. In a large serving bowl, toss together the remaining ingredients.
4. Pour dressing over salad just before serving, and toss to coat.

Nutrition Info:
- Per Servings 6g Carbs, 4.9g Protein, 20.6g Fat, 277 Calories

Tuna Salad With Lettuce & Olives

Servings: 2 | Cooking Time: 5 Minutes

Ingredients:
- 1 cup canned tuna, drained
- 1 tsp onion flakes
- 3 tbsp mayonnaise
- 1 cup shredded romaine lettuce
- 1 tbsp lime juice
- Sea salt, to taste
- 6 black olives, pitted and sliced

Directions:
1. Combine the tuna, mayonnaise, lime juice, and salt in a small bowl; mix to combine well. In a salad platter, arrange the shredded lettuce and onion flakes. Spread the tuna mixture over; top with black olives to serve.

Nutrition Info:
- Per Servings 2g Carbs, 18.5g Protein, 20g Fat, 248 Calories

Homemade Cold Gazpacho Soup

Servings: 6 | Cooking Time: 15 Minutes

Ingredients:
- 2 small green peppers, roasted
- 2 large red peppers, roasted
- 2 medium avocados, flesh scoped out
- 2 garlic cloves
- 2 spring onions, chopped
- 1 cucumber, chopped
- 1 cup olive oil
- 2 tbsp lemon juice
- 4 tomatoes, chopped
- 7 ounces goat cheese
- 1 small red onion, chopped
- 2 tbsp apple cider vinegar
- Salt to taste

Directions:
1. Place the peppers, tomatoes, avocados, red onion, garlic, lemon juice, olive oil, vinegar, and salt, in a food processor. Pulse until your desired consistency is reached. Taste and adjust the seasoning.
2. Transfer the mixture to a pot. Stir in cucumber and spring onions. Cover and chill in the fridge at least 2 hours. Divide the soup between 6 bowls. Serve very cold, generously topped with goat cheese and an extra drizzle of olive oil.

Nutrition Info:
- Per Servings 6.5g Carbs, 7.5g Protein, 45.8g Fat, 528 Calories

Salmon Salad With Walnuts

Servings: 2 | Cooking Time: 10 Minutes

Ingredients:
- 2 salmon fillets
- 2 tablespoons balsamic vinaigrette, divided
- 1/8 teaspoon pepper
- 2 cups mixed salad greens
- 1/4 cup walnuts
- 2 tablespoons crumbled cheese
- Salt and pepper to taste
- 3 tablespoons olive oil

Directions:
1. Brush the salmon with half of the balsamic vinaigrette and sprinkle with pepper.
2. Grill the salmon over medium heat for 5 minutes on each side.
3. Crumble the salmon and place in a mixing bowl. Add the rest of the ingredients and season with salt and pepper to taste.

Nutrition Info:
- Per Servings 8g Carbs, 5g Protein, 30g Fat, 313 Calories

Pork Burger Salad With Yellow Cheddar

Servings: 4 | Cooking Time: 25 Minutes

Ingredients:

- 1 lb ground pork
- Salt and black pepper to season
- 1 tbsp olive oil
- 2 hearts romaine lettuce, torn into pieces
- 2 firm tomatoes, sliced
- ¼ red onion, sliced
- 3 oz yellow cheddar cheese, shredded

Directions:

1. Season the pork with salt and black pepper, mix and make medium-sized patties out of them.
2. Heat the oil in a skillet over medium heat and fry the patties on both sides for 10 minutes until browned and cook within. Transfer to a wire rack to drain oil. When cooled, cut into quarters.
3. Mix the lettuce, tomatoes, and red onion in a salad bowl, season with a little oil, salt, and pepper. Toss and add the pork on top.
4. Melt the cheese in the microwave for about 90 seconds. Drizzle the cheese over the salad and serve.

Nutrition Info:

- Per Servings 2g Carbs, 22g Protein, 23g Fat, 310 Calories

Caesar Salad With Chicken And Parmesan

Servings: 4 | Cooking Time: 1 Hour And 30 Minutes

Ingredients:

- 4 boneless, skinless chicken thighs
- ¼ cup lemon juice
- 2 garlic cloves, minced
- 4 tbsp olive oil
- ½ cup caesar salad dressing, sugar-free
- 12 bok choy leaves
- 3 Parmesan crisps
- Parmesan cheese, grated for garnishing

Directions:

1. Combine the chicken, lemon juice, 2 tbsp of olive oil, and garlic in a Ziploc bag. Seal the bag, shake to combine, and refrigerate for 1 hour. Preheat the grill to medium heat and grill the chicken for about 4 minutes per side.
2. Cut the bok choy leaves lengthwise, and brush it with the remaining olive oil. Grill the bok choy for about 3 minutes. Place on a serving bowl. Top with the chicken and drizzle the caesar salad dressing over. Top with parmesan crisps and sprinkle the grated parmesan cheese over.

Nutrition Info:

- Per Servings 5g Carbs, 33g Protein, 39g Fat, 529 Calories

Asparagus Niçoise Salad

Servings: 4 | Cooking Time: 0 Minutes

Ingredients:

- 1-pound fresh asparagus, trimmed and blanched
- 2 ½ ounces white tuna in oil
- ½ cup pitted Greek olives, halved
- ½ cup zesty Italian salad dressing
- Salt and pepper to taste
- 3 tablespoons olive oil

Directions:

1. Place all ingredients in a bowl.
2. Toss to mix all ingredients.
3. Serve.

Nutrition Info:

- Per Servings 10g Carbs, 8g Protein, 20g Fat, 239 Calories

Creamy Cauliflower Soup With Bacon Chips

Servings: 4 | Cooking Time: 25 Minutes

Ingredients:

- 2 tbsp ghee
- 1 onion, chopped
- 2 head cauliflower, cut into florets
- 2 cups water
- Salt and black pepper to taste
- 3 cups almond milk
- 1 cup shredded white cheddar cheese
- 3 bacon strips

Directions:

1. Melt the ghee in a saucepan over medium heat and sauté the onion for 3 minutes until fragrant.
2. Include the cauli florets, sauté for 3 minutes to slightly soften, add the water, and season with salt and black pepper. Bring to a boil, and then reduce the heat to low. Cover and cook for 10 minutes.
3. Puree cauliflower with an immersion blender until the ingredients are evenly combined and stir in the almond milk and cheese until the cheese melts. Adjust taste with salt and black pepper.
4. In a non-stick skillet over high heat, fry the bacon, until crispy. Divide soup between serving bowls, top with crispy bacon, and serve hot.

Nutrition Info:

- Per Servings 6g Carbs, 8g Protein, 37g Fat, 402 Calories

Creamy Cauliflower Soup With Chorizo Sausage

Servings: 4 | Cooking Time: 40 Minutes

Ingredients:

- 1 cauliflower head, chopped
- 1 turnip, chopped
- 3 tbsp butter
- 1 chorizo sausage, sliced
- 2 cups chicken broth
- 1 small onion, chopped
- 2 cups water
- Salt and black pepper, to taste

Directions:

1. Melt 2 tbsp. of the butter in a large pot over medium heat. Stir in onion and cook until soft and golden, about 3-4 minutes. Add cauliflower and turnip, and cook for another 5 minutes.

2. Pour the broth and water over. Bring to a boil, simmer covered, and cook for about 20 minutes until the vegetables are tender. Remove from heat. Melt the remaining butter in a skillet. Add the chorizo sausage and cook for 5 minutes until crispy. Puree the soup with a hand blender until smooth. Taste and adjust the seasonings. Serve the soup in deep bowls topped with the chorizo sausage.

Nutrition Info:

- Per Servings 5.7g Carbs, 10g Protein, 19.1g Fat, 251 Calories

Warm Baby Artichoke Salad

Servings: 4 | Cooking Time: 30 Minutes

Ingredients:

- 6 baby artichokes
- 6 cups water
- 1 tbsp lemon juice
- ¼ cup cherry peppers, halved
- ¼ cup pitted olives, sliced
- ¼ cup olive oil
- ¼ tsp lemon zest
- 2 tsp balsamic vinegar, sugar-free
- 1 tbsp chopped dill
- ½ tsp salt
- ¼ tsp black pepper
- 1 tbsp capers
- ¼ tsp caper brine

Directions:

1. Combine the water and salt in a pot over medium heat. Trim and halve the artichokes; add to the pot. Bring to a boil, lower the heat, and let simmer for 20 minutes until tender.

2. Combine the rest of the ingredients, except the olives in a bowl. Drain and place the artichokes in a serving plate. Pour the prepared mixture over; toss to combine well. Serve topped with the olives.

Nutrition Info:

- Per Servings 5g Carbs, 1g Protein, 13g Fat, 170 Calories

Insalata Caprese

Servings: 8 | Cooking Time: 0 Minutes

Ingredients:

- 2 ½ pounds tomatoes, cut into 1-in pieces
- 8 ounces mozzarella cheese pearls
- ½ cup ripe olives, pitted
- ¼ cup fresh basil, sliced thinly
- Balsamic vinegar (optional)
- Salt and pepper to taste
- 3 tablespoons olive oil

Directions:

1. Place all ingredients in a bowl.
2. Season with salt and pepper to taste. Drizzle with balsamic vinegar if available.
3. Toss to coat.
4. Serve immediately.

Nutrition Info:

- Per Servings 7g Carbs, 6g Protein, 12g Fat, 160 Calories

Tomato Hamburger Soup

Servings: 8 | Cooking Time: 25 Minutes

Ingredients:

- 1-pound ground beef
- 1 can V-8 juice
- 2 packages frozen vegetable mix
- 1 can condensed mushroom soup
- 2 teaspoon dried onion powder
- 5 tablespoons olive oil
- Salt and pepper to taste
- 1 cup water

Directions:

1. Place a pot over medium flame and heat for 2 minutes. Add oil and heat for a minute.
2. Sauté the beef until lightly browned, around 7 minutes. Season with salt, pepper, and onion powder.
3. Add the mushroom soup and water.
4. Give a good stir to combine everything.
5. Cover and bring to a boil, lower fire to a simmer and cook for 10 minutes.
6. Stir in vegetables. Cook until heated through around 5 minutes. Adjust seasoning if needed.
7. Serve and enjoy.

Nutrition Info:

- Per Servings 10g Carbs, 18.1g Protein, 14.8g Fat, 227 Calories

Bacon And Spinach Salad

Servings: 4 | Cooking Time: 20 Minutes

Ingredients:
- 2 large avocados, 1 chopped and 1 sliced
- 1 spring onion, sliced
- 4 cooked bacon slices, crumbled
- 2 cups spinach
- 2 small lettuce heads, chopped
- 2 hard-boiled eggs, chopped
- Vinaigrette:
- 3 tbsp olive oil
- 1 tsp Dijon mustard
- 1 tbsp apple cider vinegar

Directions:

1. Combine the spinach, lettuce, eggs, chopped avocado, and spring onion, in a large bowl. Whisk together the vinaigrette ingredients in another bowl.

2. Pour the dressing over, toss to combine and top with the sliced avocado and bacon.

Nutrition Info:
- Per Servings 3.4g Carbs, 7g Protein, 33g Fat, 350 Calories

Thyme & Wild Mushroom Soup

Servings: 4 | Cooking Time: 25 Minutes

Ingredients:
- ¼ cup butter
- ½ cup crème fraiche
- 12 oz wild mushrooms, chopped
- 2 tsp thyme leaves
- 2 garlic cloves, minced
- 4 cups chicken broth
- Salt and black pepper, to taste

Directions:

1. Melt the butter in a large pot over medium heat. Add garlic and cook for one minute until tender. Add mushrooms, salt and pepper, and cook for 10 minutes. Pour the broth over and bring to a boil.

2. Reduce the heat and simmer for 10 minutes. Puree the soup with a hand blender until smooth. Stir in crème Fraiche. Garnish with thyme leaves before serving.

Nutrition Info:
- Per Servings 5.8g Carbs, 6.1g Protein, 25g Fat, 281 Calories

Strawberry, Mozzarella Salad

Servings: 3 | Cooking Time: 10 Minutes

Ingredients:
- 5 ounces organic salad greens of your choice
- 2 medium cucumber, spiralized
- 2 cups strawberries, hulled and chopped
- 8 ounces mini mozzarella cheese balls
- ½ cup balsamic vinegar
- 5 tablespoons olive oil
- Salt to taste

Directions:

1. Toss all ingredients in a salad bowl.

2. Allow chilling in the fridge for at least 10 minutes before serving.

Nutrition Info:
- Per Servings 10g Carbs, 7g Protein, 31g Fat, 351 Calories

Mushroom Soup

Servings: 8 | Cooking Time: 35 Minutes

Ingredients:
- 1-pound baby portobello mushrooms, chopped
- 2 tablespoons olive oil
- 1 carton reduced-sodium beef broth
- 2 cups heavy whipping cream
- 4 tablespoons butter
- 1/2 cup water

Directions:

1. In a Dutch oven, sauté mushrooms in oil and butter until tender.

2. Add the contents of seasoning packets, broth, and water. Bring to a boil.

3. Reduce heat; cover and simmer for 25 minutes.

4. Add cream and heat through.

Nutrition Info:
- Per Servings 3.6g Carbs, 8g Protein, 26g Fat, 280 Calories

Lobster Salad With Mayo Dressing

Servings: 4 | Cooking Time: 1 Hour 10 Minutes

Ingredients:

- 1 small head cauliflower, cut into florets
- ⅓ cup diced celery
- ½ cup sliced black olives
- 2 cups cooked large shrimp
- 1 tbsp dill, chopped
- Dressing:
- ½ cup mayonnaise
- 1 tsp apple cider vinegar
- ¼ tsp celery seeds
- A pinch of black pepper
- 2 tbsp lemon juice
- 2 tsp swerve
- Salt to taste

Directions:

1. Combine the cauliflower, celery, shrimp, and dill in a large bowl. Whisk together the mayonnaise, vinegar, celery seeds, black pepper, sweetener, and lemon juice in another bowl. Season with salt to taste.

2. Pour the dressing over and gently toss to combine; refrigerate for 1 hour. Top with olives to serve.

Nutrition Info:

- Per Servings 2g Carbs, 12g Protein, 15g Fat, 182 Calories

Cream Of Thyme Tomato Soup

Servings: 6 | Cooking Time: 20 Minutes

Ingredients:

- 2 tbsp ghee
- 2 large red onions, diced
- ½ cup raw cashew nuts, diced
- 2 cans tomatoes
- 1 tsp fresh thyme leaves + extra to garnish
- 1 ½ cups water
- Salt and black pepper to taste
- 1 cup heavy cream

Directions:

1. Melt ghee in a pot over medium heat and sauté the onions for 4 minutes until softened.

2. Stir in the tomatoes, thyme, water, cashews, and season with salt and black pepper. Cover and bring to simmer for 10 minutes until thoroughly cooked.

3. Open, turn the heat off, and puree the ingredients with an immersion blender. Adjust to taste and stir in the heavy cream. Spoon into soup bowls and serve with low carb parmesan cheese toasts.

Nutrition Info:

- Per Servings 3g Carbs, 11g Protein, 27g Fat, 310 Calories

Desserts And Drinks

Boysenberry And Greens Shake

Servings: 1 | Cooking Time: 0 Minutes

Ingredients:
- ¼ cup coconut milk
- 2 tbsps Boysenberry
- 2 packets Stevia, or as needed
- ¼ cup Baby Kale salad mix
- 3 tbsps MCT oil
- 1 ½ cups water

Directions:
1. Add all ingredients in a blender.
2. Blend until smooth and creamy.
3. Serve and enjoy.

Nutrition Info:
- Per Servings 3.9g Carbs, 1.7g Protein, 55.1g Fat, 502 Calories

Chocolate Cakes

Servings: 6 | Cooking Time: 25 Minutes

Ingredients:
- ½ cup almond flour
- ¼ cup xylitol
- 1 tsp baking powder
- ½ tsp baking soda
- 1 tsp cinnamon, ground
- A pinch of salt
- A pinch of ground cloves
- ½ cup butter, melted
- ½ cup buttermilk
- 1 egg
- 1 tsp pure almond extract
- For the Frosting:
- 1 cup double cream
- 1 cup dark chocolate, flaked

Directions:
1. Preheat the oven to 360ºF. Use a cooking spray to grease a donut pan.
2. In a bowl, mix the cloves, almond flour, baking powder, salt, baking soda, xylitol, and cinnamon. In a separate bowl, combine the almond extract, butter, egg, buttermilk, and cream. Mix the wet mixture into the dry mixture. Evenly ladle the batter into the donut pan. Bake for 17 minutes.
3. Set a pan over medium heat and warm double cream; simmer for 2 minutes. Fold in the chocolate flakes; combine until all the chocolate melts; let cool. Spread the top of the cakes with the frosting.

Nutrition Info:
- Per Servings 10g Carbs, 4.8g Protein, 20g Fat, 218 Calories

Raspberry Creamy Smoothie

Servings: 1 | Cooking Time: 0 Minutes

Ingredients:
- ¼ cup coconut milk
- 1 ½ cups brewed coffee, chilled
- 2 tbsps raspberries
- 2 tbsps avocado meat
- 1 tsp chia seeds
- 2 packets Stevia or more to taste
- 3 tbsps coconut oil

Directions:
1. Add all ingredients in a blender.
2. Blend until smooth and creamy.
3. Serve and enjoy.

Nutrition Info:
- Per Servings 8.2g Carbs, 4.9g Protein, 33.2g Fat, 350 Calories

Lettuce Green Shake

Servings: 1 | Cooking Time: 0 Minutes

Ingredients:
- ¾ cup whole milk yogurt
- 2 cups 5-lettuce mix salad greens
- 3 tbsp MCT oil
- 1 tbsp chia seeds
- 1 ½ cups water
- 1 packet Stevia, or more to taste

Directions:
1. Add all ingredients in a blender.
2. Blend until smooth and creamy.
3. Serve and enjoy.

Nutrition Info:
- Per Servings 6.1g Carbs, 8.1g Protein, 47g Fat, 483 Calories

Chocolate Chip Cookies

Servings: 4 | Cooking Time: 20 Minutes

Ingredients:
- 1 cup butter, softened
- 2 cups swerve brown sugar
- 3 eggs
- 2 cups almond flour
- 2 cups unsweetened chocolate chips

Directions:
1. Preheat oven to 350ºF and line a baking sheet with parchment paper.
2. Whisk the butter and sugar with a hand mixer for 3 minutes or until light and fluffy. Add the eggs one at a time, and scrape

the sides as you whisk. Mix in the almond flour in low speed until well combined.

3. Fold in the chocolate chips. Scoop 3 tablespoons each on the baking sheet creating spaces between each mound and bake for 15 minutes to swell and harden. Remove, cool and serve.

Nutrition Info:

- Per Servings 8.9g Carbs, 6.3g Protein, 27g Fat, 317 Calories

Strawberry And Basil Lemonade

Servings: 4 | Cooking Time: 3 Minutes

Ingredients:

- 4 cups water
- 12 strawberries, leaves removed
- 1 cup fresh lemon juice
- ⅓ cup fresh basil
- ¾ cup swerve
- Crushed Ice
- Halved strawberries to garnish
- Basil leaves to garnish

Directions:

1. Spoon some ice into 4 serving glasses and set aside. In a pitcher, add the water, strawberries, lemon juice, basil, and swerve. Insert the blender and process the ingredients for 30 seconds.

2. The mixture should be pink and the basil finely chopped. Adjust the taste and add the ice in the glasses. Drop 2 strawberry halves and some basil in each glass and serve immediately.

Nutrition Info:

- Per Servings 5.8g Carbs, 0.7g Protein, 0.1g Fat, 66 Calories

Ice Cream Bars Covered With Chocolate

Servings: 15 | Cooking Time: 4 Hours And 20 Minutes

Ingredients:

- Ice Cream:
- 1 cup heavy whipping cream
- 1 tsp vanilla extract
- ¾ tsp xanthan gum
- ½ cup peanut butter
- 1 cup half and half
- 1 ½ cups almond milk
- ⅓ tsp stevia powder
- 1 tbsp vegetable glycerin
- 3 tbsp xylitol
- Chocolate:
- ¾ cup coconut oil
- ¼ cup cocoa butter pieces, chopped
- 2 ounces unsweetened chocolate
- 3 ½ tsp THM super sweet blend

Directions:

1. Blend all ice cream ingredients until smooth. Place in an ice cream maker and follow the instructions. Spread the ice cream

into a lined pan, and freezer for about 4 hours.

2. Combine all chocolate ingredients in a microwave-safe bowl and heat until melted. Allow cooling. Remove the ice cream from the freezer and slice into bars. Dip them into the cooled chocolate mixture and return to the freezer for about 10 minutes before serving.

Nutrition Info:

- Per Servings 5g Carbs, 4g Protein, 32g Fat, 345 Calories

Vanilla Ice Cream

Servings: 4 | Cooking Time: 50 Minutes + Cooling Time

Ingredients:

- ½ cup smooth peanut butter
- ½ cup swerve
- 3 cups half and half
- 1 tsp vanilla extract
- 2 pinches salt

Directions:

1. Beat peanut butter and swerve in a bowl with a hand mixer until smooth. Gradually whisk in half and half until thoroughly combined. Mix in vanilla and salt. Pour mixture into a loaf pan and freeze for 45 minutes until firmed up. Scoop into glasses when ready to eat and serve.

Nutrition Info:

- Per Servings 6g Carbs, 13g Protein, 23g Fat, 290 Calories

Keto Nut Bark

Servings: 8 | Cooking Time: 40 Minutes

Ingredients:

- 1 pound chopped walnuts
- 1-1/2 teaspoons ground cinnamon
- ½ cup butter, melted
- 1 packet stevia powder
- ½ cup coconut oil

Directions:

1. Preheat oven to 350°F. Coat a 13x9-in. baking dish with cooking spray. Combine walnuts and cinnamon.

2. Mix all ingredients until well combined.

3. Press on a baking sheet and flatten with a rolling pin.

4. Allow to harden in the fridge before breaking into barks.

Nutrition Info:

- Per Servings 7.9g Carbs, 9g Protein, 68g Fat, 648 Calories

Keto Lemon Custard

Servings: 8 | Cooking Time: 50 Minutes

Ingredients:

- 1 Lemon
- 6 large eggs
- 2 tbsp lemon zest
- 1 cup Lakanto
- 2 cups heavy cream

Directions:

1. Preheat oven to 300oF.
2. Mix all ingredients.
3. Pour mixture into ramekins.
4. Put ramekins into a dish with boiling water.
5. Bake in the oven for 45-50 minutes.
6. Let cool then refrigerate for 2 hours.
7. Use lemon slices as garnish.

Nutrition Info:

- Per Servings 4.0g Carbs, 7.0g Protein, 21.0g Fat, 233 Calories

Choco Coffee Milk Shake

Servings: 1 | Cooking Time: 0 Minutes

Ingredients:

- ½ cup coconut milk
- 1 tbsp cocoa powder
- 1 cup brewed coffee, chilled
- 1 packet Stevia, or more to taste
- ½ tsp cinnamon
- 5 tbsps coconut oil

Directions:

1. Add all ingredients in a blender.
2. Blend until smooth and creamy.
3. Serve and enjoy.

Nutrition Info:

- Per Servings 10g Carbs, 4.1g Protein, 97.4g Fat, 880 Calories

Garden Greens & Yogurt Shake

Servings: 1 | Cooking Time: 0 Minutes

Ingredients:

- 1 cup whole milk yogurt
- 1 cup Garden greens
- 3 tbsp MCT oil
- 1 tbsp flaxseed, ground
- 1 cup water
- 1 packet Stevia, or more to taste

Directions:

1. Add all ingredients in a blender.
2. Blend until smooth and creamy.
3. Serve and enjoy.

Nutrition Info:

- Per Servings 7.2g Carbs, 11.7g Protein, 53g Fat, 581 Calories

Passion Fruit Cheesecake Slices

Servings: 8 | Cooking Time: 2 Hours 30 Minutes

Ingredients:

- 1 cup crushed almond biscuits
- ½ cup melted butter
- Filling:
- 1 ½ cups cream cheese
- ¾ cup swerve
- 1 ½ whipping cream
- 1 tsp vanilla bean paste
- 4-6 tbsp cold water
- 1 tbsp gelatin powder
- Passionfruit Jelly
- 1 cup passion fruit pulp
- ¼ cup swerve confectioner's sugar
- 1 tsp gelatin powder
- ¼ cup water, room temperature

Directions:

1. Mix the crushed biscuits and butter in a bowl, spoon into a spring-form pan, and use the back of the spoon to level at the bottom. Set aside in the fridge. Put the cream cheese, swerve, and vanilla paste into a bowl, and use the hand mixer to whisk until smooth; set aside.

2. In a bowl, add 2 tbsp of cold water and sprinkle 1 tbsp of gelatin powder. Let dissolve for 5 minutes. Pour the gelatin liquid along with the whipping cream in the cheese mixture and fold gently.

3. Remove the spring-form pan from the refrigerator and pour over the mixture. Return to the fridge.

4. Repeat the dissolving process for the remaining gelatin and once your out of ingredients, pour the confectioner's sugar, and ¼ cup of water into it. Mix and stir in the passion fruit pulp.

5. Remove the cake again and pour the jelly over it. Swirl the pan to make the jelly level up. Place the pan back into the fridge to cool for 2 hours. When completely set, remove and unlock the spring-pan. Lift the pan from the cake and slice the dessert.

Nutrition Info:

- Per Servings 6.1g Carbs, 4.4g Protein, 18g Fat, 287 Calories

Lemon Gummies

Servings: 4 | Cooking Time: 15 Minutes

Ingredients:

- 1/4 cup fresh lemon juice
- 2 Tablespoons gelatin powder
- 2 Tablespoons stevia, to taste
- ½ cup half and half
- 1 Tablespoon water

Directions:

1. In a small saucepan, heat up water and lemon juice.
2. Slowly stir in the gelatin powder and the rest of the ingredients. Heating and mixing well until dissolved.
3. Pour into silicone molds.
4. Freeze or refrigerate for 2+ hours until firm.

Nutrition Info:

- Per Servings 1.0g Carbs, 3.0g Protein, 7g Fat, 88 Calories

Mixed Berry Nuts Mascarpone Bowl

Servings: 4 | Cooking Time: 8 Minutes

Ingredients:

- 4 cups Greek yogurt
- liquid stevia to taste
- 1 ½ cups mascarpone cheese
- 1 ½ cups blueberries and raspberries
- 1 cup toasted pecans

Directions:

1. Mix the yogurt, stevia, and mascarpone in a bowl until evenly combined. Divide the mixture into 4 bowls, share the berries and pecans on top of the cream. Serve the dessert immediately.

Nutrition Info:

- Per Servings 5g Carbs, 20g Protein, 40g Fat, 480 Calories

Dark Chocolate Mousse With Stewed Plums

Servings: 6 | Cooking Time: 45 Minutes

Ingredients:

- 12 oz unsweetened chocolate
- 8 eggs, separated into yolks and whites
- 2 tbsp salt
- ¾ cup swerve sugar
- ½ cup olive oil
- 3 tbsp brewed coffee
- Stewed Plums
- 4 plums, pitted and halved
- ½ stick cinnamon
- ½ cup swerve
- ½ cup water
- ½ lemon, juiced

Directions:

1. Put the chocolate in a bowl and melt in the microwave for 1 ½ minutes. In a separate bowl, whisk the yolks with half of the swerve until a pale yellow has formed, then, beat in the salt, olive oil, and coffee. Mix in the melted chocolate until smooth.
2. In a third bowl, whisk the whites with the hand mixer until a soft peak has formed. Sprinkle the remaining swerve sugar over and gently fold in with a spatula. Fetch a tablespoon full of the chocolate mixture and fold in to combine. Pour in the remaining chocolate mixture and whisk to mix.
3. Pour the mousse into 6 ramekins, cover with plastic wrap, and refrigerate overnight. The next morning, pour water, swerve, cinnamon, and lemon juice in a saucepan and bring to a simmer for 3 minutes, occasionally stirring to ensure the swerve has dissolved and a syrup has formed.
4. Add the plums and poach in the sweetened water for 18 minutes until soft. Turn the heat off and discard the cinnamon stick. Spoon a plum each with syrup on the chocolate mousse and serve.

Nutrition Info:

- Per Servings 6.9g Carbs, 9.5g Protein, 23g Fat, 288 Calories

Spicy Cheese Crackers

Servings: 4 | Cooking Time: 10 Mins

Ingredients:

- 3/4 cup almond flour
- 1 egg
- 2 tablespoons cream cheese
- 2 cups shredded Parmesan cheese
- 1/2 teaspoon red pepper flakes
- 1 tablespoon dry ranch salad dressing mix

Directions:

1. Preheat oven to 425 degrees F.
2. Combine Parmesan and cream cheese in a microwave safe bowl and microwave in 30 second intervals. Add the cheese to mix well, and whisk along the almond flour, egg, ranch seasoning, and red pepper flakes, stirring occasionally.
3. Transfer the dough in between two parchment-lined baking sheets. Form the dough into rolls by cutting off plum-sized pieces of dough with dough cutter into 1-inch square pieces, yielding about 60 pieces.
4. Place crackers to a baking sheet lined parchment. Bake for 5 minutes, flipping halfway, then continue to bake for 5 minutes more. Chill before serving.

Nutrition Info:

- Per Servings 18g Carbs, 17g Protein, 4g Fat, 235 Calories

Granny Smith Apple Tart

Servings: 8 | Cooking Time: 65 Minutes

Ingredients:
- 6 tbsp butter
- 2 cups almond flour
- 1 tsp cinnamon
- ⅓ cup sweetener
- Filling:
- 2 cups sliced Granny Smith
- ¼ cup butter
- ¼ cup sweetener
- ½ tsp cinnamon
- ½ tsp lemon juice
- Topping:
- ¼ tsp cinnamon
- 2 tbsp sweetener

Directions:
1. Preheat your oven to 370ºF and combine all crust ingredients in a bowl. Press this mixture into the bottom of a greased pan. Bake for 5 minutes.
2. Meanwhile, combine the apples and lemon juice in a bowl and let them sit until the crust is ready. Arrange them on top of the crust. Combine the rest of the filling ingredients, and brush this mixture over the apples. Bake for about 30 minutes.
3. Press the apples down with a spatula, return to oven, and bake for 20 more minutes. Combine the cinnamon and sweetener, in a bowl, and sprinkle over the tart.
4. Note: Granny Smith apples have just 9.5g of net carbs per 100g. Still high for you? Substitute with Chayote squash, which has the same texture and rich nutrients, and just around 4g of net carbs .

Nutrition Info:
- Per Servings 6.7g Carbs, 7g Protein, 26g Fat, 302 Calories

Berry-choco Goodness Shake

Servings: 1 | Cooking Time: 0 Minutes

Ingredients:
- ½ cup half and half
- ¼ cup raspberries
- ¼ cup blackberry
- ¼ cup strawberries, chopped
- 3 tbsps avocado oil
- 1 packet Stevia, or more to taste
- 1 tbsp cocoa powder
- 1 ½ cups water

Directions:
1. Add all ingredients in a blender.
2. Blend until smooth and creamy.
3. Serve and enjoy.

Nutrition Info:
- Per Servings 7g Carbs, 4.4g Protein, 43.3g Fat, 450 Calories

Lime Strawberry Smoothie

Servings: 3 | Cooking Time: 3 Mins

Ingredients:
- 4 ice cubes
- 1/4 fresh strawberry
- 1 large avocado, diced
- 1 cup lime juice

Directions:
1. In a food processor, combine all ingredients and puree on High until a smooth smoothie is formed. Serve and enjoy.

Nutrition Info:
- Per Servings 4g Carbs, 3g Protein, 11g Fat, 127 Calories

Chia And Blackberry Pudding

Servings: 2 | Cooking Time: 10 Minutes

Ingredients:
- 1 cup full-fat natural yogurt
- 2 tsp swerve
- 2 tbsp chia seeds
- 1 cup fresh blackberries
- 1 tbsp lemon zest
- Mint leaves, to serve

Directions:
1. Mix together the yogurt and the swerve. Stir in the chia seeds. Reserve 4 blackberries for garnish and mash the remaining ones with a fork until pureed. Stir in the yogurt mixture
2. Chill in the fridge for 30 minutes. When cooled, divide the mixture between 2 glasses. Top each with a couple of raspberries, mint leaves, lemon zest and serve.

Nutrition Info:
- Per Servings 4.7g Carbs, 7.5g Protein, 10g Fat, 169 Calories

Hazelnut And Coconut Shake

Servings: 1 | Cooking Time: 0 Minutes

Ingredients:
- ¼ coconut milk
- ¼ cup hazelnut, chopped
- 2 tbsps MCT oil or coconut oil
- 1 ½ cups water
- 1 packet Stevia, optional

Directions:
1. Add all ingredients in a blender.
2. Blend until smooth and creamy.
3. Serve and enjoy.

Nutrition Info:
- Per Servings 8.9g Carbs, 6.5g Protein, 62.1g Fat, 591 Calories

Brownies With Coco Milk

Servings: 10 | Cooking Time: 6 Hours

Ingredients:

- ¾ cup coconut milk
- 1 teaspoon erythritol
- 2 tablespoons butter, melted
- 4 egg yolks, beaten
- 5 tablespoons cacao powder

Directions:

1. In a bowl, mix well all ingredients.
2. Lightly grease your slow cooker with cooking spray and pour in batter.
3. Cover and cook on low for six hours.
4. Serve and enjoy.

Nutrition Info:

- Per Servings 1.2g Carbs, 1.5g Protein, 8.4g Fat, 86 Calories

Five Greens Smoothie

Servings: 4 | Cooking Time: 5 Minutes

Ingredients:

- 6 kale leaves, chopped
- 3 stalks celery, chopped
- 1 ripe avocado, skinned, pitted, sliced
- 1 cup ice cubes
- 2 cups spinach, chopped
- 1 large cucumber, peeled and chopped
- Chia seeds to garnish

Directions:

1. In a blender, add the kale, celery, avocado, and ice cubes, and blend for 45 seconds. Add the spinach and cucumber, and process for another 45 seconds until smooth.
2. Pour the smoothie into glasses, garnish with chia seeds and serve the drink immediately.

Nutrition Info:

- Per Servings 2.9g Carbs, 3.2g Protein, 7.8g Fat, 124 Calories

Strawberry-coconut Shake

Servings: 1 | Cooking Time: 0 Minutes

Ingredients:

- ½ cup whole milk yogurt
- 3 tbsp MCT oil
- ¼ cup strawberries, chopped
- 1 tbsp coconut flakes, unsweetened
- 1 tbsp hemp seeds
- 1 ½ cups water
- 1 packet Stevia, or more to taste

Directions:

1. Add all ingredients in a blender.
2. Blend until smooth and creamy.
3. Serve and enjoy.

Nutrition Info:

- Per Servings 10.2g Carbs, 6.4g Protein, 50.9g Fat, 511 Calories

White Choco Fatty Fudge

Servings: 6 | Cooking Time: 10 Minutes

Ingredients:

- 1/4 cup coconut butter
- 1/4 cup cashew butter
- 2 tbsp cacao butter
- 1/4 teaspoon vanilla powder
- 10–12 drops liquid stevia, or to taste
- 2 tbsp coconut oil

Directions:

1. Over low heat, place a small saucepan and melt coconut oil, cacao butter, cashew butter, and coconut butter.
2. Remove from the heat and stir in the vanilla and stevia.
3. Pour into a silicone mold and place it in the freezer for 30 minutes.
4. Store in the fridge for a softer consistency.

Nutrition Info:

- Per Servings 1.7g Carbs, 0.2g Protein, 23.7g Fat, 221 Calories

Lychee And Coconut Lassi

Servings: 4 | Cooking Time: 2 Hours 28 Minutes

Ingredients:

- 2 cups lychee pulp, seeded
- 2 ½ cups coconut milk
- 4 tsp swerve
- 2 limes, zested and juiced
- 1 ½ cups plain yogurt
- 1 lemongrass, white part only, crushed
- Toasted coconut shavings for garnish

Directions:

1. In a saucepan, add the lychee pulp, coconut milk, swerve, lemongrass, and lime zest. Stir and bring to boil on medium heat for 2 minutes, = stirring continually. Then reduce the heat, and simmer for 1 minute. Turn the heat off and let the mixture sit for 15 minutes.
2. Remove the lemongrass and pour the mixture into a smoothie maker or a blender, add the yogurt and lime juice, and process the ingredients until smooth, for about 60 seconds.
3. Pour into a jug and refrigerate for 2 hours until cold; stir. Serve garnished with coconut shavings.

Nutrition Info:

- Per Servings 1.5g Carbs, 5.3g Protein, 26.1g Fat, 285 Calories

Coconut-melon Yogurt Shake

Servings: 1 | Cooking Time: 0 Minutes

Ingredients:
- ¼ cup half and half
- 3 tbsp coconut oil
- ½ cup melon, slices
- 1 tbsp coconut flakes, unsweetened
- 1 tbsp chia seeds
- 1 ½ cups water
- 1 packet Stevia, or more to taste

Directions:
1. Add all ingredients in a blender.
2. Blend until smooth and creamy.
3. Serve and enjoy.

Nutrition Info:
- Per Servings 8g Carbs, 2.4g Protein, 43g Fat, 440 Calories

Green Tea Brownies With Macadamia Nuts

Servings: 4 | Cooking Time: 28 Minutes

Ingredients:
- 1 tbsp green tea powder
- ¼ cup unsalted butter, melted
- 4 tbsp swerve confectioner's sugar
- A pinch of salt
- ¼ cup coconut flour
- ½ tsp low carb baking powder
- 1 egg
- ¼ cup chopped macadamia nuts

Directions:

1. Preheat the oven to 350ºF and line a square baking dish with parchment paper. Pour the melted butter into a bowl, add sugar and salt, and whisk to combine. Crack the egg into the bowl.

2. Beat the mixture until the egg has incorporated. Pour the coconut flour, green tea, and baking powder into a fine-mesh sieve and sift them into the egg bowl; stir. Add the nuts, stir again, and pour the mixture into the lined baking dish. Bake for 18 minutes, remove and slice into brownie cubes. Serve warm.

Nutrition Info:
- Per Servings 2.2g Carbs, 5.2g Protein, 23.1g Fat, 248 Calories

Coconut Raspberry Bars

Servings: 12 | Cooking Time: 20 Minutes

Ingredients:
- 1 cup coconut milk
- 3 cups desiccated coconut
- 1/3 cup erythritol powder
- 1 cup raspberries, pulsed
- ½ cup coconut oil or other oils

Directions:
1. Preheat oven to 380oF.
2. Combine all ingredients in a mixing bowl.
3. Pour into a greased baking dish.
4. Bake in the oven for 20 minutes.
5. Let it rest for 10 minutes.
6. Serve and enjoy.

Nutrition Info:
- Per Servings 8.2g Carbs, 1.5g Protein, 14.7g Fat, 170 Calories

Strawberry Yogurt Shake

Servings: 1 | Cooking Time: 0 Minutes

Ingredients:
- ½ cup whole milk yogurt
- 4 strawberries, chopped
- 1 tbsp cocoa powder
- 3 tbsp coconut oil
- 1 tbsp pepitas
- 1 ½ cups water
- 1 packet Stevia, or more to taste

Directions:
1. Add all ingredients in a blender.
2. Blend until smooth and creamy.
3. Serve and enjoy.

Nutrition Info:
- Per Servings 10.5g Carbs, 7.7g Protein, 49.3g Fat, 496 Calories

Brownie Mug Cake

Servings: 1 | Cooking Time: 5 Minutes

Ingredients:
- 1 egg, beaten
- ¼ cup almond flour
- ¼ teaspoon baking powder
- 1 ½ tablespoons cacao powder
- 2 tablespoons stevia powder
- A pinch of salt
- 1 teaspoon cinnamon powder
- ¼ teaspoon vanilla extract (optional)

Directions:
1. Combine all ingredients in a bowl until well-combined.
2. Transfer in a heat-proof mug.
3. Place the mug in a microwave.

4. Cook for 2 minutes. Let it sit for another 2 minutes to continue cooking.
5. Serve and enjoy.

Nutrition Info:

• Per Servings 4.1g Carbs, 9.1g Protein, 11.8g Fat, 159 Calories

No Bake Lemon Cheese-stard

Servings: 8 | Cooking Time: 0 Minutes

Ingredients:

• 1 tsp vanilla flavoring
• 1 tbsp lemon juice
• 2 oz heavy cream
• 8 oz softened cream cheese
• 1 tsp liquid low carb sweetener (Splenda)
• 1 tsp stevia

Directions:

1. Mix all ingredients in a large mixing bowl until the mixture has a pudding consistency.
2. Pour the mixture to small serving cups and refrigerate for a few hours until it sets.
3. Serve chilled.

Nutrition Info:

• Per Servings 1.4g Carbs, 2.2g Protein, 10.7g Fat, 111 Calories

Nutritiously Green Milk Shake

Servings: 1 | Cooking Time: 5 Minutes

Ingredients:

• 1 cup coconut cream
• 1 packet Stevia, or more to taste
• 1 tbsp coconut flakes, unsweetened
• 2 cups spring mix salad
• 3 tbsps coconut oil
• 1 cup water

Directions:

1. Add all ingredients in a blender.
2. Blend until smooth and creamy.
3. Serve and enjoy.

Nutrition Info:

• Per Servings 10g Carbs, 10.5g Protein, 95.3g Fat, 887 Calories

Chocolate Bark With Almonds

Servings: 12 | Cooking Time: 1 Hour 15 Minutes

Ingredients:

• ½ cup toasted almonds, chopped
• ½ cup butter
• 10 drops stevia
• ¼ tsp salt
• ½ cup unsweetened coconut flakes
• 4 ounces dark chocolate

Directions:

1. Melt together the butter and chocolate, in the microwave, for 90 seconds. Remove and stir in stevia.
2. Line a cookie sheet with waxed paper and spread the chocolate evenly. Scatter the almonds on top, coconut flakes, and sprinkle with salt. Refrigerate for one hour.

Nutrition Info:

• Per Servings 1.9g Carbs, 1.9g Protein, 15.3g Fat, 161 Calories

Raspberry-choco Shake

Servings: 1 | Cooking Time: 0 Minutes

Ingredients:

• ¼ cup heavy cream, liquid
• 1 tbsp cocoa powder
• 1 packet Stevia, or more to taste
• ¼ cup raspberries
• 1 ½ cups water

Directions:

1. Add all ingredients in a blender.
2. Blend until smooth and creamy.
3. Serve and enjoy.

Nutrition Info:

• Per Servings 11.1g Carbs, 3.8g Protein, 45.0g Fat, 438 Calories

Lemon Cheesecake Mousse

Servings: 4 | Cooking Time: 5 Minutes +cooling Time

Ingredients:

• 24 oz cream cheese, softened
• 2 cups swerve confectioner's sugar
• 2 lemons, juiced and zested
• Pink salt to taste
• 1 cup whipped cream + extra for garnish

Directions:

1. Whip the cream cheese in a bowl with a hand mixer until light and fluffy. Mix in the sugar, lemon juice, and salt. Fold in the whipped cream to evenly combine.
2. Spoon the mousse into serving cups and refrigerate to thicken for 1 hour. Swirl with extra whipped cream and garnish lightly with lemon zest. Serve immediately.

Nutrition Info:

• Per Servings 3g Carbs, 12g Protein, 18g Fat, 223 Calories

Lemony-avocado Cilantro Shake

Servings: 1 | Cooking Time: 0 Minutes

Ingredients:
- ½ cup half and half
- 1 packet Stevia, or more to taste
- ¼ avocado, meat scooped
- 1 tbsp chopped cilantro
- 3 tbsps coconut oil
- 1 ½ cups water

Directions:
1. Add all ingredients in a blender.
2. Blend until smooth and creamy.
3. Serve and enjoy.

Nutrition Info:
- Per Servings 8.4g Carbs, 4.4g Protein, 49g Fat, 501 Calories

Raspberry Sorbet

Servings: 1 | Cooking Time: 3 Minutes

Ingredients:
- ¼ tsp vanilla extract
- 1 packet gelatine, without sugar
- 1 tbsp heavy whipping cream
- ⅓ cup boiling water
- 2 tbsp mashed raspberries
- 1 ½ cups crushed Ice
- ⅓ cup cold water

Directions:
1. Combine the gelatin and boiling water, until completely dissolved; then transfer to a blender. Add the remaining ingredients. Blend until smooth and freeze for at least 2 hours.

Nutrition Info:
- Per Servings 3.7g Carbs, 4g Protein, 10g Fat, 173 Calories

Raspberry Nut Truffles

Servings: 4 | Cooking Time: 6 Minutes + Cooling Time

Ingredients:
- 2 cups raw cashews
- 2 tbsp flax seed
- 1 ½ cups sugar-free raspberry preserves
- 3 tbsp swerve
- 10 oz unsweetened chocolate chips
- 3 tbsp olive oil

Directions:
1. Line a baking sheet with parchment paper and set aside. Grind the cashews and flax seeds in a blender for 45 seconds until smoothly crushed; add the raspberry and 2 tbsp of swerve.
2. Process further for 1 minute until well combined. Form 1-inch balls of the mixture, place on the baking sheet, and freeze for 1 hour or until firmed up.
3. Melt the chocolate chips, oil, and 1tbsp of swerve in a microwave for 1 ½ minutes. Toss the truffles to coat in the choc-

olate mixture, put on the baking sheet, and freeze further for at least 2 hours.

Nutrition Info:
- Per Servings 3.5g Carbs, 12g Protein, 18.3g Fat, 251 Calories

Smarties Cookies

Servings: 8 | Cooking Time: 10 Mins

Ingredients:
- 1/4 cup. butter
- 1/2 cup. almond flour
- 1 tsp. vanilla essence
- 12 oz. bag of smarties
- 1 cup. stevia
- 1/4 tsp. baking powder

Directions:
1. Sift in flour and baking powder in a bowl, then stir through butter and mix until well combined.
2. Whisk in stevia and vanilla essence , stir until thick.
3. Then add the smarties and use your hand to mix and divide into small balls.
4. Bake until completely cooked, about 10 minutes. Let it cool and serve.

Nutrition Info:
- Per Servings 20.77g Carbs, 3.7g Protein, 11.89g Fat, 239 Calories

Nutty Arugula Yogurt Smoothie

Servings: 1 | Cooking Time: 0 Minutes

Ingredients:
- 1 cup whole milk yogurt
- 1 cup baby arugula
- 3 tbsps avocado oil
- 2 tbsps macadamia nuts
- 1 packet Stevia, or more to taste
- 1 cup water

Directions:
1. Add all ingredients in a blender.
2. Blend until smooth and creamy.
3. Serve and enjoy.

Nutrition Info:
- Per Servings 9.4g Carbs, 9.3g Protein, 51.5g Fat, 540 Calories

Cinnamon And Turmeric Latte

Servings: 4 | Cooking Time: 7 Minutes

Ingredients:

- 3 cups almond milk
- ⅓ tsp cinnamon powder
- 1 cup brewed coffee
- ½ tsp turmeric powder
- 1 ½ tsp erythritol
- Cinnamon sticks to garnish

Directions:

1. In the blender, add the almond milk, cinnamon powder, coffee, turmeric, and erythritol. Blend the ingredients at medium speed for 45 seconds and pour the mixture into a saucepan.
2. Set the pan over low heat and heat through for 5 minutes; do not boil. Keep swirling the pan to prevent from boiling. Turn the heat off, and serve in latte cups, with a cinnamon stick in each one.

Nutrition Info:

- Per Servings 0.3g Carbs, 3.9g Protein, 12g Fat, 132 Calories

Chocolate Hazelnut Bites

Servings: 9 | Cooking Time: 0 Minutes

Ingredients:

- 1 carton spreadable cream cheese
- 1 cup semisweet chocolate chips, melted
- 1/2 cup Nutella
- 2-1/4 cups graham cracker crumbs
- 2 cups chopped hazelnuts, toasted
- 5 tablespoons butter

Directions:

1. Beat cream cheese, melted chocolate chips, and Nutella until blended. Stir in cracker crumbs. Refrigerate until firm enough to roll, about 30 minutes.
2. Shape mixture into 1-in. balls; roll in chopped hazelnuts. Make an indentation in the center of each with the end of a wooden spoon handle. Fill with a hazelnut. Store between layers of waxed paper in an airtight container in the refrigerator.

Nutrition Info:

- Per Servings 10g Carbs, 2.7g Protein, 14g Fat, 176 Calories

Baby Kale And Yogurt Smoothie

Servings: 1 | Cooking Time: 0 Minutes

Ingredients:

- ½ cup whole milk yogurt
- ½ cup baby kale greens
- 1 packet Stevia, or more to taste
- 3 tbsps MCT oil
- ½ tbsp sunflower seeds
- 1 cup water

Directions:

1. Add all ingredients in a blender.
2. Blend until smooth and creamy.
3. Serve and enjoy.

Nutrition Info:

- Per Servings 2.6g Carbs, 11.0g Protein, 26.2g Fat, 329 Calories

Minty-coco And Greens Shake

Servings: 1 | Cooking Time: 0 Minutes

Ingredients:

- ½ cup coconut milk
- 2 peppermint leaves
- 2 packets Stevia, or as needed
- 1 cup 50/50 salad mix
- 1 tbsp coconut oil
- 1 ½ cups water

Directions:

1. Add all ingredients in a blender.
2. Blend until smooth and creamy.
3. Serve and enjoy.

Nutrition Info:

- Per Servings 5.8g Carbs, 2.7g Protein, 37.8g Fat, 344 Calories

Coco-loco Creamy Shake

Servings: 1 | Cooking Time: 0 Minutes

Ingredients:

- ½ cup coconut milk
- 2 tbsp Dutch-processed cocoa powder, unsweetened
- 1 cup brewed coffee, chilled
- 1 tbsp hemp seeds
- 1-2 packets Stevia
- 3 tbsps MCT oil or coconut oil

Directions:

1. Add all ingredients in a blender.
2. Blend until smooth and creamy.
3. Serve and enjoy.

Nutrition Info:

- Per Servings 10.2g Carbs, 5.4g Protein, 61.1g Fat, 567 Calories

Sea Salt 'n Macadamia Choco Barks

Servings: 10 | Cooking Time: 5 Minutes

Ingredients:
- 1 teaspoon sea salt flakes
- 1/4 cup macadamia nuts, crushed
- 2 Tablespoons erythritol or stevia, to taste
- 3.5 oz 100% dark chocolate, broken into pieces
- 2 Tablespoons coconut oil, melted

Directions:
1. Melt the chocolate and coconut oil over a very low heat.
2. Remove from heat. Stir in sweetener.
3. Pour the mixture into a loaf pan and place in the fridge for 15 minutes.
4. Scatter the crushed macadamia nuts on top along with the sea salt. Lightly press into the chocolate.
5. Place back into the fridge or freezer for 2 hours.

Nutrition Info:
- Per Servings 1.0g Carbs, 2.0g Protein, 8.0g Fat, 84 Calories

Coffee Fat Bombs

Servings: 6 | Cooking Time: 3 Minutes + Cooling Time

Ingredients:
- 1 ½ cups mascarpone cheese
- ½ cup melted butter
- 3 tbsp unsweetened cocoa powder
- ¼ cup erythritol
- 6 tbsp brewed coffee, room temperature

Directions:
1. Whisk the mascarpone cheese, butter, cocoa powder, erythritol, and coffee with a hand mixer until creamy and fluffy, for 1 minute. Fill into muffin tins and freeze for 3 hours until firm.

Nutrition Info:
- Per Servings 2g Carbs, 4g Protein, 14g Fat, 145 Calories

Cardamom-cinnamon Spiced Coco-latte

Servings: 1 | Cooking Time: 0 Minutes

Ingredients:
- ½ cup coconut milk
- ¼ tsp cardamom powder
- 1 tbsp chocolate powder
- 1 ½ cups brewed coffee, chilled
- 1 tbsp coconut oil
- ¼ tsp cinnamon
- ¼ tsp nutmeg

Directions:
1. Add all ingredients in a blender.
2. Blend until smooth and creamy.
3. Serve and enjoy.

Nutrition Info:
- Per Servings 7.5g Carbs, 3.8g Protein, 38.7g Fat, 362 Calories

Chocolate Marshmallows

Servings: 4 | Cooking Time: 30 Minutes

Ingredients:
- 2 tbsp unsweetened cocoa powder
- ½ tsp vanilla extract
- ½ cup swerve
- 1 tbsp xanthan gum mixed in 1 tbsp water
- A pinch Salt
- 6 tbsp Cool water
- 2 ½ tsp Gelatin powder
- Dusting:
- 1 tbsp unsweetened cocoa powder
- 1 tbsp swerve confectioner's sugar

Directions:
1. Line the loaf pan with parchment paper and grease with cooking spray; set aside. In a saucepan, mix the swerve, 2 tbsp of water, xanthan gum mixture, and salt. Place the pan over medium heat and bring to a boil. Insert the thermometer and let the ingredients simmer to 238 F, for 7 minutes.
2. In a small bowl, add 2 tbsp of water and sprinkle the gelatin on top. Let sit there without stirring to dissolve for 5 minutes. While the gelatin dissolves, pour the remaining water in a small bowl and heat in the microwave for 30 seconds. Stir in cocoa powder and mix it into the gelatin.
3. When the sugar solution has hit the right temperature, gradually pour it directly into the gelatin mixture while continuously whisking. Beat for 10 minutes to get a light and fluffy consistency.
4. Next, stir in the vanilla and pour the blend into the loaf pan. Let the marshmallows set for 3 hours and then use an oiled knife to cut it into cubes; place them on a plate. Mix the remaining cocoa powder and confectioner's sugar together. Sift it over the marshmallows.

Nutrition Info:
- Per Servings 5.1g Carbs, 0.5g Protein, 2.2g Fat, 55 Calories

No Nuts Fudge

Servings: 15 | Cooking Time: 4 Hours

Ingredients:
- ¼ cup cocoa powder
- ½ teaspoon baking powder
- 1 stick of butter, melted
- 4 tablespoons erythritol
- 6 eggs, beaten
- Salt to taste

Directions:
1. Mix all ingredients in a slow cooker.
2. Add a pinch of salt.
3. Mix until well combined.
4. Cover pot.
5. Press the low settings and adjust the time to 4 hours.

Nutrition Info:
- Per Servings 1.3g Carbs, 4.3g Protein, 12.2g Fat, 132 Calories

Vanilla Jello Keto Way

Servings: 6 | Cooking Time: 6 Minutes

Ingredients:
- 1 cup heavy cream
- 1 teaspoon vanilla extract
- 2 tablespoons gelatin powder, unsweetened
- 3 tablespoons erythritol
- 1 cup boiling water

Directions:
1. Place the boiling water in a small pot and bring to a simmer.
2. Add the gelatin powder and allow to dissolve.
3. Stir in the rest of the ingredients.
4. Pour the mixture into jello molds.
5. Place in the fridge to set for 2 hours.

Nutrition Info:
- Per Servings 5.2g Carbs, 3.3g Protein, 7.9g Fat, 105 Calories

Mint Chocolate Protein Shake

Servings: 4 | Cooking Time: 4 Minutes

Ingredients:
- 3 cups flax milk, chilled
- 3 tsp unsweetened cocoa powder
- 1 avocado, pitted, peeled, sliced
- 1 cup coconut milk, chilled
- 3 mint leaves + extra to garnish
- 3 tbsp erythritol
- 1 tbsp low carb Protein powder
- Whipping cream for topping

Directions:
1. Combine the milk, cocoa powder, avocado, coconut milk, mint leaves, erythritol, and protein powder into a blender, and blend for 1 minute until smooth.
2. Pour into serving glasses, lightly add some whipping cream on top, and garnish with mint leaves.

Nutrition Info:
- Per Servings 4g Carbs, 15g Protein, 14.5g Fat, 191 Calories

Coconut Macadamia Nut Bombs

Servings: 4 | Cooking Time: 0 Mins

Ingredients:
- 2 packets stevia
- 5 tbsps unsweetened coconut powder
- 10 tbsps coconut oil
- 3 tbsps chopped macadamia nuts
- Salt to taste

Directions:
1. Heat the coconut oil in a pan over medium heat. Add coconut powder, stevia and salt, stirring to combined well; then remove from heat.
2. Spoon mixture into a lined mini muffin pan. Place in the freezer for a few hours.
3. Sprinkle nuts over the mixture before serving.

Nutrition Info:
- Per Servings 0.2g Carbs, 1.1g Protein, 15.2g Fat, 143 Calories

30 Day Meal Plan

	Breakfast	Lunch	Dinner
Day 1	Pesto Stuffed Mushrooms	Cranberry Sauce Meatballs	Cheesy Cheddar Cauliflower
Day 2	Chocolate Mousse	Chicken Enchilada Dip	Balsamic Zucchini
Day 3	Zucchini And Cheese Gratin	Bacon Mashed Cauliflower	Buttered Broccoli
Day 4	Curry ' N Poppy Devilled Eggs	Shrimp Fra Diavolo	Spinach And Ricotta Gnocchi
Day 5	Sour Cream And Carrot Sticks	Crispy Keto Pork Bites	French Fried Butternut Squash
Day 6	Coconut And Chocolate Bars	Yummy Shrimp Fried Rice	Russian Beef Gratin
Day 7	Parmesan Crackers	Coconut Curry Mussels	Baked Pork Meatballs In Pasta Sauce
Day 8	Cheesy Green Bean Crisps	Jalapeno Beef Pot Roasted	Spanish Frittata
Day 9	Tofu Stuffed Peppers	Thyme-sesame Crusted Halibut	Caesar Salad With Smoked Salmon And Poached Eggs
Day 10	Onion Cheese Muffins	Pork Burgers With Caramelized Onion Rings	Creamy Soup With Greens
Day 11	Zucchini Gratin With Feta Cheese	Steamed Chili-rubbed Tilapia	Watermelon And Cucumber Salad
Day 12	Fat Burger Bombs	Onion Swiss Steak	Corn And Bacon Chowder
Day 13	Beef Italian Sandwiches	Cedar Salmon With Green Onion	Pesto Tomato Cucumber Salad
Day 14	Cheesy Lettuce Rolls	Beef With Dilled Yogurt	Easy Tomato Salad
Day 15	Italian-style Chicken Wraps	Moroccan Beef Stew	Coconut Cauliflower Soup

	Breakfast	**Lunch**	**Dinner**
Day 16	Cheesy Chicken Fritters With Dill Dip	Vegetable Tempura	Creamy Cucumber Avocado Soup
Day 17	Easy Vanilla Granola	Roasted Asparagus With Spicy Eggplant Dip	Parmesan Roasted Cabbage
Day 18	Stuffed Portobello Mushrooms	Spicy Cauliflower Steaks With Steamed Green Beans	Walnut Tofu Sauté
Day 19	Morning Granola	Mushroom & Jalapeño Stew	Brussels Sprouts With Tofu
Day 20	Zucchini Noodles	Mushroom & Cauliflower Bake	Scrambled Eggs With Mushrooms And Spinach
Day 21	Zesty Frittata With Roasted Chilies	Creamy Vegetable Stew	Sautéed Celeriac With Tomato Sauce
Day 22	Avocado And Tomato Burritos	Cauliflower Risotto With Mushrooms	Curried Tofu
Day 23	Pumpkin Bake	Butternut Squash And Cauliflower Stew	Colorful Vegan Soup
Day 24	Sausage Roll	Coconut Cauliflower Rice	Stir-fried Buttery Mushrooms
Day 25	Keto Enchilada Bake	Simple Steamed Salmon Fillets	Guacamole
Day 26	Morning Coconut Smoothie	Cod With Balsamic Tomatoes	Fried Tofu With Mushrooms
Day 27	Vegetarian Burgers	Bacon And Salmon Bites	Greek-style Zucchini Pasta
Day 28	Creamy Hoki With Almond Bread Crust	Red Curry Halibut	Zoodles With Avocado & Olives
Day 29	Blackened Fish Tacos With Slaw	Lemon-rosemary Shrimps	Avocado & Cauliflower Salad With Prawns
Day 30	Sicilian-style Zoodle Spaghetti	Lemon Marinated Salmon With Spices	Mustard-crusted Salmon

Appendix : Recipes Index

Printed in Great Britain
by Amazon

27030397R00071